Marginal Workers, Marginal Jobs

University of Texas Press, P.O. Box 7819,
University Sta., Austin, TX 78712

Marginal Workers, Marginal Jobs

The Underutilization of American Workers

by Teresa A. Sullivan

Foreword by Philip M. Hauser

University of Texas Press Austin & London

Library of Congress Cataloging in Publication Data

Sullivan, Teresa A., 1949–
  Marginal workers, marginal jobs.
  Bibliography: p.
  Includes index.
  1. Underemployment—United States. I. Title.
HD5716.2.U5S94   331.1'1'0973   77-26727
ISBN 0-292-75038-2

Printed in the United States of America

For reasons of economy and speed, the tables and charts in this
volume were printed from camera-ready copy provided by the
author.

For Mary Elizabeth Finnegan Sullivan,

my Mother

Contents

Tables

Charts

Foreword

Marginal Workers, Marginal Jobs is the first book-length report on the use of the labor utilization framework, which is designed to measure underemployment as well as unemployment. Persons in the work force, as reported in this volume, are dichotomized into workers adequately and inadequately utilized. Four categories of underutilization are measured—the unemployed; the part-time employed who want more work; the working poor, full-time workers with poverty income; and the mismatched, persons with work that does not utilize their education or highest skills. The part-time employed wanting more work are the visible underemployed; the last two categories are the invisible underemployed.

The labor utilization framework was primarily intended to measure underemployment in the less developed countries, where unemployment is merely the tip of the iceberg in labor underutilization. The original conceptualization of the framework has been modified and sharpened by experimental work done in Thailand, Indonesia, Singapore, Malaysia, the Philippines, Taiwan, Hong Kong, and South Korea, as well as in the United States.

In this book, Teresa Sullivan not only demonstrates the usefulness of measuring underemployment in the U.S. and therefore in other more developed countries but also ingeniously uses the framework in a theoretical sociological context for testing a number of significant hypotheses. Dr. Sullivan has therefore made a dual contribution. She has, first, demonstrated that it is possible to obtain a reasonable and useful measurement of underemployment in the U.S. This is a significant result, especially in view of the Comprehensive Employment and Training Act, passed in 1973, which requires the U.S. Department of Labor to measure underemployment in addition to unemployment. Second, Dr. Sullivan has skillfully demonstrated how labor force data can be used to enhance sociological as well as economic knowledge.

In the experimental work done with the labor utilization framework, there have been both unfavorable and favorable reactions. Some economists, especially, have been negative because the framework does not emerge as a clear product of economic theory or as an answer to some important economic questions. Moreover, the labor utilization framework has been criticized for having arbitrary cut-offs in its operationalization of visible and invisible underemployment. As this volume testifies, the measurement of labor utilization is useful *sui generis* even if it leaves some economic questions unanswered. No one measurement approach can be expected to satisfy all objectives. What can be claimed for the labor utilization framework is that, with little additional input, it supplies more useful information than the standard labor force approach.

With respect to the criticism that labor utilization framework cut-off points are arbitrary, it should be emphasized that the same is true of the current standard measurement of the labor force and of unemployment. Those of us who developed the standard labor force approach, including the measurement of unemployment, necessarily had an arbitrary definition of unemployment. The unemployed, with detailed specific criteria, were in essence defined as those seeking work during the reference week, excluding all persons who worked at any time during the reference week. It would have been just as possible, with quite different results, to define the unemployed as all those seeking work at the end of the week or as those who spent more time seeking than working during the week. All social measurement necessarily involves arbitrary definition. The key consideration is that the definition provide reliable and meaningful information and a consistent measurement of change over time.

Dr. Sullivan is to be commended for her skillful and innovative investigation. She has retrieved knowledge, previously buried in computer tape of the 1960 and 1970 U.S. censuses, that promises to be useful not only to academicians but also to the public and private sectors of the nation for policy and programmatic purposes.

Philip M. Hauser
Lucy Flower Professor Emeritus
of Urban Sociology and
Director Emeritus,
Population Research Center,
Chicago

Preface

These days, it is nearly impossible to teach an undergraduate course, talk with your neighbors, or even read the newspaper without uncovering anxiety about jobs—finding a job, finding a *good* job, finding a *secure* job. College students, especially, are concerned about the jobs that they will be qualified for and that will be open for them. The job has taken on functions far beyond earning one's daily bread—expectations of what a "good" job brings are rivaling the expectations an earlier generation had for a "good" marriage. "Occupational subcultures" are examined for their relation to alcoholism, credit abuse, religious activity, and general life-style. Work is looked to for fulfillment, creativity, and emotional growth, and is generally linked to one's continuing health, education, and welfare. All of this is in addition to the usual job requirements: a steady income stream that is reasonably secure.

Needless to say, many jobs (like many marriages) do not live up to all the expectations put on them. Grumbling about one's job is one of life's subtle pleasures, and certainly not a matter for public policy. However, genuine labor market hardship is a matter of public policy and has been—depending on your classification of policies—at least since the 1930's Depression and officially so since 1947. This monograph treats government data as a prerequisite for sound policy.

Specifically, I deal with data about the adequacy of employment. Current data cover unemployment in detail but provide relatively little information about the problems of the *employed*. Unemployment remains a serious labor market hardship, but it is not the only one. Finding a job is important, but so are finding a *good* job and finding a *secure* job.

After the Great Depression of the 1930's, government agencies spent years experimenting with the concepts and measures of unemployment. Every few years since 1940, the first census year in which the "labor force" approach was used to measure unemployment, there have been changes in the definition and measurement of unemployment. It would not be surprising if a similar process of experimenting, followed by years of tinkering, were needed to develop measures of adequate employment and underemployment. This study is neither the last word on the subject, nor the first word—but it does come during the early experimenting stage. I hope that it can contribute to the dialogue.

One theme of this study is developing better government labor statistics. There are several sections dealing with data adequacy and definitional problems. Some of these sections prove that it is possible to turn even an interesting subject such as underemployment into dry description and analysis, but the conceptual experimentation I mentioned above requires careful, even painstaking, attention to data quality and other details.

Unlike unemployment, which can be defined in comparatively straightforward terms, underemployment must be studied in reference to a normative standard. The norm used here is not optimal employment, but minimally adequate employment. Adequate employment is defined by hours of work, income, and skills. An adequately employed person works a full workweek at a wage above the poverty level, and in an occupation suitable for his or her education. Voluntary part-time workers are also considered adequately utilized. Optimal employment, on the other hand, would have to consider the *best* job for each worker (in terms of productivity, personal fulfillment, or some other standard). Many persons who consider themselves underemployed are not classified that way by these criteria. Some who are underemployed by these criteria may not consider themselves to be so.

The second theme of this study is the composition of the underutilized, defined by the relatively objective standard outlined above. It is from this theme that the "marginal workers" emphasis comes. But many underutilized workers are not marginal, at least not by any a priori category we can determine. This suggests that there are a number of "dead end" jobs—marginal jobs—that even the preferred workers must take. Census data are not sufficient to examine marginal jobs in depth, although one chapter is dedicated to a preliminary investigation.

An earlier version of this study was accepted as a doctoral dissertation at the University of Chicago in December, 1975. While I take responsibility for the study's shortcomings, much of the credit belongs to a supportive network of helpful teachers and colleagues. The inspiration for the study came from a graduate seminar on the labor force that Professor Philip M. Hauser offered at the University of Chicago. Professor Hauser's initial conceptualization of the Labor Utilization Framework and his constant encouragement and enthusiasm made this study possible. The other members of the doctoral committee were Professors Evelyn M. Kitagawa, Morris Janowitz, and Leo A. Goodman from the University of Chicago and Professor Joseph Ben-David from Hebrew University, Jerusalem. Their sound criticism and encouragement were invaluable.

Professor Harley L. Browning of the University of Texas at Austin was a faithful, reliable critic and colleague. I am indebted to him and a number of faculty at the University of Texas, especially Professors Omer Galle, Robert Glover, Allan King, and Ray Marshall. Professor Wilhelm Flieger of the University of San Carlos, Philippines, and Professor Clifford C. Clogg of the Pennsylvania State University offered me substantial help in thinking through the ideas in this study. Like many other students at the Population Research Center, I benefited both from Dr. Clogg's advice and from his own substantial contribution to labor utilization studies. I am grateful to Dr. Patricia Anderson of Kingston, Jamaica, for challenging my data accuracy and quality. Professors

Ivar Berg and T. Aldrich Finegan, both of Vanderbilt University, and Sar A. Levitan of George Washington University, were stimulating and challenging readers.

My support during the research was provided by a National Science Foundation Graduate Fellowship. Grants from the Population Council, New York, and the Department of Sociology and the Division of the Social Sciences at the University of Chicago provided computer time. The Population Research Center at the University of Chicago and the Population Research Center at the University of Texas at Austin provided library assistance and clerical help. Typists who helped included Susan Dlugach, Beverly A. Moore, Harvene McGee, and Colleen Count. Donald Tom was my research assistant during the revision of the manuscript. Maria Luchesi Ring helped prepare the index. I learned a great deal from the careful editing of Mary Beissner.

A project similar to this study was funded by the Asia Foundation through the Council for Asian Manpower Studies. Travel funds from that grant helped me compare the underemployment and data collection problems in the United States with those in Southeast Asia. The Institute for Latin American Studies at the University of Texas at Austin made it possible for me to explore some preliminary results at the Conference on Labor Anthropology in Mexico.

To my patient husband, H. Douglas Laycock, I owe special thanks. In the course of this project, he endured months of scribbled postcards from Asia, two interstate moves, the storage of stacks of computer output and tapes, and endless labor force discussion. His faith never wavered, even when mine did.

Chicago, Illinois
August, 1977

Marginal Workers, Marginal Jobs

CHAPTER I

Approaching Labor Underutilization and Labor Marginality

Unemployment and underemployment are hardly modern phenomena. A Biblical description could apply to some contemporary hiring halls:

And about the eleventh hour he went out and found others standing; and he said to them, "Why do you stand idle all day?" They said to him, "Because no one has hired us."[1]

But although unemployment and underemployment persist, they are less visible to the public. When the commodity market and labor exchange were in the same village square, merchants and consumers could not avoid witnessing involuntary idleness. Today's differentiated economic structure disguises inadequate labor conditions. Most of us know relatives or friends who have trouble finding adequate jobs, but it is easy to dismiss this anecdotal evidence when we do not know how many others are in similar straits.

Ironically, official data as well as the economic structure have tended to hide inadequate employment. One unintended consequence of current labor statistics is that reporting data about one sort of inadequate labor situation has disguised the existence of other sorts. That is, although the unemployed workers are reported in monthly labor statistics, the workers hired "at the eleventh hour" for temporary or low-level jobs are not.

A new interest in data about inadequately employed workers arose during the recession of the mid-1970's, when it seemed that high unemployment rates might be the tip of an iceberg of underemployed labor. The Comprehensive Employment and Training Act of 1973, or CETA, mandates the Secretary of Labor to develop data for measuring underemployment.[2]

One provision of this statute further stimulated local government officials to demand underemployment data. The act provides that some federal manpower funds be disbursed in proportion to the extent of unemployment, although this excludes large numbers of underemployed workers not included in unemployment surveys. Later, a smaller allocation was also proposed in proportion to the number of adults in low-income families.[3] But this was not sufficient, for some officials argued that their local industries respond to recession by underemploying through partial layoffs, work sharing, and wage cuts. The unemployment rate is not sensitive to these changes, and the number of low-income families may also be a datum that is insensitive to these changes.[4] New kinds of data are needed.

Despite these expressions of official concern, progress has been slow. Two years after CETA, the Labor Department reported, "Considerable conceptual work must be done in the development of statistics on economic hardship. When satisfactory definitions and criteria have been developed, ways to use these in analyzing economic hardship and underemployment can be examined."[5] Two economists, commenting on the low priority of new statistics, concluded from this that economic policy makers in the administration were opposed to an index that might concentrate attention on structural economic problems.[6]

On the other hand, the act creating the National Commission on Employment and Unemployment Statistics indicated renewed congressional interest.[7] The commission is charged with reassessing labor market statistics, especially the accuracy with which they measure labor market hardship. On July 29, 1977, President Carter appointed Professor Sar A. Levitan to serve as chairman of the commission.

For five years now, there has been official concern about statistics on underemployment. Admittedly the degree of interest has varied among levels of government and among agencies. But the response from social scientists is only now gaining momentum. This study was designed to add to that momentum by sketching some directions for conceptual development, offering a measurement framework, and analyzing national data on employment adequacy. Although it is not yet feasible to provide the local area data needed for revenue sharing, the analysis of national data is an important first step.

Labor Adequacy: The Neglected Inquiry

At first blush, the absence of recent sociological studies of labor adequacy is surprising. Occupation is an individual's single most important social position. It is a proxy for prestige, an indicator of social class, and an index of mobility. Occupations are identified with characteristic life-styles, with age and sex roles, and even with so-called occupational personalities. So exceptional cases, the marginal, unstable, or nonexistent occupational identities, should be of both substantive and methodological interest. To what extent does a discontinuous occupational identity imply lower-class status? Does labor marginality affect social mobility? Is labor underutilization distributed among the population much as poverty, illiteracy, and other disadvantaged positions are?

Sociologists have done little work along these lines, even though studies of labor supply have been an area of sociological inquiry for some time.[8] Sociologists, especially those trained in demography, have studied the labor force. Studies of labor force participation rates, especially of women, are regularly undertaken.[9] What has been neglected is the quality and stability of the participation. Even recent reviews of needed research rarely mention underemployment.[10] If labor underutilization is treated at all, it is peripherally, often as a symptom of a related phenomenon.[11] In many studies, including those of labor mobility, underemployed workers are excluded with a ritual disclaimer about the problems they cause.[12]

Economists have also tended to neglect underemployment, at least in developed countries. As one economist recently wrote: "One finds no discussion in the literature, moreover, about the possible design of a consistent underemployment index. In the absence of such an index, a survey of trends in underemployment is obviously impossible."[13]

Psychology shares in the neglect: "The problems of unemployment and underemployment would seem to fall generally within the realm of industrial psychology. For the most part, however, traditional organizational and industrial psychology have failed to deal successfully with such problems. The underemployed and the unemployed are, by definition, people who lie outside of the organizational setting."[14] Anthropologists have only recently begun to express interest in underemployment, especially in developing countries.[15]

By comparison, unemployment has been extensively studied.[16] The unemployment rate has become an important economic indicator and, frequently, a political datum. Through its high visibility, the unemployment rate may serve as a diversion from other issues of labor utilization.

Other phenomena, no matter how interesting, may appear to be anecdotal sidelights by comparison to a hard, cold unemployment rate. For example, in the 1958 recession Daniel Bell noticed "downgrading," or the practice of demoting skilled, senior workmen to lower-paid jobs when their junior colleagues had been laid off. "As the number of workers was cut, senior men took on menial tasks at lower pay. The downgrading seems to have affected the men more than any other blow."[17] But little systematic evidence was collected, then or now, to document the extent or effects of downgrading, or other forms of underemployment.

The study of unemployment is certainly important. In welfare terms, those with no work at all are in the direst straits. But our picture of labor utilization in the United States is incomplete with measures of unemployment alone. To emphasize labor force participation and unemployment may mean premature closure on other problems of labor utilization. To put it differently, social scientists are studying what they can measure. Further work requires better measurement, and better measurement requires clearer conceptualization.

Labor Underutilization—a Transitory Phenomenon?

Some of the relative neglect of labor underutilization may stem from a theme, found even in the early literature, that inadequate employment tends to be transitory. This was believed true of individuals who would either look for better jobs until they were satisfied or leave the labor force altogether. But more importantly, a similar adjustment process was believed to go on within the society as a whole. High aggregate levels of inadequate employment were seen as the "growing pains" of the Industrial Revolution.

Durkheim called it "the anomic division of labor." "It often happens in a commercial, industrial, or other enterprise that functions are distributed in such a way that they do not offer sufficient material for individual activity."[18] He believed that increased coordination in organic solidarity would eliminate the abnormality. "These new conditions of industrial life naturally demand a new organization, but as these changes have been accomplished with extreme rapidity, the interests in conflict have not yet had the time to be equilibrated."[19]

The process of economic development transforms the labor force, much as a mini–Industrial Revolution might. It was not surprising then that the concept of underemployment was applied by analogy to developing countries. Development specialists have observed that labor inadequacy does increase during development, despite increased savings and investment.[20]

What has been more controversial is the extent to which labor inadequacy exists in societies not undergoing rapid economic change. Some early analysts denied that underemployment could even exist in traditional economies. In 1936 Joan Robinson wrote: "An economy consisting of self-supporting families working their own land always enjoys full employment, since each individual is free to work as long as he considers the reward he obtains a sufficient inducement for his efforts."[21] She implied that in traditional agriculture neither unemployment nor underemployment were of concern.

Critics responded that labor marginality was primarily a problem of traditional societies because the social factors in subsistence agriculture "disguised" unemployment. Indeed, they argued, where there is no subsistence agriculture there can be no underemployment.[22] At any rate, either on the theory that underutilization was to be found in traditional societies *before* development or that it would occur *during* development, the bulk of the work on disguised unemployment has been conducted in developing countries.[23]

But if the studies flourished in developing countries, they seemed to languish in developed ones. The major exception was in times of depression, when interest in inadequate employment was revived. During the 1930's, Joan Robinson described both unemployment and disguised unemployment, in this case the adoption of inferior occupations, in the industrial economy. The recession in the 1970's stimulated the contemporary interest in underemployment in developed countries. Although it is not yet extensive, there is a body of contemporary literature that is discussed in chapter 3.

The clearest interest in the role of underemployment in advanced economies can be found in Marxist thought. Marx understood that inadequate employment was common during depressions ("gluts"), but for him this was not an indication that the problem was transitory, but rather an indicator that it would continue. He expected the "gluts" to become more severe, and he expected that technological changes to deal with the "gluts" would make employment prospects worse: "The whole form of the movement of modern industry depends, therefore, upon the constant transformation of a part of the labouring population into unemployed or half-employed hands."[24]

Marx argued that a "reserve army" of the unemployed would bid down wages and compete for scarce jobs. But it seems fair to infer that the underemployed would be the auxiliary troops, and that the magnitude of labor inadequacy would increase with industrialization. Not surprisingly, several contemporary treatments of underemployment come from Marxist and radical economists. Some of this literature is also included in chapter 3.

All of this suggests that some of the delay in studying underemployment is due to doubt about its significance as well as to where it can be found. Is it found in traditional agriculture? During early industrialization? In services? And can it be found at any time of the business cycle?

This study side-steps, for the moment, the question of how permanent labor inadequacy may be. Instead, it assumes that labor inadequacy exists in every society, because in every society the social organization of work will have imperfections. At the minimum, some short-term, "frictional" unemployment and underemployment should be expected. And so, underemployment in a developed country is a legitimate area of inquiry. Whether transitory or permanent, it deserves investigation.

More generally, it is likely that labor underutilization exists in all societies, although its *magnitude, composition*, and *characteristic forms* may differ. Possibly the characteristic type of underemployment changes with economic development. Without assuming any necessary, linear, evolutionary path for developing countries, perhaps one could delimit characteristic patterns of labor inadequacy resulting from different industry mixes, trade patterns, and economic growth records. Part of the conceptual clarification needed for studies of underemployment is a sense of how to approach the questions of magnitude, composition, and forms of underutilization. These ideas are explored in the next section.

A Conceptual Approach to Labor Utilization

✗ So far the terms underemployment and labor inadequacy have been used synonymously, without further clarification. Now a different term will be used. In this study, "labor underutilization" is the collective term for unemployment and underemployment. "Underemployment" refers to three types of inadequate employment: inadequate hours of work, inadequate level of income, and mismatch of occupation and skills. These categories are discussed in greater detail in succeeding chapters.

Compared with fertility and mortality, economic activity is inherently more culture-bound and presents greater variability for the analyst to explain. There are three sorts of variability with which the analyst must deal: the magnitude, the composition, and the forms of underutilization. These sources of variability imply the criteria of aggregation and mutual exclusivity.

Magnitude refers to the absolute number of persons who are underutilized, and it is usually related to the size of the adult population. Where economic differentiation has progressed beyond traditional agriculture, magnitude may be related to the size of the labor force. Orders of magnitude should be internationally comparable regardless of type of economy.

In classical studies, population size was closely linked to the magnitude of labor underutilization. Malthus and Ricardo formulated the problem in terms of too many workers for the available jobs. When workers were scarce, wages rose. Higher labor demand influenced a larger supply through greater migration in the short run, and higher birth rates in the long run. As the labor supply increased, the wage declined. Poverty, or wage underemployment, was the prevailing form of underutilization. Disease and starvation provided the effective mechanisms for diminishing the labor supply. Then wages rose and the process began anew. X

One reason that studies of underutilization have focused on developing countries is their rapid population increase. "Overpopulation" has been linked to labor underutilization at least since the time of Malthus. After World War II, although "death control" was widely adopted throughout the world, birth control was accepted more slowly. Larger birth cohorts meant surplus labor within ten to fifteen years. As a result, both labor supply and labor underutilization were formulated as problems of overpopulation. Implicitly, a homogeneous labor supply was often assumed.

Most industrial countries have passed through the demographic transition, so that overpopulation is infrequently perceived to be a problem. Except during recessions, an oversupply of labor is rarely a pressing concern. If developing countries' experience has led underutilization to be perceived as a function of oversupply, it may seem irrelevant to industrial countries. In advanced countries, it is argued, the labor market adequately regulates supply and demand, and the unemployment figure is the index of disequilibrium.

Defining underutilization as a function of overpopulation diverts attention from advanced countries, but by implication it also distorts the realities of industrial labor markets. The simplifying assumption becomes homogeneity of demand, if not of supply. When underutilization is viewed in terms of inadequate or inappropriate demand, it becomes obvious that "underemployment" may exist even if the only unemployment is frictional, regardless of labor supply. Indeed, underemployment and labor shortages, even general shortages, may coexist, especially when poverty wages are the prevailing form of underemployment.

Magnitude of underutilization is treated here as an empirical question. It may be viewed as indicating maladjustments between supply and demand, but it does not require the assumption that either is homogeneous. Possibly it is more fruitful to think about characteristic social and economic organizations as well as population size, instead of just the shorthand terms "demand" and "supply."

Malthus and Ricardo did not discuss the composition of marginal workers because they postulated a relatively homogeneous, unskilled population. Industrialization brought greater economic differentiation, however, and the simple identification of workers with the adult population was replaced by the conceptual differentiation of the adult population into the economically productive and the economically unproductive. As Joan Robinson put it, "Every man is occupied for twenty-four hours a day, so that the total amount of occupation can never be increased, yet *employment* can be said to increase if a man's time is transferred from an occupation in which its productivity is lower to one where it is higher"[25] (emphasis hers). This partition of the adult population directed the interest in marginal workers to those classified as economically active. The magnitude of underutilization continued to be an issue, but the issue of composition had become inextricably bound to it.

Composition refers to the kinds of people affected by underutilization. Age, sex, and ethnicity are likely to be categories of interest. Other salient categories might be the highly skilled, the physically handicapped, or veterans. Family welfare is adversely affected by the underutilization of the household members, and so household position is an important category. Compositional detail permits cross-national comparison of utilization by demographic categories.

The composition of the underutilized must reflect to a greater or lesser extent the composition of the labor force. One aspect of labor force composition is the proportion of "marginal workers." In this study, "labor marginality" is used to describe general categories of less-preferred workers who are likely to be underutilized. Labor marginality is a probabilistic term. For example, workers aged 65 and over are marginal workers. They are likely to be underutilized, but how many actually are underutilized is an empirical question. Thus magnitude and composition interact.

The requirements for magnitude and composition suggest a measurement that can be *aggregated* across large social units or disaggregated to smaller units. Presumably individual workers are the principal unit of analysis; if so, this would permit aggregation into households, families, group quarters, and so forth, which are alternative units of analysis.

Forms of Underutilization

At the outset, one should be warned that generalizations about the forms of underutilization do some damage to the richness of the empirical variations. Any system of labor statistics may be *mathematically* exhaustive, in the sense of completely classifying the population. But no system is likely to be *conceptually* exhaustive in the sense of listing all possible forms of underutilization. The best recourse for the analyst is to have a theoretical grounding for the underutilization forms summarized in statistical reports.

The forms of underutilization arise from the organizational heterogeneity that exists among cultures, and within cultures as well. For any given culture, the greater the heterogeneity of economic organizations, the greater the number of possible forms of labor underutilization. In agricultural countries, especially among extended family groups, work-sharing arrangements for all may be preferred to idleness by a few. Beyond kinship structures, villages and other primary organizations are likely to emphasize work sharing. In so-called dual economies, the urban wage market may be prone to all the sorts of labor underutilization found in industrial countries, while rural areas have a different set of utilization conditions. Even industrialized countries, though resembling each other, have unique characteristics. For example, industrial layoffs are more common in the United States than in Europe. The Japanese life-tenure system offers job tenure but may lead to quite distinctive patterns of underutilization over the life cycle. Thus another source of variability in labor utilization will be the characteristic form of underutilization and the changes in form from culture to culture and within a culture over time. An analysis of unemployment alone, and even analyses of general underemployment, miss important differences in the quality and content of utilization.

Advanced economies are characterized by a high degree of economic differentiation that is reflected in the sectoral shift from agriculture, the separation of home from workplace, and the use of money and credit as exchange media. One result of this differentiation is the separation of production and consumption functions. And this makes it possible to seek the forms of underutilization in the adequacy of the household-economy interchanges.

In the household-economy interchange, the economy offers a labor contract—that is, employment itself—and remuneration. The household offers time and skills. Inadequate exchange may occur in four basic ways: unemployment, an income inadequate to meet the household's adaptive imperative, inadequate hours of work, or inadequate use of skills.[26] These four inadequate exchanges constitute the basic forms of underutilization in an advanced economy.

These four possibilities correspond closely to situations described in the classical studies. Marx discussed unemployment, and both Marx and Durkheim described "half-employed" hands. Ricardo identified the "working poor," and Robinson's "disguised unemployed" are very close to the "mismatched."

Unemployment is the most extreme form of labor underutilization and does not coexist with other forms—that is, one cannot be simultaneously unemployed (without employment) and underemployed (with employment, albeit inadequate employment). Underemployment may occur in several ways, and this creates the possibility that a single person may be multiply underemployed. But a heterogeneous category, "multiply underemployed," disguises the empirical variations. A more acceptable approach is a hierarchy of forms of underutilization based on a meaningful continuum. Family welfare, manpower policy objectives, or the maintenance of human capital might be appropriate continua. This implies that the forms of underutilization be mutually exclusive.

A single worker could be prey to several forms of underutilization simultaneously. To discuss this problem, I introduce a new concept, private underutilization. Private underutilization may be further divided into gross and net underutilization.

GROSS AND NET PRIVATE UNDERUTILIZATION

Private underutilization is the loss of individuals' time, income, or talents through underutilization. Underutilization may occur in any of the following ways. First, there may be total unemployment of some or all of the workers offering to work. Second, workers who offer more hours of work than the market demands are underutilized by hours of work. Another term for them is involuntary part-time workers. A third possibility is wage employment that is below subsistence level, whether the low wage be due to low productivity, employer niggardliness, or whatever. A fourth possibility is mismatch, or the inadequate use of skills that workers offer the economy. These skills might be obsolete, or common skills in oversupply, or even advanced skills for which supportive technology and complementary skills are inadequate. (For example, a surgeon might be prepared to do an intricate operation if only adequately trained staff were available to assist.)

Gross private underutilization is the aggregated inadequate utilization of all forms occurring to any worker or household. Gross private underutilization includes all the workers or households falling into each of the four categories. That is, the underemployed are counted in every category into which they fall. For example, involuntary part-time workers may also earn low wages and be mismatched. Only unemployment precludes multiple classification, by definition.

Net private underutilization is gross private underutilization adjusted through a mutually exclusive hierarchy of the underutilized. In this study, worker welfare is the criterion for ordering the hierarchy of underutilization. Unemployed workers are considered the most underutilized, and so unemployment is tabulated first. Workers with inadequate hours of work are counted next, because low wages may also result from too few hours of work. In terms of welfare, these workers may be subject to a double disadvantage. Full-time workers who nevertheless earn inadequate incomes are the third category. Finally, the full-time workers who are employed at adequate wages, but who are mismatched, are tabulated. Another hierarchy, of course, could be used. The magnitudes reported in this study measure net private underutilization.

But individuals are not the only ones who lose from underutilization. Although this study deals with net private underutilization, it seems useful to introduce a concept to describe the loss to society.

SOCIAL UNDERUTILIZATION

Social underutilization is the loss to society resulting from underutilized workers. In its simplest form, social underutilization may be expressed in total labor time lost, foregone earnings, or inadequate returns to education. Some of these measures have already been suggested in the literature.[27] Each of these measures is really a restatement, in terms of time or money, of the effects of gross or net private underutilization.

From a sociological perspective, there is a richer, more complex concept of social underutilization, albeit one that is difficult to quantify. This perspective requires the sociological insight that society is more than the sum of its parts. The criterion of worker welfare is supplemented by the criterion of societal well-being. Social underutilization in this sense includes "reverse mismatch," that loss in labor quality that results from workers who are underqualified for their jobs. These workers are, so to speak, "overutilized." A worker welfare criterion might not include them in net private underutilization, but they are part of the loss to society from inadequate utilization.

Conceptually at least, social underutilization might include an inadequate commitment of workers to the economy. (In Parsons' terminology, this would be an inadequate A_L-L_L interchange.) Thus, social underutilization could reflect the employer's frustration at low productivity, "featherbedding," or laziness. Of course the cost to society would also include the aggregated private underutilization. Measures of social underutilization are not developed here but are mentioned for a more complete conceptual statement.

Summary and Preview

Labor underutilization is an age-old problem, but one which social structure tends to conceal. Ironically, even social science data and analysis have tended to conceal the problem. This is partly because of uncertainty about the persistence and significance of underemployment, and partly an overemphasis on unemployment, a concept that was already measured and for which abundant data were available.

Rather than viewing labor inadequacy as a function of supply and demand, it may be useful to view it as a by-product of the social organization of work. Its magnitude, composition, and forms will vary depending on the characteristic social organizations of work.

For the United States, those forms are likely to include unemployment, involuntary part-time work, low income despite a full workweek, and occupational attainment that does not use one's skills. These forms may be aggregated by overall incidence—which is here called gross private underutilization—or they may be aggregated for individuals by using a mutually exclusive index. That is called net private underutilization. Private underutilization, or the loss to individuals, is conceptually distinct from social underutilization, which is the loss to society.

"Marginality" is introduced as a probabilistic term that describes categories of people who are *likely* to be underutilized. This study is an empirical investigation of the overlap between the marginal categories and the measured underutilization. The next chapter considers what those marginal categories are in American society. Chapter 3 addresses the construction of an index of net private underutilization. In later chapters the "expected" underutilization is compared with the actual underutilization for a series of marginal workers.

CHAPTER 2
Who Are the Marginal Workers?

Commenting on their colleagues, two sociologists wrote that they "may begin with a problem or set of questions about the nature of a particular social pattern, not with certain well-defined hypotheses to be tested."[1] Speaking specifically about studies of labor force irregularity, Eli Ginzberg once wrote that hypothesis generation seemed to "proceed with an axe rather than a scalpel," because it is an area "not in fashion, in which the theoretical apparatus is relatively primitive and for which the data have not even been gathered."[2]

Both comments apply to some extent to the hypothesis generation in this study. This study began with a set of questions about underutilization: how is marginality related to underutilization? Who are the underutilized? In this chapter, these questions lead to an examination of marginality and to four hypotheses to test the overlap between marginality and underutilization. In this exploratory study, the hypotheses are more likely to bear marks of the axe than of the scalpel.

Marginality as an Independent Variable

The recent literature on underemployment, while richly suggestive, has been difficult to test—not only because the data were lacking, but also because theoretical statements were not phrased in testable form. Much of the literature resorts to tautological labeling, so that the underutilized are labeled "marginal workers" and their jobs, "marginal jobs."[3] To separate the concepts of marginality and underutilization, one needs a theoretically informed concept of marginality, one that implies a probabilistic empirical relationship. That is, although not every member of Category X may be underutilized, one can establish the odds of underutilization for a person in X at a given time. In terms of this study, this means that the a priori categories of marginality are independent variables and underutilization is the dependent variable.

Clearly, the independent variable categories should not be inferred from underutilization data. For example, the independent categories could not be the unemployed, the working poor, and so forth, for they are underutilized by definition. A simple linear relationship inferred from published findings about the unemployed would also be inadequate. Consider the proposition: "For any

Group X, the higher the unemployment, the higher the other forms of under-utilization." This proposition may be true for some groups, but underutilization measures were proposed partly because the unemployment rate *hides* under-employment. And so the proposition, "The lower the unemployment, the higher the other forms of underutilization," is equally plausible. We must "stand back" from the variables of immediate interest to examine conditions contributing to marginality. Presumably one could be marginal to society in a number of ways. Several of these ways will be investigated here as operational definitions of marginality.

Sufficient Conditions for Marginality

Judging from a wide-ranging literature review, it seems reasonable to assert that any of four conditions is sufficient to make a worker *or his job* marginal:[4]

1. Disabilities that, objectively or subjectively, make one less competitive in a labor market—for example, physical handicaps.
2. Ascriptive characteristics that carry low status.
3. Achieved characteristics that are inferior to other workers' achievements, especially years of schooling.
4. Structural characteristics of the worker's occupation or industry that make it unstable, irregular, or less competitive.

Before marshaling the evidence supporting the inclusion of these four conditions and defending the omission of others, a brief digression is in order about the interpretation of marginality.

IS MARGINALITY VOLUNTARY OR INVOLUNTARY?

Because manpower programs are often seen as an alternative to welfare, the question of whether the underutilized are "deserving" will come up, just as it does with welfare recipients. So it is important to discuss the degree of volition involved in marginality. Or, to turn the argument around, categorical welfare aid may be used to indicate some types of marginality.

In this study, marginality is defined through a few fairly objective indicators of the four conditions above. The first three conditions define persons who are marginal to the social structure, but for quite different reasons. The conditions can be distinguished by the degree of public recognition of marginality and by the degree of "fault" imputed to the marginal worker. The primary purpose of this section is not to endorse faultfinding, but to show how compositional detail may interact with the conventional wisdom to influence data interpretations. If workers are perceived to be marginal *by choice*, the policy impact of underutilization—even involuntary underutilization—is greatly diminished. In fact, underutilization may be seen as a well-deserved negative sanction for deviant behavior.

Physically disabled workers, whose illness or defect is usually attributed to chance, are acknowledged more or less explicitly to be marginal to the labor force by the categorical welfare aid given in lieu of earnings. In the public idiom, "It's not their fault." Mental, behavioral, and emotional disabilities are less likely to be perceived as involuntary, despite efforts to have the public view alcoholism, addiction, and other disorders as diseases.

The case for ascriptive characteristics is mixed. The marginality of the elderly and children is usually seen as legitimate and is often recognized by transfer payments. Race and sex, on the other hand, are ascriptive characteristics which, while "not one's fault," may be proxies for real or imagined work behaviors. Stereotypes of work behaviors can become the justifications for employment discrimination. ("Blacks are lazy." "Women get pregnant and quit.")

The category whose members appear most "blameable" consists of those deficient in achieved status. In particular, it is easy to dismiss the uneducated as undeserving. The government has slowly recognized that some barriers to educational opportunity are beyond one's control and has provided job training under various programs. Ironically, the "blame the victim" tendency may be strengthened by such programs. The reasoning is that one must be unusually shiftless to have avoided even government training courses.

The final category refers to persons who may not be socially marginal but whose jobs are marginal to the economic structure. The degree of volition in this category is difficult to assess. Since the Depression of the 1930's, many persons have come to recognize that impersonal economic forces make some jobs marginal. This is most apparent in a recession, but it is also evident when a single firm collapses or an entire industry is depressed. Such marginality appears to be involuntary. On the other hand, assuming a free labor market, these workers could find employment in more vigorous concerns or in new occupations. Their reluctance to maximize their employment returns could be seen as voluntary marginality.

Is marginality voluntary or involuntary? The identification of a priori conditions is designed to minimize the question of volition in order to trace patterns of marginality in the population. There is "deviant marginality"—that is, some individuals really are shiftless, lazy, unambitious, or unbalanced. But just as measures of net private underutilization do not require an adjustment for labor force commitment, the components of marginality do not require psychological qualification (see the section "Labor Force Commitment," below). Nevertheless, as long as work serves as a major proxy for personality and status, implicit assumptions about volition are likely to color the *application* of the findings.

A DETAILED LOOK AT MARGINALITY

The evidence in this section is designed to show that each condition is sufficient to make a worker marginal to the labor force. Findings from studies of unemployed or part-time workers are introduced only as supplementary evidence.

Disability

Animal behavior studies for many species indicate that an injured or sick animal is likely to be rejected, even killed, by its healthy relatives. Similar behavior has been found among some human groups, where it is sometimes justified as a eugenic measure. Such rejection is far from universal, but it offers a graphic first suspicion that the physically different are somehow marginal, outside the mainstream of society.

Most human history indicates that persons with mental, emotional, or behavioral disturbances share the stigma of the physically disabled. Institutionalization symbolizes and aggravates their marginality. Institutionalized persons are excluded from the labor force, and so they are not considered further here. But even workers who have slight incapacities, or who have a history of hospitalization, are probably marginal in important respects.

Not all disabilities are so serious as to preclude any work at all, but the "otherness" of disability is still with the disabled worker. Marx included the "mutilated" and the "sickly" in the reserve army of the unemployed. When labor is plentiful, there is little incentive to hire or train them.[5] Even when hired, the disabled tend to have erratic and precarious work records—not because they are unreliable, but because of employers' preferences, restrictive insurance regulations, or the kinds of jobs they get.[6]

The advertisements to "hire the handicapped" allude to their special problems in finding work. It seems fair to conclude that disabled persons are marginal to the labor force to the extent that "disability" may be one a priori component of marginality.

A possible source of faulty reasoning should be noted. Some writers speak of "underutilization by malnutrition" to describe persons whose work is unproductive through inadequate human capital maintenance.[7] *In situ*, the causality is almost inherently circular. But for purposes of this study it would be backward logic to argue, "Group X is underutilized because of disease, and *therefore*, they are disabled." Despite the imperfections of the operational definition, I have tried to treat disability as a logically prior condition, and to treat the forms of underutilization as identifying symptoms, not causes.

Ascriptive Characteristics

It is part of the conventional wisdom to associate ascriptive characteristics with labor underutilization. Even without sound data about underemployment, a national commission concluded that "unemployment and under-employment among the nation's minorities, particularly among non-whites, is a most critical domestic problem in the United States today."[8] Marx scarcely questioned his implicit definition of preferred workers when he described capitalists cutting their wage bills by replacing "mature labour-power by immature, male by female, that of adults by that of young persons."[9] United States civil rights legislation forbids job discrimination based on race, sex, and age, an indication that Congress believes these statuses related to labor market hardship. If preferred workers are white, male, and in the prime working years, then everyone else is, by contrast, marginal to the labor force.

The much-publicized Bakke lawsuit, in which a white male charged reverse discrimination, in some ways underscores the point. Affirmative action programs were proposed to open the door for less-preferred workers. By implication, those omitted from affirmative action (or those who are the victims of reverse discrimination) are the preferred workers. However, it should be noted that the Bakke case does not deal with employment discrimination, but with medical school admissions.

Beyond the conventional wisdom, evidence of labor force marginality comes from studies of prestige, worker satisfaction, income, and discrimination. Stratification studies show that women and blacks are clustered in the lowest-status jobs, where employment tends to be unstable.[10] Young workers, at least temporarily, tend to hold low-status jobs. And each of these groups tends to have a lower earnings profile than that of white middle-aged males.

Blacks with equal education are less likely than whites to have equal occupational attainment; those with equal occupations tend to earn less than whites.[11] This appears to be a pure discrimination effect, for it holds true even when quality of education is considered. And age may make matters worse— older black workers are likely to have wider gaps from whites at the end of their careers than the same workers did at the beginning of their careers.[12]

Old workers—this investigation emphasizes those over the customary retirement age of 65—are subject to discrimination. Investing in their training is uneconomical, and it is difficult to dock their wages if their productivity declines.[13] Social Security, old age assistance, and private pension plans indicate an expectation that older workers will be marginal labor force members and will require income supplements.

A survey of job satisfaction found significantly higher levels of dissatisfaction among the young, the nonwhites, and women.[14] These workers tend to be in the lower-status jobs in which job satisfaction is lower and extrinsic rewards (e.g., remuneration) are most salient.[15] If we regard adequate extrinsic rewards as the minimum requirements for a "good job," then the low morale among the young, nonwhites, and females may be an indicator both of their marginality and their underutilization.

Achievement
The human-capital approach in economics has stressed the importance of academic and on-the-job training for improving human capital. The other side of the coin is "unimproved" human capital. Structural unemployment theorists argue that undereducated persons are marginal to the labor force.[16] Many of the uneducated withdraw from the labor force. Although by definition they cannot be either unemployed or underemployed (see chapter 3), their withdrawal further illustrates their marginality to the labor force. Within the labor force, their marginality is "structural" because there is a lower demand structure for unskilled labor. It is also "structural" in terms of the educational upgrading of the general American labor force. Diplomas and certificates serve employers as relatively costless screening devices, and devices that avoid raw discrimination on ascriptive bases.

Many of the poorly educated will be screened out either by achievement or by ascriptive characteristics, especially blacks, teenagers, and many older workers with obsolete skills or little formal training. Fortunately the data permit cross-classification of ascriptive and achieved characteristics.

Marginal uneducated workers should not be confused with the mismatched. The uneducated workers are marginal, but not necessarily underutilized. Mismatched workers are underutilized, but not necessarily marginal. In terms of my analysis, the uneducated worker is *prima facie* marginal to the society, while the educated worker is very much aligned to the cultural ideal. The mismatched worker may not be marginal, despite possible status discrepancy in his or her present job. On the other hand, the uneducated worker is "protected" from mismatch. This is the only case in which a marginal status eliminates a possible form of underutilization.

Structural Marginality

Marginal jobs are usually unstable or intermittent, relatively unskilled, and low paying. They provide little or no security for the worker. Marginal economic structures are those which are not in the mainstream of economic life because they are obsolete, uncompetitive, or poorly organized. Although there are marginal jobs found in mainstream economic structures, they will be hard to find with the data set used here.

The marginal occupation can best be described by contrast to the preferred occupations: it is not white collar, it is not in professional or technical services, and it does not require high-level skills. In structural unemployment theory, technologically obsolete occupations, including most manual labor, are marginal. In stratification studies, the low-status occupations (usually unskilled or service work) are considered marginal. The major occupational groups incorporate this hierarchy, so the lower blue-collar classifications are a rough approximation to the marginal occupations (e. g., labor except farm, and private household workers). But some low-status jobs are stable; many are well paying. So occupational prestige is not a proxy for marginality. Indeed, some relatively prestigious jobs involve a high degree of financial risk, and to that extent are prone to instability.[17] Adam Smith conjectured that there would be chronic underemployment in the "glamour" occupations, where some individuals have high visibility and remuneration, because entrants would overestimate their chances for success.[18]

Professional athletes and creative and performing artists may be such occupations. These occupations are not marginal to the economy, but a high percentage of their members are marginal *to the occupation*. Unfortunately, in this study the only empirical measure of this kind of marginality would be underutilization, and that resurrects the circular argument I have been trying to avoid.

The marginal firm is the one most vulnerable to the market. Robert Averitt describes it as a "periphery firm":

> The periphery firm is relatively small. It is not integrated vertically, and it may be an economic satellite of a center firm or cluster of center firms.

Periphery firms are less geographically dispersed, both nationally and internationally. Typically they produce only a small line of related products . . . (they) usually inhabit relatively unconcentrated markets.[19]

By contrast, large and profitable firms have steady jobs that are highly skilled and well paid, and where some form of tenure or job protection is customary.[20]

It is not possible to determine from census data the size or success of a given firm, but it does appear that "class of worker" is one proxy variable. Unpaid and self-employed workers are most likely to be in an unprotected, vulnerable peripheral firm. City, state, and federal employees, although in "not-for-profit" firms, are working for large, stable concerns and often have job protection through civil service. "Private wage and salary" workers are a more heterogeneous group. Even here, though, those in farm labor and domestic services are most likely to be independent contractors and, therefore, somewhat insecure. At the time the census data were collected, these workers were not covered by minimum wage and farm woikers were not included in labor legislation. These are rough-and-ready measures, but they surpass the analyses in the literature that are either descriptive, ideal-type analyses or ethnographic studies.

Organization and technology are the keys to identifying marginal industries. Not all agriculture is marginal, but the family farm is more likely to be marginal than the corporate ranch. Within the industrial sector, seven major industry groups account for most low wages: textile mills, apparel, lumber and wood products, furniture and fixtures, rubber and miscellaneous plastic products, leather and leather products, and miscellaneous manufacturing. Low productivity, low-skilled work, and highly competitive market positions seem to make these industries marginal.[21] Within the service sector, labor-intensive industry groups are more likely to be marginal than capital-intensive ones. However, although the idea of a marginal industry is fairly easy to understand, empirical determination from census data is difficult and the analysis will be limited.

Empirical Support

Although systematic, national-level studies about underutilization are only now gaining attention, there is a sociological tradition of case studies of underutilized workers and of marginal workers. Booth and the Webbs did such studies in England; the Chicago school of sociology did studies of occupations and marginal groups in the United States.

It makes sense to ask whether, in overview, the marginal categories just developed could account for the persons included in recent case materials on "marginality" and underutilization. The Negro men in *Tally's Corner* would be included on ascriptive and achievement bases. The white marginal workers studied by Padfield and Williams for the National Alliance of Businessmen would be included under the achievement and economic structure criteria. A few former convicts could be included under the "behavioral disability" grouping. (There was no way to control for behavioral disabilities in this study.) The work-incentive trainees studied by Leonard Goodwin would have been included. The program itself was designed to upgrade their work skills, but both the trainees and their young sons were already marginal on ascriptive bases.[22]

Dual-Market Theory and Marginality

Dual-market theory and the present marginality approach coincide on several points, but they differ sufficiently to deserve a brief comparison. Dual-market theory, which is only superficially similar to the dual-economy theory in development economics, is concerned primarily with the American economy. It postulates two distinct labor markets, one with stable jobs and the other with unstable jobs. Underutilization is found in the secondary, unstable market. Intersectoral allocation relegates minority groups, the elderly, teens, and women to the secondary market, where behavioral factors reinforce the allocation.[23] The analytic distinction between marginality and underutilization is implied but not cast into bold relief as it is in this study. Further, the marginality analysis presented here is more general and more parsimonious in several ways.

First, the marginality approach does not require, as dual-market theory does, the existence of separate and discontinuous labor markets. Dual-labor-market theory has been generalized from studies of ghetto labor markets, some of which were conducted by economists who have also designed indices of underutilization.[24] They found job structure and job behavior in the ghetto quite different from the rest of the city. Although ghetto residents might be excluded from many desirable jobs, a single stratified labor force might explain their marginality as well as a theory of noncompeting or separate markets. The marginality concept is consistent with a single labor market or two labor markets, but the former is more parsimonious.

Second, a marginality approach does not require behavioral mechanisms to explain the stratification. The dual-labor-market theory implies that behavioral patterns are widening the split between the two markets. Gordon notes the heavy emphasis "placed on the historical importance of changing individual attitudes as a primary source of the dualism."[25] Employers are thought to employ "statistical discrimination" to minimize the costs of employment screening. Primary workers are thought to organize to protect their own jobs and exclude others, while the secondary labor market is expected to reinforce secondary workers' habits of work instability and apathy. The marginality approach does not deny attitudinal factors but seeks to establish a relationship without resort to them.

Third, marginality is a more general term that can be applied in countries where the peculiar historical and social effects of the United States do not apply. Sociologically speaking, marginality may be identified in any society, but the bases for it are likely to differ. In the United States, race is an important form of marginality. In other countries, religion, caste, or clan may be more important. To test whether the marginal workers are the ones underutilized, it is necessary to separate the concepts of marginality and utilization.

Both approaches admit the possibility that there are both marginal workers and marginal jobs. Those elements are separated for analysis in this study; dual-labor-market analysts have not clearly distinguished the elements. As Gordon summarizes: "In some instances, analysts suggest that the division corresponds only to differences in job characteristics and that the intersectoral distribution of individuals in various groups—like race and sex groups—does not provide a very accurate picture. . . . In contrast, others seem to equate the dual market structure with occupational segregation by demographic characteristics."[26] A comparison of "findings" between the two approaches is not really possible until such ambiguities are resolved.

Ascriptive characteristics are usually treated one at a time. Some studies have shown that nonwhite teenagers and women are relatively "more marginal" than their white counterparts. I have not seen a previous attempt to test the possible cumulative effects of marginal statuses (see the section "Hypotheses" below). This seems to be important in adequately assessing the labor chances of marginal workers.

The approach taken here to marginal jobs is also somewhat different from that of dual-market theory. As mentioned above, marginal workers are separate from marginal jobs, although a high degree of correspondence between the two is expected. Second, no historical or dialectical process, deliberate or not, is postulated. A radical economist explains structural marginality in this way: "It becomes increasingly likely that employers will seek to balkanize the labor market, creating highly stratified clusters of jobs quite distinctly separated from each other."[27] A somewhat different explanation uses commitment to the labor force as its principal variable; in dual-market and radical theories, lower commitment becomes both a cause and effect of channeling into marginal economic structures. The question asked here is more modest: is structural marginality related to underutilization?

Some Omitted Marginal Conditions

A review of the literature reveals several possible categories omitted from the definition of marginality.

GEOGRAPHIC LOCATION

Should inner-city ghetto residence be used as one component of marginality? Willard Wirtz and others limited their analyses to ghetto areas (see chapter 3), and much of the dual-labor-market theory was generalized from studies of

Harlem and ghetto areas of Boston, Chicago, and Detroit.[28] This component was not used for several reasons. First, to use ghetto residence alone ignores widespread economic disadvantage in nonmetropolitan areas, especially the South.[29] A geographic component should be more broadly based. Second, the components already identified probably include most ghetto labor force members. Certainly the groups Herbert Gans called the "downwardly mobile" and "the trapped" are included. The nonmigrant from a depressed area is also included, at least in theory. Net private underutilization uses persons as the unit of analysis, so a better approach to get geographical detail is to cross-tabulate the data by geographic location.

LABOR FORCE COMMITMENT

Limited commitment to the labor force has been omitted from the definition of marginality for several reasons. First, it would be asymmetrical to measure commitment in marginality but not in net private underutilization. The volitional aspect of commitment confuses the interpretation of the data. Second, if the hypothesized reasons for including commitment are true, then the commitment component is redundant. Theorists who use labor force commitment as an explanatory variable make it part of a causal circle.[30] Being in a marginal group reduces commitment, and lower commitment makes the group more marginal. If this cycle exists, then we already have a proxy measure in marginality components. Any further measure of commitment would be redundant.

HOUSEHOLD POSITION

So-called "secondary workers," meaning married women and household dependents, are considered "marginal" workers by some analysts. In most cases, this argument collapses into the labor force commitment argument, *supra.* Discrimination against non–household heads has been alleged,[31] but there is little evidence that this is a problem beyond discrimination based on age and sex.

MIGRATION

Migration is a neglected component of the human-capital approach, perhaps because it is somewhat misleading to think of migration as "improving" human capital. Human capital, unlike physical capital, is mobile, and migration may bring the available human capital into closer proximity to complementary factors of production. In terms of our framework, migration could be related to two sorts of marginality: the migrant who moves apart from a recognized career line, and the resident of a depressed area who refuses to move.

Immigrants are often unfamiliar with their new territories and their rate of acculturation depends on local language or customs. These are persons who are likely to be marginal to the society and to the labor force.[32] This applies both to international and interregional migrants who move apart from career lines. If a corporation transfers an executive between cities, he is a migrant in the career line and not marginal to the labor force, although he may be socially marginal for a while. His dependents, however, are not moving within their career lines, and they become marginal. There is evidence, for example, that although migration may improve social mobility for males, it seems to lower labor force participation by married women. It seems likely that married women migrants who participate in the labor force might also be more marginal.[33]

The argument of migrant marginality is important because it runs counter to an older argument that migration was always equilibrating supply and demand. Unfortunately the data do not permit a full test of migrant marginality as the case is laid out here.

The nonmigrant can be discussed analytically but not empirically, for he is impossible to identify as marginal. In terms of economic maximization the nonmigrant is one whose geographic mobility would improve his economic position. Chances are good that this person is well integrated socially and not at all marginal in that sense to his community. Inferences based on the nonmigrant's residence are too simplistic and ignore the personal ties, racial discrimination, and so forth, that are deterrents to migration.

Hypotheses

The general question studied here is the relationship of marginality to underutilization. Each of the four components is sufficient, and so one set of hypotheses relates each component, in turn, to underutilization.

I. The idiosyncrasy hypothesis: if one is disabled, then one is more likely to be underutilized

II. The discrimination hypotheses:

    A. If one is very young or over 65, one is more likely to be underutilized

    B. Nonwhites are more likely to be underutilized than whites

    C. Women are more likely to be underutilized than men

III. The achievement hypothesis: less-educated workers are more likely than educated workers to be underutilized

IV. The structural hypothesis: workers in marginal occupations, firms, and industries are more likely to be underutilized than those in other economic activities

In addition, some marginality components have subcomponents that may be internally related. In the discrimination hypotheses, subcomponents of marginality may interact. In particular, the literature seems to indicate that Negro teenagers are in a very marginal position.[34] So an additional subhypothesis is added:

IID. Persons who are marginal on more than one component are more likely to be underutilized. The attempt to identify interactions represents a significant extension over the descriptive tradition in manpower studies.

Concluding Comments

The brief exposition of dual-market theory showed the extent to which ideas of marginality and underutilization are knotted together. This chapter began unraveling the strands for logical and analytic clarity in assessing composition.

Composition of the underutilized is so important, both to policy planners and to social scientists, that it was singled out in chapter 1 as characteristic of a general approach to underutilization. This chapter contains four hypotheses about the composition of the underutilized in the United States. The physically disabled, women, racial minorities, and the young and the old are defined as marginal workers. They are exposed to the highest risk of underutilization. Marginal jobs are defined as those that are unstable, intermittent, or in other ways outside the economic mainstream. Persons who hold these jobs, even if they do not share the personal characteristics of marginal workers, are expected to be underutilized.

This chapter has laid out the independent variables for the study. The next chapter will discuss the dependent variable, underutilization, and ways to measure it.

CHAPTER 3

How Do You Measure Underutilization?

The unemployment rate has spawned as much controversy as the intelligence quotient, and objections to the measurement instrument are still raised, even though unemployment data have been collected in the United States for nearly forty years.[1] Any underutilization index is equally controversial, and for the same reason: slippage between a pure concept and its operational definition is inevitable. We can grasp the abstract meaning of unemployment, intelligence, or underutilization, but it is much more difficult to ensure that the measures accurately reflect the abstraction. It would be astonishing if the first generation of underutilization measures did not evoke serious objections.

For this study, a compelling objection to a specific measure would be its incompatibility with the general approach outlined in chapter 1. That is, any measure is deficient if it precludes either aggregative summary or compositional detail, or if it does not identify forms of underutilization. Three measures reviewed in this chapter are deficient in one or more ways: the disguised unemployment measure, the surplus labor measure, and observational measures. A few miscellaneous measures that do not fall into these categories are also examined.

Demographic measures, broadly conceived, seem to be compatible with the approach to underutilization outlined earlier. Among the demographic measures, however, the gainful worker and labor force techniques by themselves are unsatisfactory. Eight indices loosely based on the labor force approach are more promising measures. These measures differ from one another in their target populations, their constituent components, and their generalizability. The Labor Utilization Framework is flexible and analytic, and it will be used in succeeding chapters.

The approach chosen here, because it is interested principally in the incidence and distribution of symptoms of underutilization through population subgroups, is quite different from techniques designed to study the *causes* of underemployment. The data collected with this technique may be useful in inferring causes of underemployment.[2] The Labor Utilization Framework, however, is not intended to be an all-purpose instrument. It cannot be used, for example, to measure rates of return to education. (Over time, mismatch rates may give an approximate return in terms of *occupational achievement*.) Thus, the appropriateness of the measure for testing all economic theories was not a criterion for selection. Economists, for example, may still find it useful to pursue studies of marginal productivity as a means to defining underemployment.

Disguised Unemployment and Marginal Productivity

The research that has been conducted on "disguised unemployment" bears little relationship to the phenomenon for which Joan Robinson coined the term—the temporary adoption of inferior jobs. In development economics, "disguised unemployment" is reserved to describe a situation in which the marginal productivity of some labor in the noncapitalist sector is negligible or zero. That is, it refers to redundant labor that could be removed with no reduction in output. (Some authors relax their *ceteris paribus* assumptions to allow the routine reorganization of work; most do not permit the introduction of new techniques.) Theoretically, the development economists are referring to labor available for higher-productivity employment. In practice, the disguised unemployment approach has been used neither in advanced countries nor in manufacturing and services in developing countries. Overwhelmingly, its empirical applications have been limited to traditional agriculture.[3]

A marginal productivity approach differs fundamentally from a utilization approach.[4] A utilization approach focuses on the *inadequacy* of household-economy interchanges, presumably with reference to some societal standard. Net private underutilization is inadequacy from the worker's viewpoint. A marginal productivity approach assumes that a worker is paid what he is worth to the employer, but the adequacy of employment is not at issue. Even if the worker's wage is very low, it carries no implication of "underutilization"; by definition the worker is being utilized in line with the service he provides the economy. What might be "underutilization" is viewed only from the employer's view. If, for example, union contracts force him to hire and pay additional workers more than their worth to him, they would be underutilized. The marginal productivity concept seems to be incompatible with the concept of net private underutilization. Nor is it compatible with social underutilization, because that concept contains worker "ill fare" as one component.

Development economists emphasized that low marginal productivity in agriculture was *not* mere name-calling, a label for worker inefficiency or incompetence (although the literature sometimes implied that it was). Instead, they argued that the very same worker would be more productive in a different sector. The emphasis on sectoral transfer to achieve higher productivity was elegantly formulated by Eckaus and Leibenstein, among others.[5]

For our purposes, the disguised unemployment approach provides too little detail about underemployed workers to be a useful measure. It can provide data on magnitude, but not composition. Economists have criticized it for its empirical vagueness and its theoretical shortcomings. The disguised unemployment theory is difficult to test and its methodology has caused a good bit of controversy. Only one article reports a negative marginal product.[6] All other estimates were positive.[7]

In fact, there are data refuting the theory. Schultz[8] used data from the 1916–17 and 1919–20 influenza epidemics in India to show that there had been no disguised unemployment, and indeed, whenever "surplus" labor is removed, total output is likely to fall. "Target production," or the balancing of labor and output, is a term used by economic anthropologists to explain the fall in total output.[9] Target production is an example of economic rationality among peasants. (To phrase it differently, it would be irrational for them to work for nothing, a point made by Cho and Myrdal.)[10] Although the target production phenomenon does not invalidate disguised unemployment theory, it does complicate empirical tests of marginal productivity.

Presumably wages would provide a better variable for theory testing than total output. Yet even where agricultural wage markets have been studied, the market wage exceeds that hypothesized in the marginal productivity literature. The principal explanation for the excessive wage is patron-client dependency exchanges, where the commodities exchanged are the employer's prestige and the worker's motivation.[11] If there are dependency exchanges, then an empirical validation of the theory is not possible, but neither is a refutation.

However, even if all the difficulties of empirical verification were surmountable, the theoretical attacks have probably been more damaging. One attack argues that the surplus is nonremovable, either because family ties prevent its removal, or because the total underemployment is fractionated among several workers (each of whom is otherwise critical), or because disguised unemployment is seasonal.[12] Related to this is the notion that the family surplus worker would not remove himself if he could, because on the family farm he receives the *average* product of labor regardless of his *marginal* product.[13]

A second line of attack questions the very notion of surplus. Viner argues that agriculture can always be made more labor intensive, and recent studies tend to document the absorptive capacities of agriculture.[14] A second way of arguing that there is no surplus is to examine the urban wage rate. Surplus labor must have a zero opportunity cost, and this is incompatible with the relatively high urban wage rate. (This attack is weak, however, because it ignores income efficiency.)[15]

The third attack on the disguised unemployment theory emphasizes labor efficiency. In the gloomiest variant of this attack, Mellor and Stevens suggest that even the average product, let alone the marginal product, may be insufficient for subsistence.[16] To put it differently, a population might starve to death even at full employment. This is the most dramatic juxtaposition of the marginal productivity and net private underutilization approaches, for it shows the weak relationship between worker welfare and marginal productivity.

In Myrdal's variant of the efficiency argument, he argues that most disguised unemployment treatments leave out the qualitative dimensions of labor.[17] He traces the preoccupation with the labor quantity to the survival of the colonizers' belief in a backward-sloping supply curve. Today's situation in most developing countries is quite the opposite: industrial and urban job sites are flooded with applicants.[18] The lengthy employment queues signal us that sheer quantity of labor is no longer the overriding issue, but they also remind us that there are few places left to which one can "remove" redundant labor.

These other criticisms aside, the disguised unemployment measure gives insufficient detail for this study. A crude magnitude is often given in disguised unemployment studies, but it is difficult to identify those workers with low marginal products or those who are removable. As for the forms of underemployment, one occasionally finds a partition of disguised unemployment. The parts identified are usually attributed to the hypothesized economic causes of disguised unemployment.[19] For example, some disguised unemployment may be due to low productivity. A taxonomy based on *causes*, rather than symptoms, is difficult to operationalize because of the multiple-concept slippage that occurs. In the example, "low productivity" could be defined in terms of human capital, physical capital, and input ratios, each of which would require its own empirical indicators. Testing the hypothesis is impossible when the taxonomy itself is based on hypothesized causes. By contrast, a symptom (e.g., "low income") permits classification and identifies a target group for further research into causes. For these reasons, the disguised unemployment measure is insufficient.

Surplus Labor Measure

The surplus labor approach is more empirically based but less theoretically informed than the disguised unemployment approach. The surplus labor approach requires a work standard to be established for a given project, geographical area, and so forth. For example, one might set as a standard that no more than ten man-hours be required to harvest a hectare. The units of analysis may be the number of laborers, man-days, or man-hours. Any labor supplied over and above the standard is surplus labor.

There are two variants of the surplus labor approach, depending on how one establishes the standard. The so-called static variant uses labor productivity levels that might "reasonably" be expected in local circumstances.[20] The "dynamic" standard is set using *projected* or *desired* levels of productivity that often incorporate projected technical improvements. With either approach, the quantity of surplus labor is given by (Labor Supply–Labor Standard) = Labor Surplus.[21]

Both variants suffer from theoretical and technical ambiguities. First, who is the labor supply? Most surplus labor studies use the Malthus-Ricardo assumption of universal, homogeneous, adult labor. Sometimes women's labor is excluded. Either assumption is unrealistic, for even granting that the supply of adult male labor may be relatively invariant, wages and working conditions probably affect the number of women, youths, and elderly workers who supply labor. It seems especially ironic that the "dynamic" labor assumption ignores the dynamic aspects of labor supply.

The second ambiguity lies in determining the amount of labor currently supplied. Unless the job for which the labor standard has been set is defined with precision, records of labor supply will be inaccurate. For example, suppose the standard were defined as "n workers to harvest this year's sugar cane." May they do other chores? Defining one task as "work" overlooks a great many other activities, including economically productive activities and activities that are ethnodefined as "work." Even ignoring tendentious error and faulty memory, defining what is "work" is problematic.

The third ambiguity lies in setting the "labor requirements." It is a haphazard procedure with countless possible assumptions about technical improvements, nutritional adequacy, skill levels, and so forth, and so the results are neither comparable nor cumulative. Presumably the "labor requirement" includes only productive, adequately utilized labor. Thus Turnham praises the labor surplus approach for attempting "to allow for disguised unemployment, i.e., where part of the time spent at work, or some part of the employed labor force, is effectively non-productive."[22] This is a back-door approach to measuring disguised unemployment: the difference between all labor supplied and the productive labor needed must be disguised unemployment. Unfortunately, the approach is built upon so many ambiguities as to make the estimate unreliable.

The labor surplus approach does yield a magnitude, albeit an imprecise one and one that assumes a future reality. More importantly, it cannot be disaggregated or analyzed by component. Smith writes: "[The surplus labor concept does not] yield a breakdown by 'symptomatic' category for although at the national level it conceptually embraces unemployment, it cannot distinguish and measure separately these various elements. And what may be especially significant for purposes of policy prescription, it is incapable of distinguishing the different kinds and conditions—sex, age, location, etc.—of the individuals who experience these forms of labour underutilization."[23]

Observational Approaches

The least theoretical and most empirical of the approaches discussed so far are the "observational techniques," included here with anthropological approaches. In many cases an observational approach is deliberately atheoretical, designed to give the observer a subjective sense of inadequate employment in the texture of village life. The strength of the observation study is its fidelity to reality. For example, an observational study of farm families in Egypt, despite methodological shortcomings, provided data about the seasonal rhythm of agriculture—useful data for supplying alternative employment in the off-season.[24] Clearly defined "occupations" may not exist. Instead, peasant farmers eke out a living through a variety of barely profitable activities that can be described in ethnographies.[25] Observation provides useful input to policy planners because it is a reminder of local idiosyncrasies.

Although observation studies are useful adjuncts to underutilization measurement, they are not an acceptable substitute. Observation studies may clarify the meaning of work, suggest proxies for some variables, or provide peasant time budgets, but such studies cannot provide generalized data about the magnitude, composition, and forms of underutilization.

Most anthropological studies of labor underutilization have a strong "debunking" theme. They continue the substantivist-formalist debate in economic anthropology. Many of these studies challenge the disguised unemployment concept and the assumptions upon which it is based. The anthropological approach could be converted into a challenge to national labor statistics, but the criticism is rarely spelled out.

Demographic Approaches

"Demographic measure" refers to a labor statistic based upon census or survey data using the individual or household as the analytic unit. Various demographic approaches measure gainful workers, the labor force, and subemployment. There are also a few survey-based, experimental demographic measures.

Demographic measures are the most compatible with the general approach to utilization outlined in chapter 1. They are relatively easy to aggregate and disaggregate because they use individuals or households as units of analysis. The measures discussed below differ primarily in their ability to distinguish forms of underutilization.

GAINFUL WORKERS

From 1870 to 1930, census enumerators asked each respondent ten years of age or older if he or she "usually" pursued a gainful occupation for money or goods, or if the respondent assisted in producing marketable goods and services. Persons answering "yes" were classified as gainful workers. Although this procedure measured changes in the occupational skills mix and industrial composition, it provided no measure of current occupational behavior because workers reported their "usual" (not present) occupation, or if retired, their previous occupation. Such a question taps status rather than activity. Because there was no information about actual employment, there could be no measure of current unemployment. Entrants with no occupation were the only persons usually counted as "unemployed."[26] Very little data were provided about inadequate utilization. Gainful worker analysis is no longer recommended by the United Nations although data are still collected about current (not "usual") occupations.

THE LABOR FORCE

The labor force measure was introduced into the United States near the end of the 1930's. It differs fundamentally from gainful worker measures by using a behavioral referent with a time referent. The significant question is, "What were you doing last week (or during another reference period)?" A status criterion supplements the activity criterion for defining the "employed" and "unemployed."

The abstract "labor force" is defined as that portion of the population who are economically productive, and it is defined through a series of nested dichotomies of the population at risk. The currently defined population at risk for the United States labor force is all noninstitutionalized adults aged 16 and over. Children and inmates of jails, hospitals, and other institutions are automatically outside the labor force. The remaining "not in the labor force" (NILF) adults are the residual of the classification procedure.

Labor force members are either employed or unemployed during the reference period. "Employed" persons work at least one hour for pay or profit or fifteen hours in unpaid work. Persons with a job but not at work are "employed" under the status criterion. If one is not employed but actively seeking work, or awaiting the result of a job search, or waiting to report to a job within 30 days, then one is unemployed. Persons neither employed nor unemployed are not in the labor force. This approach gives a "snapshot" of actual economic activity for a specific time period.

The labor force is used in descriptive demographic statistics such as the labor force participation rate, the ratio of the labor force to the population at risk. The crude activity rate is the ratio of the labor force to the total population. Eliminating children below working age from the denominator converts the crude activity rate into the labor force participation rate. Age-specific participation rates are used to construct tables of economically active life. The unemployment rate is the percentage of unemployed persons in the labor force at a given time; the employment rate is its complement. One dependency ratio may be computed by dividing the number not in the labor force by the labor force.

Problems in the Labor Force Approach
The labor force approach does reasonably well what it was designed to do—it measures unemployment. It is not, however, an all-purpose tool. For our purposes, its major flaw is that it identifies only one sort of underutilization. A second criticism is its inappropriateness for developing countries.

The Labor Force. "Labor force" and "economically active population" are criticized as concepts that apply only to countries with a fair amount of economic differentiation.[27] The definition of "productive" work is a particular problem. The labor force is sensitive to age structure and female participation, both in terms of "actual" activity and measured activity. Especially in traditional agriculture, activities of children and women may be "productive" but uncounted because of response error or enumerator bias. A related criticism, more applicable to advanced countries, is linked to attacks on Gross National Product (GNP) measurement. It argues that the work of housewives and volunteer workers is "productive" and should be included in GNP. Therefore, housewives and volunteers should be included in the labor force. Unfortunately, this criticism returns us to equating the adult population with the economically active population.

The present study is designed to measure underutilization in an advanced country, and so the immediate effect of this criticism can be neutralized. It is a more salient criticism for measures of underutilization designed to be useful at every level of development. Nevertheless, the labor force concept is used in most countries of the world, and so a measure based on the labor force would cause minimal disruption to statistical agencies and data users.

The Employed. The most heterogeneous labor force category is the "employed," which includes all employed persons regardless of the quantity or quality of employment. The "unemployed" category is a residual in the sense that only those with no employment at all are eligible to be unemployed. One criticism of the current labor force approach is that the term "employed" is too general and heterogeneous given the limited definition of "unemployed." It is the "employed" category that hides the extent of underemployment. A measure of underemployment based on the labor force approach may remedy this defect in one of two ways. One could redefine "unemployed"—for example, count as unemployed those who looked for work at any time in the reference period. This has the disadvantage of being noncomparable to current statistics. Or, one could treat "employed" as the residual category and further subdivide it. The latter approach is recommended in this study.

Multiple Jobs. United States labor force surveys report hours worked at all jobs, but attribute income and occupation to the principal job. There is a very imperfect relationship between the number of jobs and the number of workers. Although not a very telling criticism of the labor force concept itself, this criticism illustrates its limitations. For example, the number of unemployed workers cannot be routinely interpreted as the number of jobs that must be created. On the other hand, the "employed" worker may make ends meet only by juggling several jobs.

Discouraged Workers. Another criticism of the current labor force approach is that manpower wastage is hidden among "not in the labor force" (NILF) adults. "Not in the labor force" is a heterogeneous category, lumping together housewives, students, and retired and disabled workers as well as discouraged workers. Discouraged workers are no longer in the labor force because they have ceased the active search for work. Some underutilization measures, though not the one recommended in this study, include "passive unemployment" or "discouraged workers" as an element.

Unpaid family workers are a special case of this problem. In some countries, unpaid family workers who do not work enough hours to be counted as "employed" are counted as "unemployed." In the United States, they are "not in the labor force." This is a second possible source of underutilization that can be "hidden" among NILF adults.

Assessment. An analysis of the labor force concept should not neglect its important contributions, but neither should they be overstated. As Herman Miller wrote, "The labor force concept is still extremely useful as an economic indicator but it has serious defects as a social indicator, for which it is often used, because it takes no account of the adequacy of the income from employment."[28] The indices discussed below address this inadequacy as well as several others.

Indices of Subemployment and Underutilization

Eight indices of subemployment or of underutilization have been proposed in the recent literature.[29] The indices differ in purpose and in constituent components, but they are similar in being related (at least loosely) to the labor force approach and in attempting to tap the dimensions of inadequate employment. Each index contains a number of mutually exclusive components or symptoms of underutilization. The components common to all eight are unemployment, involuntary part-time work, and inadequate income. With each index, a target population is identified and classified by a series of operational definitions for the components. A summary figure, "the number subemployed," is the sum of the persons classified in the components.

The first index, called the Wirtz Index here, was constructed to reflect conditions in 10 urban slum areas. The index was a personal project of then-Secretary of Labor Willard Wirtz, and its first results, based on a survey in November, 1966, were transmitted in a confidential memo to President Lyndon B. Johnson.[30] The Wirtz subemployment index ranged from 24.2% in Boston to 47.4% in San Antonio. In Winter, 1967, an urban employment survey task force was started, and by June, 1968, six teams had been fielded to follow up the Wirtz initiative. Despite the interesting data collected—for example, the information that 30% of the not-in-the-labor-force adults in Atlanta and Chicago wanted a job "now"—the field research was abruptly terminated in June, 1970.[31] When a 1972 congressional report reviewed the Wirtz subemployment index for 51 cities, 31% of the workers in urban poverty areas were subemployed.[32]

The second measure, introduced in 1972, was the Spring-Harrison-Vietorisz (SHV) Index, which attempted to "gauge the degree of labor market failure."[33] According to this measure, 60% of inner city residents do not earn enough for a decent level of living. Two additional measures were introduced in 1973. Herman P. Miller's index, using data from the 1970–71 Census Employment Survey, showed 15% to 25% subemployed in the same cities cited in the SHV Index. Miller's index measures those "employed in jobs that do not permit them or their families to live at minimum levels of decency for this society."[34] Levitan and Taggart introduced the Employment and Earnings Inadequacy Index to "measure the number of persons who experience difficulties in competing for gainful employment paying an adequate wage." Their trial data base was the 1972 March Current Population Survey and they found 14.9% sub-employment in the United States.[35]

Three more indices were proposed by Vietorisz, Mier, and Giblin in 1975. The Exclusion Index measures "the extent to which the labor market does not provide the needed number of adequate jobs and thereby precludes opportunities for individuals to engage in steady, productive work." The trial data base was the 1970 Detroit Census Employment Survey sample. At a $2-an-hour wage standard, 50% of the Detroit workers were subemployed.[36]

The Inadequacy Index, proposed by Vietorisz and his colleagues, tries "to delineate critical jobs which could serve to upgrade the social and economic status of entire families."[37] This statement is misleading because primary workers and not jobs are the analytic unit. This index tries to examine the link between the labor market and family poverty. When it was applied to the Detroit Census Employment Survey, 34.7% of household heads (or unrelated individuals) were subemployed at the $2-an-hour wage standard.

Vietorisz, Mier, and Giblin introduce, but do not test, an underutilization index. In speaking of this index, they write:

> In addition to the usual components of subemployment, however, there are two other potential components which require consideration as manpower underutilization measures. One of these is manpower wastage owing to work in jobs below qualifications. . . . Similarly when a job technically requiring only a high school education is made subject to college credentials, wastage also occurs. . . . We have not so far attempted to estimate an underutilization index because our resources precluded the assembling of the necessary data.[38]

Thus no data are available for this index. The only further particulars are an admonition that such an index must be corrected for different degrees of attachment to the labor force by different classes of workers.

While these indices were being elaborated in the United States, an eighth index was proposed by Philip M. Hauser and was tested in Southeast Asia. It is called the Labor Utilization Framework (LUF), and its purpose is to measure net private underutilization (as defined in chapter 1). Preliminary data for the LUF are available from Hong Kong, Indonesia, Malaysia, the Philippines, Singapore, Taiwan, and Thailand. The present study applies the LUF to United States data.[39]

The stated purposes of each of these indices seem similar even if the phrasings differ. The important differences are choice of a target population and how the choice affects the interpretation of the index, the components of the index and how they are operationalized, and the generality of the index. Each area of difference is discussed in some detail below, and then some comments are added about indexing problems.

TARGET POPULATION

The target population, or "population at risk," in United States labor force measurement is the noninstitutionalized population aged 16 and older. Most of the indices reviewed here have substantially different target populations as summarized in table 3.1.

There are two major divergences: the exclusion of some workers from the target population and the inclusion of some nonworkers. One author uses political expedience to justify some arbitrary exclusions. Miller says, "The intent is to demonstrate that even if we restrict the count of the subemployed only to those groups that reasonable people could agree should be included . . . we end up with a much larger number and a much more serious problem than the unemployment figures themselves would suggest."[40]

Slightly different rationales are used by other writers. Levitan-Taggart and Miller exclude students aged 16–21 and persons over 65 from the target population. Some of their reasoning is strained—for example, Levitan and Taggart's remark that a student's "standard and style of living [are] frequently different."[41] Other reasons boil down to: (1) the limited commitment to the labor force and the preference for part-time work assumed to be true of students and the elderly; (2) the possibility of non-work-related income supports, such as parental aid and scholarships for students, and Social Security and pensions for the elderly.

Levitan-Taggart and Miller also exclude workers living in households with above-average income, and in common with the Inadequacy Index they exclude secondary workers. The target populations for Wirtz and SHV indices are even more confusing because they exclude certain age and status groups from some types of subemployment but not from others. The Wirtz Index excludes females from one component. Only the LUF uses the entire labor force as its target population.

The exclusions from the labor force as population at risk involve several disadvantages. The advantages of the exclusions are better obtained through other procedures. Consider the following points.

Disadvantages of Exclusions
The proposed indices are crude measures because the population at risk in the numerator is smaller than that in the denominator. (There are two exceptions: the Inadequacy Index uses as its denominator household heads and unrelated individuals who are in the labor force or who are discouraged workers. The LUF uses the labor force as its population at risk in both the numerator and denominator.) Except for the LUF and the Inadequacy Index, the indices exclude some persons from the numerator but not from the denominator. As proposed, the faulty denominators will cause an understatement of the extent of subemployment. If the denominators were refined, the resulting statistics would be even harder to interpret vis-à-vis current statistics.

Second, altering the target population is an improper adjustment for labor

Table 3.1. *Detailed comparison of target populations (population at risk) in eight*

Conditions for inclusion	Hauser Labor Utilization Framework (1972)	Wirtz Subemployment Index (1966)	Potentially Spring-Harrison-Vietorisz Index (1972)
1. Aged 16 and over (14 and over in 1960)	+	+/−	+
2. If aged 16–21, not a student	−	−	−
3. Not over 64	−	+/−	+/−
4. Head of a household or unrelated individual	−	+/−	−
5. Not a resident of a household with an above-average family income in the previous year	−	−	−
6. In the labor force	+	+/−	+/−
7. Time referent= previous week	+/−	+/−	+/−
Data available for:	U.S., 1960 & 1970; Hong Kong, Philippines, Thailand, Taiwan, Malaysia, Indonesia, Singapore	10 ghetto areas	Inner city poverty areas

Note: + applies to all components of the index; +/− applies to some components

inderutilization indices

iderutilized workers must meet these criteria

Levitan-Taggart Index (1973)	Miller Index (1973)	Exclusion Index (1975)	Inadequacy Index (1975)	Vietorisz Under-utilization Index
+	+	+	+	+
+	+	−	−	?
+	+	−	−	?
−	+/−	−	+	?
+	+	−	−	?
+/−	+/−	+/−	+/−	+/−
+/−	+/−	+/−	+/−	+/−
United States, 1968–1972	Inner city poverty areas	Detroit census survey	Detroit census survey	Not available

of the index; − applies to no components of the index; and ? is uncertain.

force attachment. The a priori exclusion is unjustified by any theory or concept. Presumably, some workers are excluded because they are believed to be less committed to the labor force. But labor marginality, labor force attachment, and labor underutilization are logically distinct notions, and their linkages must be established empirically. Altering the target population prevents any test of the overlap between labor marginality and labor underutilization—a major aim of this study. Worse, inferring present-day labor force attachment from previous records of inadequate employment smacks of "blaming the victim." What passes for today's limited commitment may be the result of yesterday's discrimination. Under such schemes, underemployment measures might exclude major groups already suffering underemployment.

This issue of labor force attachment is never clearly confronted in the literature. A worker is said to be less committed to the labor force if, for example, he wants to work only part-time. Both the worker who wants full-time work and the worker who wants thirty hours work are underutilized if only twenty hours work are available to them. Some critics have argued that any subemployment index must distinguish the two cases. Vietorisz et al. define an underutilization index as one which makes this distinction. The criticism fails to distinguish net private underutilization from social underutilization. For net private underutilization it is only necessary to know how many of the labor force are underutilized, who they are, and in what underutilization category they fall. Knowing that two persons are involuntary part-time workers is sufficient. Thus measures of net private underutilization are self-weighting. Social underutilization is the measure of loss to society, and for this measure one must know how many hours of work were lost—in this case, thirty hours. Social underutilization measures probably should be weighted.

But even if one is quantifying social underutilization, adjusting the target population is unjustified and unnecessary. It is unjustified because even though some elderly workers want part-time work, others want full-time work. Some 16–21-year-old students want summer jobs, but some work year-round. Some secondary workers earn only pin money, but some are indispensable to their family's income. It is unnecessary because a better adjustment is already made in United States statistics, which classify unemployed and part-time workers by the amount of work they are seeking. This, and not a limited target population, is the way to approach labor force attachment, and it does so without confounding labor marginality with labor underutilization.

Third, altering the target population obscures the postulated interpretations of the proposed indices. The selection of a target population implies an analytic unit. Levitan and Taggart's aim was to "measure the number of *persons*," but they limit some components by *household* income or *household* position. In the same way, the Miller Index mixes family and individual considerations. The Inadequacy Index proposes to "delineate critical jobs," and the Exclusion Index purports to measure "the needed number of adequate jobs," but household heads are the analytic unit for the former and individual workers for the latter. Neither index handles multiple job holding, so their generalizations about *job* adequacy are questionable.

Fourth, even the political expedience of altering the target population is dubious. Governments may be wary of measures which show "too much" underutilization, but there are several ways to keep the results believable without sacrificing conceptual clarity. The first is to alter the "standard of adequacy" on each component. Minimum income figures can be adjusted, or a range of measures, each using a different cutoff, can be presented. The second is to adjust properly for labor force attachment—for example, to report separate statistics for the full-time labor force and the (voluntarily) part-time labor force. The worst way is to manipulate the target population, for this does violence to the very notion of net private underutilization. It establishes a caste system that implies that the underutilization of some workers is more grave than that of others. As I have noted above, no theoretical justification for this caste system has been made. Finally, an index that is noncomparable to the current statistics arouses suspicion and complicates interpretation.

THE LABOR FORCE AS TARGET POPULATION

To return to the Labor Utilization Framework, it offers the advantages claimed by the other indices without incurring the disadvantages. It is a refined measure because the denominator—the labor force—is also the "population at risk" in the numerator. (Like the unemployment rate, it is not a true rate because of the time referent, which is discussed below.) It is amenable to proper adjustments for labor force attachment. It permits interpretation for individuals, but the individual data can also be aggregated into household data. Separate tabulations are easily made for household heads, nonstudents, and persons over 65, if there are sound reasons to do so. Finally, the LUF is politically acceptable because it permits easy comparison with current measures.

The further advantage of the LUF in an advanced country is that its comparability with labor force measures makes it highly sensitive to cyclical fluctuations. Further, time-series data for the LUF are possible. The only adjustment necessary in the United States is to lower the minimum age to 14 for dates prior to 1966.

DISCOURAGED WORKERS

Every index except the LUF includes a measure of discouraged workers. Discouraged workers are those who would be listed as unemployed, but they have given up the active search for work. By the behavioral criterion for inclusion, they are no longer participants in the labor force. A measurement of discouraged workers must mingle attitudinal criteria with the more objective behavioral and status criteria used in the other underutilization components. There is a wide range of operational definitions.[42] The Wirtz Index counts one-half of the male nonparticipants aged 20–64 as discouraged workers. The exclusion and inadequacy indices count those who "desire work," and the Miller Index counts those who "are not looking because they believe no work is available." The SHV Index counts those who give "inability to find work" as the primary or secondary reason for not seeking work. Finally, the Levitan-Taggart Index includes those who desire work but are not looking due to either job market or personal reasons. All except the Miller Index, then, add the discouraged workers into the denominator.

The LUF excludes discouraged workers. This does not deny that their problem is an objective one of manpower wastage.[43] But conceptual clarity requires that underutilization not be an umbrella concept incorporating all ills. In advanced countries, where the "labor force" is a meaningful construct, it is sensible to consider separating underutilization—that is, unemployment and underemployment—within the labor force from other labor problems in the adult population. Probably the best way to handle the problem is to present summary discouraged worker data alongside underutilization data but without adding discouraged workers into the index.

COMPONENTS

Each index includes measures of unemployment, involuntary part-time work, and low income. The operationalization and the mutual exclusivity of the components differ from index to index, but there is substantial conceptual agreement on these components. Only the LUF includes the mismatch of occupation and skills, and only the LUF excludes discouraged workers as a component. The Wirtz Index is unique in including a component for census undercount.

Every index includes the unemployed, using the official definition, although restrictions on target population affect the number of unemployed in the Levitan-Taggart, Miller, and Inadequacy indices. Unemployment data are presently published every month.

Another datum that has been published since 1962 is the reason for part-time work. Involuntary part-time workers are those who work part-time for economic (not personal) reasons—for example, because of partial layoffs or supply bottlenecks (see appendix B for a full explanation). Every proposed index defines the involuntary part-time worker as one working fewer than 35 hours a week for economic reasons. The Exclusion and Inadequacy indices also include persons working fewer than 50 weeks a year for economic reasons. This counts underutilized seasonal workers, but it does so by distorting the reference period. Seasonal adjustment is an alternative way of identifying seasonal workers without relying on retrospective data. Levitan and Taggart have two involuntary part-time work components based on household position: "(1) currently employed household heads earning less than a poverty income *because of intermittent employment*, less than full-time work, *and/or low wages*, and (2) . . . part-time workers in the survey week, not included in the previous category, who want full-time jobs but cannot find them, were laid off during the survey week, or have some other economic impediment requiring part-time employment" (emphasis and numerals added).[44] The emphasized portions are not operationalized because Levitan and Taggart use "less than 35 hours of work for economic reasons" as their classificatory variable.

Underemployment by low wages is the component with the greatest operational variations. For every index except the Levitan-Taggart, low earners must be full-time workers, so the measure is one of the "working poor." The principal variations lie in the standard used and the adjustment made for family size. The Wirtz, Levitan-Taggart, and Miller indices limit the target group for this component to household heads or unrelated individuals.

One standard is the Social Security Administration poverty index, described in appendix C, which incorporates adjustments for age and sex of household head, urban-rural residence, and family size. The LUF Index uses the family's poverty as its standard for primary earners and an individual poverty level for secondary workers. The Levitan-Taggart measure uses the poverty level for household heads, but its target population excludes those workers in families earning more than the average family income.

Two indices use alternative standards. The SHV Index uses either the Bureau of Labor Statistics "lower level" annual budget for a family of four or $4,000 a year (for 1972). The latter figure corresponds to the then-proposed minimum wage level of $2 an hour. The Miller Index uses family heads or unrelated individuals working full-time for less than the minimum wage *or* those working full-time for less than the poverty level adjusted for family size. It is not clear from the literature when one alternative is preferable to another. (Miller also introduces an alternative target population for this component, without saying when this alternative should be used. This population excludes all persons living in families with higher than average incomes for the metropolitan areas in which they reside.)

Finally, the Exclusion and Inadequacy indices use a parametric definition of low income. They permit the analyst to choose an "appropriate" level from a range of cutoffs. This is a flexible standard, but it has the disadvantage of precluding a simple summary figure. Further, it facilitates choosing the magnitude of subemployment in advance and then announcing the corresponding cutoff point. An a priori income standard is preferable. The Inadequacy Index would adjust the parametric standard for family size; the Exclusion Index would not.

Census Undercount
The Wirtz Index contains a census component described as "conservative and carefully considered." It was computed by estimating the number of missed males and assuming that one-half this number are subemployed. The Wirtz Index is limited to slum areas, which are believed to have the worst undercount problem. The Miller and SHV indices are similarly limited but do not correct for undercount.

Although a general "error term" is a useful precaution with all census or survey data, quantifying subemployment within a "missing population" is guesswork. Once LUF data are collected, it would be possible to state how many, say, 20–24-year-old Negro men were underutilized, and this would permit an estimate of the underutilization occurring among those not counted. To build the estimate into the index removes the usefulness of the index for estimating.

Mismatch

Only the LUF contains a mismatch component, although several authors, as noted, allude to the need for this component. Mismatch data for the United States have not previously been presented, so mismatch should not be included in this survey of literature. Its conceptual background is presented in chapters 2 and 4 and its operational definition in appendix D.

Time Referents

A word is in order about mixed time referents. None of the proposed indices uses the customary one-week reference period for every component. Specifically, the income component is nearly always based on the previous year's income. Presumably this is a problem of operationalization; in principle one could use weekly income, but income flows tend to be erratic over short time periods.

PROBLEMS OF GENERALIZABILITY AND INDEXING

The indices that mix target populations within components—the Wirtz, SHV, and Miller indices—do not generalize easily to any population. The Levitan-Taggart Index generalizes to the labor force plus discouraged workers, and the Inadequacy Index to heads of households who are in the labor force or who are discouraged workers.

The LUF is more general than any other index. It generalizes to the labor force, but it may be tabulated for certain groups, for example, those in families with below-average incomes. Furthermore, because time-series data are available for the labor force, reanalysis of old surveys is possible. (This study includes a reanalysis of 1960 census data.)

Of the indices noted, only the LUF can be used to construct comparable descriptive demographic statistics. For example, the labor force participation rate can be partitioned into an adequate participation rate and an inadequate participation rate. Dependency ratios can be defined as a function of adequate participation. Even life tables of adequate economic activity become possible. There is a problem in using it in developing countries to the extent that the labor force concept is inadequate for them. Even here, the LUF could be useful because of its international and historical comparability. And many observers assume that the labor force concept will become more useful as economic differentiation continues.

Several other problems have been raised concerning international comparability. Presumably the cutoff points for each component (e.g., minimum income) will differ from country to country. Then how can an international comparison be made? Does the pattern of mutual exclusivity used in the United States make sense for policy planners elsewhere? Is it sensible to index underutilization simply by addition, or should there be a system of weighting? One of the advantages of the LUF is its international comparability, and so although this study is directed at measurement in advanced countries, a brief answer to these questions is in order.

The question about relative cutoffs is a special case of the general problem, balancing local details with international comparability. International comparisons of unemployment are already hindered because of differing operational definitions among countries. Underutilization cutoffs would lose some comparability, but this does not mean that they would be meaningless. *Given the local context*, one may still interpret the meaning of involuntary part-time work or an inadequate income despite a full workweek. The pattern of mutual exclusivity suggested by the LUF is similar to that used in every proposed index except for one. Levitan reverses the position of involuntary part-time workers and low earners. But in terms of summary data, mutual exclusivity is more important than the ordering.

As for indexing, each proposed index, including the LUF, sums the components. If the index is interpreted as a measure of net private utilization, no weighting is necessary, because persons are the unit of analysis. (It could be argued that the SHV, Levitan-Taggart, and Exclusion indices measure a mixture of private and social underutilization and require weighting.)[45]

Other Approaches

A few other approaches to underemployment measurement are found in the literature. Myrdal and the Eleventh International Conference of Labour Statisticians independently proposed a series of ratios which, when multiplied together, yield aggregated magnitudes. The formula of the International Labor Organization (ILO) is

$$\frac{\text{man-hours}}{\text{working members}} \times \frac{\text{output}}{\text{man-hours}} = \frac{\text{output}}{\text{working members}}$$

The two forms of underutilization are called visible and potential underemployment. Myrdal labels his three ratios participation, duration, and labor efficiency. Participation incorporates unemployment. His formula is

$$\frac{\text{working numbers}}{\text{labor force}} \times \frac{\text{man-hours}}{\text{working numbers}} \times \frac{\text{output}}{\text{man-hours}} = \frac{\text{output}}{\text{labor force}}$$

The major shortcoming of these two approaches lies in not cross-classifying forms of underutilization by population composition categories. Output is difficult to measure—as difficult as "productive work" in the labor force approach—and less salient than income to worker welfare. Cutoff points must be set for hours of work and output just as with the LUF.[46]

Another approach for the developing countries, the so-called CAMS-ODA approach, reclassifies the entire adult population by sector of employment, type of income, and household or nonhousehold employment. It allows for multiple job holding and uses either households or individuals as the analytic unit. It avoids the labor force concept entirely, although it can be combined with the LUF to give a fuller picture of economic activity.[47]

A final approach mentioned in the literature, although not used extensively, is the adjusted median income approach. The adjusted median income is intended to represent the income a particular individual would receive if his or her returns were identical with the national median income for people of "comparable" demographic characteristics and economic activity. While this method can account for population differences, it expresses all the components of underutilization in terms of income.[48]

Conclusions

The Labor Utilization Framework (LUF) is the preferred measure of underutilization for this study because it provides a better assessment of the magnitude, composition, and forms of underutilization than do disguised unemployment, surplus labor, or observational approaches. The LUF is preferred to similar indices because its target population, the labor force, makes it more general and easier to interpret and permits international and longitudinal comparability. The LUF provides more complete conceptual coverage because, unlike the other measures, it includes mismatch. The LUF is subject to many of the same shortcomings as the labor force approach, but its advantages outweigh the shortcomings.

CHAPTER 4

Data, Methods, and Time Effects

This chapter presents an overview of the data sources for this study, and the principal variables constructed from the data sets. It also discusses the methods used in data analysis and concludes with a comparison of underutilization in 1960 and in 1970. A more technical discussion of the data is found in appendix A. Appendices B, C, and D contain detailed information about the operational definition of the components of the underutilization index.

Data

DATA SOURCES

The population for this study was the civilian labor force on April 1, 1960, and April 1, 1970. Estimates of the labor force are usually drawn from surveys of households. The sample used here was all labor force members living in certain households enumerated in the 1960 and 1970 U.S. Census of Population. Not all households are asked to provide detailed labor force information in the census. In 1960, 25% of all households received a detailed questionnaire that included labor force questions. In 1970, there were two detailed questionnaires, one answered by 15% of households and one by 5%. The principal data source for this study was a sample of a sample—a subset of all the households that answered the detailed questionnaires. The subset reported here represented one in every thousand households enumerated in the U.S.[1] The total number of workers aged 16 and over in these households was 67,750 in 1960 and 79,899 in 1970.

Raw numbers given in tables should be read as thousands of workers, because the sample used represented one one-thousandth of the labor force. Thus, this sample represented a labor force of approximately 68 million in 1960 and 80 million in 1970.

Between 1960 and 1970, the civilian labor force definition was modified to exclude 14- and 15-year-olds. Some data presented here correspond to the 1960 definition, although where possible comparability to the 1970 definition was preserved.

The supplementary data sources were published census and Current Population Survey (CPS) data and the CPS tape for March, 1970 (see appendix B).

Disability data for 1960 were not available, and so a 1962 survey of disability was used for approximate data. A similar disability survey from 1971 is also used.

The chief sources of error in the data are expected to be underenumeration, especially among marginal groups, and response error. Imputed data or allocations may also be a source of error. These sources of error, along with sampling variability, are discussed in more detail in appendix A.

VARIABLES

Independent Variables
The independent variables are the indicators of marginality outlined in chapter 2. For the idiosyncrasy hypothesis, the indicator is a physical disability variable used for the first time in the 1970 census. Conceptually, several other indicators of disability could be salient to underutilization, although they are not available in the census. Limited survey data about mental and behavioral disabilities are also reported in the chapter on the idiosyncrasy hypothesis.

Age, sex, and race, often called the "master social positions," are the principal indicators of marginality for the discrimination hypothesis. A plausible case could be made to include nationality in the operational definition, but its role in marginality is not so well established in the literature as that for age, sex, and race.

Inadequate training, measured by completed years of school, is the principal indicator for the achievement hypothesis. The 1970 census included for the first time data about vocational education, which may be a better proxy variable. Marginal workers are those with little education of either type.

Finally, the indicators of marginal economic structure are drawn from occupation, class of worker, and industry data. The most marginal occupational groups are expected to be labor, farm labor, services, and household services. By contrast, white-collar workers, craftsmen, and operatives are expected to be better utilized. Class of worker data is used as a rough proxy for marginal firms. City, state, and federal workers are expected to be well utilized, with self-employed and unpaid workers most underutilized. Agriculture, manufacturing industries with low levels of unionization, and personal service industries are expected to be the most marginal industries and to show the highest underutilization.

Dependent Variable
The dependent variable, net private underutilization, is the sum of four components: unemployment, underutilization by hours of work, underutilization by level of income, and mismatch of occupation and education. Because this is net underutilization, a tabulation hierarchy was introduced that counted the unemployed first and then involuntary part-time workers. Full-time workers with inadequate earnings were tabulated next, and mismatch was calculated for adequately compensated, full-time or voluntary part-time workers. Chapter

1 introduced these components, and chapter 3 indicated the degree of consensus on them.[2] A fuller discussion of the components is given here, and the details of the operational definitions are given in appendices B, C, and D.

Unemployment. In chapter 1, private underutilization was defined as the inadequate economy-household exchange. The contract for employment is the first sort of exchange; its absence is unemployment. Unemployment may also be conceptualized as the limiting case of the remaining forms of exchange; unemployment implies no hours of work, no present work-related income, and no use of skills. Unemployment is coded in the Public Use Samples, using the official definition.

Between 1960 and 1970 the official definition was changed, so there is some loss of comparability between the two dates. Unemployed civilians in 1960 were neither "at work" nor "with a job but not at work" during the week preceding the census, but were "looking for work" within the past sixty days. Also coded as unemployed were persons waiting to be called back from a job layoff or furlough. The principal changes made in 1970 involved work availability. The unemployed were neither "at work," nor "with a job but not at work," but they were looking for work within the past four weeks, and they were "available for work." Persons waiting to report to a new job within thirty days were added to the unemployed.[3] CPS unemployment data are seasonally adjusted; the adjusted unemployment rate for the first quarter of 1970 was 3.8%, and for the second quarter, 4.3%. The figure reported here for April 1, 4.4%, is not seasonally adjusted, but the use of two April census dates provides a crude seasonal adjustment.

Hours of Work. Although Marx wrote of "half-employed hands," a greater evil of the early Industrial Revolution was the 12-to-14–hour working day. The secular decline in hours of work is due to rising productivity, protective legislation, and worker organization. In turn, shorter hours support rising wage levels by giving workers the leisure to be consumers. Some "full" workweeks appear to be voluntary part-time work—the most notable example is the twenty-five–hour workweek resulting from collective bargaining in New York City electrical contruction.[4] Nevertheless, the "half-employed" hands are still with us, although, for a variety of reasons, involuntary part-time employment or part-time unemployment is expected to be the smallest component of underutilization.

Partial layoff or "work sharing" was fairly common during the Depression and is still more common in Europe than in the United States. Work sharing is no longer common in the United States for at least two reasons. First, it is uneconomical because unit costs rise and output falls when the workweek is shortened.[5] Understaffing for full workweeks may be preferable. Second, unions have preferred total layoffs based on seniority to work sharing. In one study of 1,743 labor agreements, 80% had layoff provisions but only 4.2% had work-sharing clauses; 164 union contracts put a floor under hours.[6] These institutional arrangements tend to raise unemployment relative to involuntary part-time work. The trade-off between total and partial layoff is likely to continue wherever complex routine, continuous process technology or "real-time" data processing affect the pace of work.

A second type of involuntary part-time work, the inability to find full-time work, is most commonly reported in industries that accommodate part-time workers. These workers are found disproportionately in clerical work, retail sales, and services, but this is more an indication of the location of part-time jobs than of industry preference.

Involuntary part-time work is included in nearly every treatment of underemployment.[7] It is considered second only to unemployment in gravity because it puts the worker at a double disadvantage: with too few hours of work, even an adequate hourly wage may not bring adequate earnings. The operational definition of underutilization by hours of work is given in appendix B.

Level of Income. Underutilization by level of income goes by several other names—"disguised underemployment," "working poverty," "structural underemployment," and "hidden underemployment." In every case, the concept implies an inadequate return for work. There are many possible causes, but our interest here is primarily in its incidence and composition. To the employer, an hour of work by an inefficient employee may be worth one-tenth hour of a productive worker's time. Certainly low productivity may "cause" underutilization in this sense. The point of this study is not to argue that low wages are either justified or unjustified, but to examine the overlap between social marginality and underutilization, and between economic structure and underutilization.

In this study, the underutilized by level of income are already working a full workweek. The census questionnaire asks for total income in the preceding year. This includes income from several jobs for moonlighting workers. By contrast, many labor force surveys ask only for income from the principal job. It is necessary to assume that, for the sample as a whole, last year's income is a reasonably good guide to current income, and last week's full-time workers were also full-time workers last year. Only work-related income was considered in the underutilization tabulation.

The most conservative, reliable income cutoff figure for the United States is the Social Security Administration poverty index. Not all industries are covered by minimum wage, and alternative minimum budget figures are not adjusted for such factors as family size and residence, as the poverty index is. Because it is based on a study of nutrition, the poverty index is more closely related to maintaining human capital than other indices. But underutilization by level of income is not a direct measure of current or future work efficiency. The operational definition of level of income is given in appendix C.

Mismatch. Mismatch is unique to the LUF scheme, although the problem of "educated underemployment" has become an issue of some concern.[8] A University of Michigan survey found that 14.9% of Americans regarded themselves "significantly overeducated" for their jobs—defined as two or more educational levels above the level needed. Another 21.3% considered themselves "slightly overeducated" or one level of education beyond that required for their jobs. About 45% felt perfectly matched, 12.9% were slightly undereducated, and 6.2% felt significantly undereducated.[9] (Incidentally, a measure of social underutilization should probably include the possible loss to society from persons underqualified for their jobs. This study is principally concerned with net private underutilization.)

To what extent is this a "real" problem? In economic terms, mismatch represents at least some overinvestment in education. Depending on the kinds of skills going unused, mismatch also represents foregone services at a high level. The foregone services may be interpreted as unused current capacity, or as foregone investment. Foregone research, for example, may be reflected later in slower technological and economic growth.

Of course, there are many reasons for pursuing higher education that are not job related. Education may be valued as a consumer good as well as an investment. But the economic wastefulness of mismatch can be compared to an inflationary spiral, as well as to overinvestment. Mismatch may be a sociological equivalent of inflation, especially if there is a scramble to acquire more and more credentials merely to assure a better place in the job queue. Like inflation, mismatch may have many causes.

Employers, in an attempt to minimize their information costs in hiring, may select employees on the basis of diplomas. For some employers, this selection procedure may be a response to the "debasing of the currency"—employers may have come to expect that a high school diploma certifies attendance, not literacy, and that even high grades result from grade inflation. Although the Supreme Court's decision in *Griggs* v. *Duke Power Company* would seem to bar the use of irrelevant credentials, it would be difficult in many clerical and sales jobs to show any academic credential to be irrelevant.[10] And just as monetary inflation is dependent on money supply, mismatch is dependent to some extent on labor supply. The combination of large cohorts of young workers who have higher educational attainment leads to large numbers of applicants. If the employer merely chooses the "best qualified," he may have selected someone who is overqualified, but he has done it without requiring an irrelevant credential. In the short run, this process leads to mismatch and to the "defensive degree," the master's or doctorate acquired as insurance for a good job.

Beyond economic effects, mismatch is a "real" problem because, following W. I. Thomas, things perceived as real are real in their consequences. The Michigan study found the overeducated to be much more dissatisfied than other workers. In some developing countries, unemployment and underemployment of college graduates have become politically destabilizing. Unlike the other forms of underutilization, mismatch is more likely to affect those who are already middle-class and have a high sense of political efficacy. Alternatively, mismatch may disproportionately affect the upwardly mobile. Either way, it is a problem. If it affects the educated regardless of class, it may be a political problem. If there is a composition difference—if mismatch is really blocked mobility—then mismatch becomes an indicator of inequality that overrides equal educational opportunity.

Although mismatch may be a "real" problem in the sense that theorists and attitudinal data aver it to be so, adequate indicators are hard to find. Economists of education have used the rate of return to college investment as an indication of the adjustment between the supply and demand of college graduates. Salaries for college-educated workers have declined somewhat in the United States, but a lower rate of return to investment is not the same thing as underutilization. Certainly the salaries received by the college-educated are not so low as to put them among the underutilized by level of income. For our purposes here, an indicator of underutilization that goes beyond income must be used.

Attitudinal data, although useful, are too subjective to be reliable indicators. Other forms of underutilization point to but do not quantify the problem. Higher unemployment among college graduates (7.4% in 1971 and 9.3% in 1972) is an indicator that jobs are difficult to find. One-quarter of college graduates employed reported that their jobs were not related to their fields of study, but this does not necessarily indicate mismatch.[11]

The Bureau of Labor Statistics (BLS) uses projections of the supply of educated manpower and of the demand for trained personnel. Using this technique, a surplus of 140,000 college graduates a year from 1980 to 1985, or 10% of the projected supply, is projected.[12] Unfortunately, the rate and extent of "credentialism" cannot be projected, and so this method is imprecise. For example, occupations that hire larger numbers of young workers are likely to "upgrade" more rapidly. Besides, this technique gives neither current data nor compositional detail. General projections cannot hint whether the mismatched are more likely to be minority group members or the "first-generation" college graduates in their families.

BLS also reports the number of college graduates employed in jobs that do not usually require a college degree. This is closer to a current quantification of the problem, but it does not include possible mismatch by persons with a few years of college. Nor are there reliable data about educational "requirements" for an occupation (except for those with licensing requirements). The best proxy for requirements is the current education distribution within occupations. The operational definition used here is based on that distribution and is described in detail in appendix D.

This proxy, although prone to many pitfalls, at least avoids a certain nominalism involved in the use of major occupational groups. "It is only in the world of census statistics, and not in terms of direct assessment, that an assembly line worker is presumed to have greater skill than a fisherman, an oysterman . . . For the category of operatives, training requirements and the demands of the job upon the abilities of the workers are now so low that one can hardly imagine jobs that lie significantly below them on any scale of skill."[13] Instead, the detailed occupation classification is the initial source of data.

Occupation is chosen as the variable to relate to education because of its widespread use as a measure of stratification and attainment. An inability to convert education into occupational attainment is the indicator chosen here to measure mismatch.

It would be possible to use another variable, such as industry, to measure mismatch, but the link between education and occupation is stronger. Industries tend to subtend a variety of occupations, and so occupation would become an intervening variable anyway. One would expect industrial mismatch levels to be stable except in industries whose technology is rapidly changing, whose occupation composition is changing, or whose hiring patterns draw disproportionately from the young. Indeed, intraindustry upgrading has been fairly low.[14] Occupation upgrading has been more pronounced, and so separate mismatch cutoffs must be set up for 1960 and 1970. (This is analogous to deflating the poverty index for 1960.)

Certain occupations may be relatively impervious to upgrading. Those that already require a graduate degree—the learned professions—may have a greater number of graduates who had already completed other graduate degrees. For example, law school applicants may earn a "defensive" master's degree to improve their competitive position. Because lawyers and other professionals already have the highest average education coded in the census, potential mismatch among them cannot be detected. This artificial upper limit may bias the level of mismatch downward.

Mismatch poses a number of interesting measurement problems. After the empirical findings about mismatch are discussed, we will return to the topic of mismatch in chapter 11.

Methods

The four hypotheses in this study vary in the number and type of independent variables related to underutilization. Marginal status on any independent variable is hypothesized to be sufficient for underutilization, and so each independent variable is examined individually. The statistical description used is determined by the level of measurement of the variable and the number of "marginal" values the variable may take.

The discrimination hypothesis requires multivariate analysis because it predicts that the presence of two or more marginal statuses intensifies underutilization. The choice of a multivariate method for this hypothesis depends upon the level of measurement of the dependent variable. The dependent variable, utilization, will usually be dichotomized into adequate and inadequate utilization.

Applying Goodman's hierarchical log-linear models is useful when both independent and dependent variables are nominal level (qualitative). It requires none of the conventional assumptions and provides tests of significance for both partial association and interactions, as well as measures of association

Table 4.1. *Civilian labor force by type of industry and type of utilization, 1960* (
(Thousands of workers aged 16 and older, with percentages)

| | 1970 | | |
Type of utilization	Total (1)	Agriculture (2)	Nonagricult (3)
Civilian labor force	79,899 (100.0%)	2,293 (100.0%)	77,606 (100.0%)
Adequately utilized	61,256 (76.7%)	1,307 (57.0%)	59,949 (77.2%)
Inadequately utilized	18,643 (23.3%)	986 (43.0%)	17,657 (22.8%)
By unemployment[a]	3,519 (4.4%)	79 (3.5%)	3,440 (4.4%)
By hours of work[b]	1,455 (1.8%)	161 (7.0%)	1,294 (1.7%)
By level of income	5,432 (6.8%)	492 (21.5%)	4,940 (6.4%)
By mismatch[c]	8,237 (10.3%)	254 (11.1%)	7,983 (10.3%)

[a] Unemployed workers without industrial classification included in nonagricultur
[b] Adjusted. See appendix B.
[c] Adjusted. See appendix D.

Source: U.S. Bureau of the Census, *1960* and *1970 Public Use Samples.*

0

	1960		
otal 4)	Agriculture (5)	Nonagriculture (6)	
7,750 (100.0%)	4,192 (100.0%)	63,558 (100.0%)	
0,757 (74.9%)	2,091 (49.9%)	48,666 (76.6%)	
6,993 (25.1%)	2,101 (50.1%)	14,892 (23.4%)	
,342 (4.9%)	116 (2.8%)	3,226 (5.1%)	
,591 (2.4%)	186 (4.4%)	1,405 (2.2%)	
,421 (12.4%)	1,577 (37.6%)	6,844 (10.8%)	
3,639 (5.4%)	222 (5.3%)	3,417 (5.4%)	

ustry.

analogous to partial, multiple, and multiple-partial coefficients. Single variable and interaction effects are tested by comparing the goodness of fit between the actual data and hypothetical models fitted to the marginals. The statistic used, χ^2, is sensitive to sample size, and so a very conservative significance level is used.[15]

Because even the Goodman method shows so many significant effects, relative measures of association such as the comparative odds-ratio are stressed. It shows the direction and magnitude of interactions already identified as significant.[16] An example of odds-ratio analysis is used later in this chapter. Further discussion of methods is found in appendix A.

Time Effects

Table 4.1 presents the civilian labor force for 1960 and 1970 by type of industry and type of utilization. Columns 1 and 4 show the differences in utilization between 1960 and 1970. Despite an 18% increase in labor force size over the decade, underutilization declined by 1.8%. This appears to be due to a marked decrease in the working poor, which more than offset the doubling of mismatch. We postpone the discussion of industry differences until chapter 10.

When table 4.1 is analyzed using Goodman's models, the interaction between time and utilization is significant, although barely so, and much less significant than the interaction of time and industry, or of industry and utilization. Table 4.2 tests for the strength of the time-utilization relationship within categories of the control variable. Odds-ratios greater than one indicate a positive association between 1970 and more adequate utilization. The group that was the worst off in 1960, farmers, shows the most positive association for 1970. However, as the weighted average and zero-order ratios show, even in 1960 agriculture was a small part of the labor force.[17] What accounts for the improvement? This question is somewhat peripheral to our main interests, but it deserves a brief word. The country was in a recession in 1960, and in 1970 it was just ending a prolonged spell of prosperity. Table 4.3 presents some economic indicators for the two dates. The growth in employment between 1960 and 1970, juxtaposed with the growth in output per worker, is particularly remarkable. But this association is reversed in agriculture, where output grew even though employment shrunk.

Utilization of labor may be a useful intervening variable for explaining this apparent anomaly. The growth in overall employment was accompanied by increased adequacy in employment, a circumstance that may have interacted with increased output. Despite the fall in farm employment, there was improved output and utilization of the remaining workers. So it appears that economic indicators and utilization data may be mutually illuminating, a proposition that is testable by time-series analysis.

It might be expected that the components of the LUF will respond differently over time. Unemployment and involuntary part-time employment respond to the business cycle. Underutilization by level of income can be expected

Table 4.2. *Odds-ratios for year and utilization by sector*
*(*N, *in thousands of workers)*

Sector	Odds-ratio (1970:1960) (adequate:inadequate)	N
Nonagriculture	1.04	141164
Agriculture	1.33	6485
Weighted average	1.05	. . . . .
Zero order	1.10	. . . . .

Source: Table 4.1.

Table 4.3. *Selected economic indicators for 1960 and 1970*

	1970	1960
Total private output per man-hour (1967 = 100)	104.3	78.2
Farm	119.6	64.9
Nonfarm	103.4	80.3
Employment (1967 = 100)	104.8	89.5
Farm	88.5	139.6
Nonfarm	105.8	86.5
Compensation per man-hour (private) (1967 = 100)	124.6	71.7
Implicit price deflator	113.5	89.5
Consumer price index (1967 = 100), all items	116.3	88.7

Source: U.S. President, *Manpower Report of the President,* 1973.

to show a secular decline, while mismatch—at least for the near future—is likely to show some secular increases. These issues deserve further consideration if underutilization indices are used as indicators for public policy.[18]

Summary

The principal data sets for this study are the 1960 and 1970 Public Use Samples, supplemented by the March, 1970, Current Population Survey and published census and survey data. The independent variables are divided into those used to identify "marginal workers" (disability, age, race, sex, education) and those used to identify "marginal jobs" (occupation, industry, etc.). The dependent variable is utilization. For most purposes, it is analyzed as a dichotomous variable, adequate or inadequate utilization. The elements of the underutilization index, and measurement problems of each one, are discussed.

A first look at the data shows a decline in underutilization between 1960 and 1970, one that is disproportionately enjoyed by agricultural workers. The decline in underutilization parallels an improvement in the economy reflected in other economic indicators.

Further detail on adequacy of data, the analytic techniques, and the operational definition is given in the technical appendices.

CHAPTER 5
The Idiosyncrasy Hypothesis: Employment of the Disabled

Handicapped, or just "odd" people—according to the broadest interpretation of the idiosyncrasy hypothesis—are among the workers most likely to be underutilized in the labor market. They get what might be called the leftovers in available jobs. The idiosyncrasy hypothesis treats physical, mental, and emotional disorders as if they were distributed randomly throughout the population, impediments to employment even before age, race, sex, or social class are considered. Without considering these other factors, are persons with physical handicaps and similar idiosyncrasies more likely to be underemployed and unemployed? This is the idiosyncrasy hypothesis, for which this chapter musters only slight evidence.

The problem is sometimes stated by assuming the hypothesis. That is, one argues, "If you are unemployed or underemployed, then there must be something wrong with you." This is the converse of the idiosyncrasy hypothesis, and it says that identifiable idiosyncrasies "account for" underutilization. After classifying the underutilized by known impairments, proponents of the converse hypothesis tend to label the residual underutilized workers as "work-resistant," "undisciplined," or just "lazy." No doubt there are lazy and undisciplined workers; on the other hand, an argument that some personal shortcoming accounts for every worker's underutilization is nearly impossible to verify.

This chapter treats the converse hypothesis as an alternative to the idiosyncrasy hypothesis, with physical disabilities examined to see if they "account for" underutilization. The data do not permit us to count "lazy" underemployed or unemployed workers. However, even if you were to consider every part-time disabled worker to be underutilized, the physically disabled would account for only 14% of the underutilized. This is weak support for the converse hypothesis, unless one is willing to accept a large and heterogeneous residual.

A second alternative hypothesis considered here is the redundancy hypothesis. It states that disabilities are most likely to occur among workers who are already marginal for other reasons. This means that some other characteristic, such as minority group membership, is associated both with disability and with underutilization. The association is a statistical one; it does not imply that minority status *causes* disability or underutilization. The correlation could occur because minorities are more likely to be in dangerous jobs or less likely to have adequate medical care. The redundancy hypothesis explicitly notes that disability is not randomly distributed through the population. No formal test of this hypothesis is attempted here, but there is a discussion of disability as a redundant marginal status.

All three hypotheses—the idiosyncrasy hypothesis, its converse, and the redundancy hypothesis—speak to the composition and magnitude of underutilization, without specifying mechanisms of underutilization. Employer discrimination is one possible mechanism. Other possible mechanisms are an inability to perform some kinds of work and decreased aspirations among the disabled.

This chapter continues with an overview of physical disabilities in the United States population and in the labor force, and a discussion of the available data. A limited ten-year comparison is made. The extent and forms of underutilization among the disabled are discussed, and the adequacy of the idiosyncrasy, converse, and redundancy hypotheses is assessed. In the final part of the chapter, some observations are made about other "idiosyncrasies," such as mental and emotional disorders.

Physical Disability in the American Population

In 1970, about 12 million Americans were physically disabled. Many of them were capable of holding jobs; some were partially disabled and some had temporary impairments. About 7 million of the total were partially disabled; of them, 2.6 million had had their disabilities for 10 years or more. About 1.2 million had been disabled from 5 to 9 years, and 1.5 million had been disabled for less than one year.

About 10.8% of the total population aged 18–64 reports some work disability. The incidence of work disability is highest among the aged, among males, and among Negroes. Disability increases steadily with age. Among age groups, the percent with a work disability ranges from 5.7% among persons aged 18–24 to 26.0% of those aged 60–64. Men report a work disability incidence of 11.7%. Among women the comparable percentage is 9.9%, but this may reflect a response bias. Because of the historically lower participation rates of women, disabled women might not report themselves as "work disabled" if they have never considered entering the labor force. The percentage of work-disabled Negroes is 14.5%, compared with 11.2% of Spanish-origin Americans and 10.3% of all whites. One of the highest percentages of work disability, as might be expected, is found among older Negro males. Among those aged 60–64, 34.6% are work disabled.

In 1961–62, 7.3% of the civilian labor force over 17 was disabled. This was about 5,190,000 persons, of whom 8.8% were unemployed; the unemployment rate for the entire labor force was 5.1%. Just as in 1970, work limitation increased with age. Men had more work limitations, but women reported more chronic conditions. In 1970, 7.7% of the civilian labor force over 17 was disabled, about 5,713,000 persons.[1] Unemployment in 1970 is discussed in more detail below.

DATA SOURCES

There are two principal sources for data on physical disability. One is the 1970 census, both published tabulations and Public Use Samples. The other is the Health Interview Survey of the National Center for Health Statistics. Data from the survey are reported for 1961–62 and 1971. The institutionalized population is excluded from both data sources.

Census Data
Five percent of the respondents in the 1970 census were asked: "Does this person have a health or physical condition which limits the *kind* or *amount* of work he can do at a job? Does his health or physical condition keep him from holding *any* job at all?" (emphasis in the original). The results of these questions, cross-tabulated by demographic and labor force variables, were published in a census subject report.[2] Data about the underutilization of the disabled were taken from the 1970 Public Use Samples (see chapter 4). However, there was no way to estimate the underutilized by hours of work. There are no data available giving reasons for part-time work among the disabled. Correlations reported in this chapter are based on percentages of the full-time labor force that are underutilized. For this purpose, the unemployed are considered part of the full-time labor force. Questions about work disability were not asked in the 1960 census, and so directly comparable 1960 data are not available.

There are two shortcomings in the census data. First, there was a sizable response error. About 4,873,000 Americans reported themselves "completely disabled": that is, they indicated that their health or physical condition kept them from holding any job at all. Nevertheless, a substantial number of them also reported themselves "looking for work." This boosted their labor force participation and unemployment rates. Another substantial number of completely disabled persons reported themselves "with a job but not at work." Perhaps the respondents did not understand the question, or perhaps they were still looking for a job which they might be able to hold. At any rate, their replies, given the current labor force framework, are logically inconsistent. Except where noted, figures here are for the "partially disabled." Unemployment rates for the completely disabled must be interpreted in the light of probable response error.

The second problem is age reporting of the disabled. The subject report presents data for persons aged 18 to 64. The Public Use Samples report disability data for persons aged 14 to 64. Disability questions were recoded as "not applicable" to the elderly before the release of the tapes. In 1970 the labor force was composed of persons aged 16 and over, but persons 16 and 17 are omitted from the subject report. Admittedly, the incidence of disability among them is probably low. However, both the subject report and the census tapes omit the aged, for whom disability may become an increasing impediment to employment.

Survey Data
The Health Interview Survey is a continuing national survey conducted by household interviews. In 1961–62, 125,000 persons in 38,000 households were surveyed; in 1971, 134,000 persons in 42,000 households were included in the sample.[3] The data differ from census data in several respects. A reference period of two weeks, rather than the customary one week, was used. Persons aged 17 years and over were surveyed, although the minimum labor force age was 14 years in 1961 and 16 in 1971. These data may be relatively larger than census data because the elderly are included.

Other Shortcomings
One problem with both data sources is the changing lower age limit used. The magnitude of error introduced at this end of the life cycle is probably small, both because of the lower participation rates of teenagers and their lower likelihood of work disability. More serious is the consistent underreporting of chronic conditions. Part of the increase in reported work disability between 1961–62 and 1971 may have been due to reduced response error. Liberalization of disability benefits may have broadened the public's understanding of "disability," and changes in questionnaire design may have improved response completeness. Considerable methodological research has been done with the Health Interview Survey. Response error on the census question is being studied in the census evaluation program. There is evidence of an increase in work disability from Social Security surveys. Between 1966 and 1972, the number unable to work regularly or at all increased.[4]

DISABILITY AND LABOR FORCE PARTICIPATION

The participation levels of partially disabled workers aged 18–64 are somewhat higher than those for the whole population. However, the participation level varies by type of disability. Among disabled persons aged 17–64 in 1971, 80.9% of the hearing impaired and 61.7% of the visually impaired "usually" worked, compared with 74.1% of those with the absence of a major extremity and 38.5% of those partly or completely paralyzed.[5] As table 5.1 shows, roughly three-fourths of partially disabled adult Americans are also workers. (The figures for the totally disabled, as the review of data quality indicated, are too unreliable for inference.) Still, the disabled account for less than 9% of the labor force.

As earlier chapters suggested, nonparticipation probably bears some relationship to inadequate participation. Barriers to participation are also likely to be barriers to adequate participation. Of all nonparticipating adult males in 1970, about 17.2% were disabled or in ill health. But their nonparticipation is difficult to interpret. Nearly 29,000 partially disabled males and 220,200 partially disabled females have never worked at all. They may be "discouraged entrants," or they may require intensive rehabilitation and training to qualify for a job. Among experienced workers who are currently not participating, some may be discouraged workers who have finally given up the search for employment. The data do not indicate how many fall into this category. Other experienced workers may have retired early because of disability. More liberal disability benefits have been used as an explanation for the decline in participation rates among black males, especially in the 45–54 age group, during the period from 1955 to 1972.[6]

The idiosyncrasy hypothesis treats disability as an a priori condition. It assumes that the disabled worker will have great trouble finding a job, especially a good job. But for workers who become disabled while already holding a good job, disability retirement may be an alternative to occupational downgrading and underutilization. If disability benefits become more liberal, and if relatively larger proportions of the disabled acquire their disability after accumulating some work record, then the relationship between disability and underutilization may be expected to weaken as more of the disabled leave the labor force.

TYPE AND SEVERITY OF DISABILITY

The relationship of disability to underutilization is probably conditioned by the type and severity of the disability. For example, table 5.1 shows that employed white males are somewhat more likely to be "at work" than are white females and Negroes. It is possible that the disabilities of white males are less serious for the performance of their jobs than the disabilities of Negroes are for theirs. White males are more likely than Negroes to hold white-collar jobs, and a disability that might not hinder an office worker might idle a semiskilled operative. This does not explain, however, the difference between "at work" white males and females, for white females tend to be white-collar workers.

Perhaps it is the case that although more males are disabled, their average disability is not so serious as the average female disability. A direct test of this idea is impossible, but some indirect data tend to refute it. Among disabled white males, 14.7% have been disabled for one year or less, compared with 16.9% of white females. Almost 40% of disabled white men have been disabled ten or more years, compared with 34% of white women. Our conclusions about the relationship of disability to underutilization would probably be improved with data about the type and severity of disability.

Underutilization of the Physically Disabled

Table 5.2 compares the utilization of the total civilian labor force with the full-time civilian labor force, which is subclassified by disability status. All figures are adjusted to the 18–64 age range for greater comparability to the disability

Table 5.1. *Physically disabled persons by race, sex, labor force status, and degree of disability, 1970* (*Thousands of persons aged 18–64, with percentages*)

Labor force status	Both sexes (1)	White Male (2)	Female (3)	Both sexes (4)	Negro Male (5)	Female (6)
			Partial disability[a]			
Total, all statuses	6,286.7 (100.0%)	3,913.6 (100.0%)	2,373.1 (100.0%)	796.9 (100.0%)	397.7 (100.0%)	399.2 (100.0%)
Not in the labor force	1,537.7 (24.5%)	405.7 (10.4%)	1,132.0 (47.7%)	221.4 (27.8%)	61.5 (15.5%)	159.9 (40.1%)
In the labor force	4,749.0 (75.5%)	3,507.9 (89.6%)	1,241.1 (52.3%)	575.5 (72.2%)	336.2 (84.5%)	239.3 (59.9%)
Civilian labor force	4,676.1 (100.0%)	3,436.3 (100.0%)	1,239.8 (100.0%)	565.2 (100.0%)	326.0 (100.0%)	239.2 (100.0%)
Employed	4,442.3 (95.0%)	3,284.2 (95.6%)	1,158.1 (93.4%)	523.6 (92.6%)	303.3 (93.0%)	220.3 (92.1%)
At work	4,220.8 (90.3%)	3,136.6 (91.3%)	1,084.2 (87.4%)	494.0 (87.4%)	286.8 (88.0%)	207.2 (86.6%)
With a job, not at work	221.5 (4.7%)	147.6 (4.3%)	73.9 (6.0%)	29.6 (5.2%)	16.5 (5.0%)	13.1 (5.5%)
Unemployed	233.8	152.1	81.7	41.6	22.7	18.9

	Total disability[b]					
Total, all statuses	4,045.5 (100.0%)	1,659.3 (100.0%)	2,386.2 (100.0%)	827.5 (100.0%)	324.5 (100.0%)	503.0 (100.0%)
Not in the labor force	3,706.0 (91.6%)	1,447.2 (87.2%)	2,258.8 (94.7%)	761.5 (92.0%)	287.8 (88.7%)	473.7 (94.2%)
In the labor force	339.5 (8.4%)	212.1 (12.8%)	127.4 (5.3%)	66.0 (8.0%)	36.7 (11.3%)	29.3 (5.8%)
Civilian labor force	240.1 (100.0%)	210.7 (100.0%)	29.4 (100.0%)	65.7 (100.0%)	36.4 (100.0%)	29.3 (100.0%)
Employed	149.7 (62.3%)	132.5 (62.9%)	17.2 (58.5%)	37.4 (56.9%)	20.3 (55.8%)	17.1 (58.4%)
At work	... ...	... ...	... ...	... ...	... ...	... ...
With a job, not at work	149.5 (62.3%)	132.3 (62.8%)	17.2 (58.5%)	37.4 (56.9%)	20.3 (55.8%)	17.1 (58.4%)
Unemployed	90.4 (37.7%)	78.2 (37.1%)	12.2 (41.5%)	28.3 (43.1%)	16.1 (44.2%)	12.2 (41.6%)

[a] See text.
[b] See text.

Source: U.S. Bureau of the Census, *Persons with Work Disability*, table 4.

Table 5.2. *Total and full-time civilian labor force by disability status and labor utilization, 1970 (Thousands of workers aged 18–64, with percentages)*

	Total CLF (1)	Full-time CLF		
		Total (2)	Disabled[a] (3)	Able-bodied (4)
Total, all types	74336 (100.0%)	64202 (100.0%)	4636 (100.0%)	59566 (100.0%)
Adequately utilized	56649 (76.2%)	48984 (76.3%)	3309 (71.4%)	45675 (76.7%)
Inadequately utilized	17687 (23.8%)	15218 (23.7%)	1327 (28.6%)	13891 (23.3%)
By unemployment	3035 (4.1%)	3035 (4.7%)	408 (8.8%)	2627 (4.4%)
By hours of work	1479[b] (2.0%)	....	....	....
By level of income	5134 (6.9%)	5134 (8.0%)	500 (10.8%)	4634 (7.8%)
By mismatch	8039[b] (10.8%)	7049[c] (11.0%)	419[c] (9.0%)	6630[c] (11.1%)

[a]Persons aged 18–64, classified in the labor force, with the answer "yes" to the question, "Does this person have a health or physical condition which limits the kind or amount of work he can do at a job?"
[b]Adjusted using March, 1970 Current Population Survey. See appendix B.
[c]Unadjusted for part-time mismatch.

Source: U.S. Bureau of the Census, *1970 Public Use Samples.*

data. Regardless of the comparison made, the disabled labor force had higher underutilization—5.3% higher than full-time, able-bodied workers; 4.9% higher than all full-time workers; 4.8% higher than all civilian workers. (The disabled are also part of the comparison group in the latter two comparisons.)

FORMS OF UNDERUTILIZATION

Judging from both table 5.1 and table 5.2, it seems fair to conclude that disabled persons, except for white males, have a higher incidence of unemployment than the labor force as a whole. The unemployment rate of the disabled given in table 5.2 is 215% that of the total labor force, and 187% that of the full-time labor force. By 1975, an unemployment rate of 8.5% had been recorded for the entire labor force, but in 1970, rates over 8% were uncommonly high. The unemployment rate for all disabled aged 18–64 (not just full-time workers) was 7.2%.

The correction for involuntary part-time work could not be made, but indirect evidence may be useful. In the nonstudent, able-bodied labor force aged 18–64 in 1970, 15% were part-time workers. Of the disabled nonstudent workers in the same age group, 22.3% were part-time workers; one-fourth of them were working fewer than 29 hours a week. More disabled workers than able-bodied workers are employed part-time; is this by preference or is it involuntary? If involuntary, is it due to physical limitations or to economic conditions? Our data permit only speculation. Assume that the ratio of involuntary part-time workers to all part-time workers is the same for disabled workers as it is for the civilian labor force. Under the circumstances, the equal-ratio assumption seems to be a conservative one. Then 148,000 or 3.2% of all disabled workers would be underemployed by hours of work. This would make the disabled rate for inadequate hours of work 160% that of all workers.

Using the same age grouping, percentage of disabled who are "working poor" is 157% that of the civilian labor force. The significance of this figure is heightened when we consider that the working poor includes only full-time workers, and a higher proportion of disabled workers are part-time workers. When the income of all disabled workers, full-time and part-time, is considered, 957,000 disabled workers fall below the cutoff level; 67% of them are "severely underutilized" by level of income, for they earn less than 75% of the poverty level. The number reported in table 5.2 is smaller because so many of the disabled poor work only part-time.

Only in mismatch are the disabled relatively better off. The mismatch percentage among the disabled is 82% that of the full-time, able-bodied labor force (using unadjusted figures). Three possible explanations may be given for this relatively low figure. First, the disabled could have a higher occupational profile than the population as a whole. Table 5.3 compares the occupational distribution of disabled workers in 1961 and 1962 with that of the 1970 civilian labor force. The index of dissimilarity, although small, indicates a difference in distribution—but not in the hypothesized direction. The disabled have a somewhat lower profile. Higher proportions of the disabled are found in farm work and service work. The higher proportion in clerical work is more than offset by the lower proportion of disabled professionals. Consequently, relative to the whole labor force, mismatch cutoffs are lower, and if educational levels were equal, the percentage of mismatched disabled workers should be higher than it is.

Before going on to alternative explanations for lower mismatch, it is worthwhile to compare the occupational profile of the disabled in 1961 with that in 1970. There is almost as much difference between the 1961 and 1970 disabled workers as there is between the 1961 disabled workers and the 1970 total workers! There was a substantial occupational shift among disabled workers, but it did not reflect the national trends. Disabled workers were somewhat more likely to be in semiskilled, unskilled, and farm labor in 1970 than in 1961, although less likely to be domestic workers. The percentage of skilled blue-collar and lower white-collar workers declined more than the offsetting increase in professionals. Of the 1.8 index point decline between the 1961 disabled and the 1970 total population, 0.5 points came among the disabled, and 1.3 points between the disabled and the total population.

A second explanation may be sought for lower mismatch percentages. Perhaps the disabled have a lower educational attainment than the civilian labor force. Table 5.4 lends support to this possibility. The index of dissimilarity for men is 12.4; for women it is 15.6. Disabled men and women are less likely to have had at least an eighth grade education. The same disability that impairs work may also impair education, or parents may be less motivated to secure education for their disabled children. Too, older people tend both to have less education and to have a work disability. For whatever reason the education differential exists, it helps to explain the lower rate of mismatch among the disabled.

A third possible reason for lower mismatch among the disabled lies in the nature of the underutilization index. A higher proportion of the disabled are included in the other categories, and so fewer are available for the mismatch criterion. About 184,000 workers who were both disabled and mismatched were already part-time or working poor.

If the estimate of 148,000 underutilized by hours of work is accepted, the total number of inadequately utilized is 1,475,000, or 30.8% of the disabled labor force. This number accounts for only 8.3% of the inadequately utilized in the civilian labor force. Thus, although the incidence of all categories except mismatch falls harder on the disabled, the disabled workers explain a very small percentage of United States underutilization.

It is also possible to summarize the utilization of the disabled without estimating involuntary part-time work. Table 5.2 presented summary figures for full-time workers, aged 18 to 64, in the civilian labor force and in the disabled force. The minimum change needed to make the distributions equal is one out of fifteen workers. Is this a sufficient difference to support the hypothesis? In the next section, we turn to a consideration of the strength of the support.

Table 5.3. *Civilian and partially disabled labor force in 1970 and disabled labor force in 1961–62, by occupation*

(Percentages)

Occupational group	Civilian labor force, 1970 (1)	Disabled labor force, 1970 (2)	Disabled labor force, 1961–62 (3)
Professional, technical, managers (except farm)	26.3	21.4	19.1
Clerical and sales	14.3	15.8	16.5
Craftsmen, farm managers	21.9	19.9	22.0
Operatives, service workers	27.2	30.0	28.2
Laborers, except farm	6.1	6.9	4.8
Farm laborers	4.1	5.9	3.8
Private house-hold workers	0.1	0.1	5.3
Total	100.0	100.0	99.7[a]
	$\Delta_{12} = 6.9$	$\Delta_{23} = 8.2$	$\Delta_{13} = 8.7$

[a] Rounding error.

Sources: 1970: U.S. Bureau of the Census, *Persons with Work Disability*, table 6; 1961–62: U.S. Public Health Service, *Disability, 1961–1962*, table 12.

Table 5.4. *Percent distributions of experienced civilian labor force and disabled labor force by sex and educational attainment, 1970 (workers aged 18–64, in percentages)*

Years of school completed	Male		Female	
	Experienced civilian labor force (1)	With work disability[a] (2)	Experienced civilian labor force (3)	With work disability[a] (4)
Less than 8 years	10.0	16.5	6.7	13.6
8 years	9.2	12.6	6.8	11.1
1–3 years high school	19.7	22.1	19.0	24.3
4 years high school	33.2	28.0	42.6	33.4
1–3 years college	13.5	12.1	14.0	10.9
4 years college	14.4	8.6	10.9	6.5
Total	100.0	100.0	100.0	100.0
		$\Delta = 12.4$		$\Delta = 15.6$

[a] Any sort of work disability, partial or complete.

Source: U.S. Bureau of the Census, *Persons with Work Disability*, table 7.

First, it is appropriate to offer some data about forms of underutilization among the disabled in 1961–62.

The currently employed and the currently unemployed in 1961–62 showed some differences in disability status. Among the employed, 10.5% had work limitations, while 16.7% of the unemployed had such limitations. About 0.8% more of the unemployed than of the employed reported limitations in their non-work-related activities. Among disabled unemployed workers—who are already underutilized by our index—another 17.3% had family incomes of $2,000 or less.

Hours of work data were not available for the disabled in 1961–62. An approximation for the underutilized by level of income is possible, however. In 1961–62, 10.4% of the civilian labor force had incomes less than $2,000, and 17.6% of the employed disabled workers had annual incomes of less than $2,000. The equivalent percentage in 1970—when the poverty level was higher—was 7.3% for disabled employees. The reported 1961–62 incomes are family incomes and not limited to work-related incomes; this makes the reduction in low incomes more dramatic. These approximations are tabulations of income among all employed workers, not just full-time workers. Both the 1961 percentage and the 1970 percentage would be reduced if part-time workers were eliminated from the numerator.

Figures for mismatch are not available for 1961–62, nor is the educational distribution of the disabled. The occupational distribution of the disabled in 1961–62 has already been discussed. The higher proportion of professional and lower proportion of private household workers in 1970 make a somewhat higher mismatch likely in 1970, but this might be offset by the increased percentage of disabled workers in blue-collar occupations.

Comparing all disabled workers in 1961–62 with those in 1970, it seems that the general trends to reduced unemployment and underutilization by level of income were sustained for this subpopulation. The disabled population differ in mismatch trends; even from the scanty evidence here, one would not expect mismatch to have doubled since 1961 among the disabled, as it did among the general population.

THE IDIOSYNCRASY HYPOTHESIS

Another way of stating the idiosyncrasy hypothesis is to say that underutilization is associated with disability. Suppose we compare the adequately and inadequately utilized in columns 3 and 4 of table 5.2 (the disabled and able-bodied). Chi-square shows a significant difference, but this can be discounted because of the large sample size. Phi is a statistic that corrects for sample size; its value, .03, indicates very little association. Gamma, with a value of .14, is positive, so it indicates some likelihood that disability is associated with inadequate utilization, but the relationship is weak. Similar measures of association are also weak. There is insufficient evidence to accept the idiosyncrasy hypothesis, although it is true that the disabled are somewhat more likely than the able-bodied to be underutilized.

THE CONVERSE HYPOTHESIS

At least as far as physical disability data are concerned, there is little evidence that disability "accounts for" large proportions of underutilization, either in 1961–62 or in 1970. In 1970, the full-time disabled accounted for 7.2% of the labor force and 8.7% of the inadequately utilized. This is overrepresentation, but not proof of the hypothesis. By knowing underutilization status, you cannot improve your prediction of what someone's disability status is.

THE REDUNDANCY HYPOTHESIS

The idiosyncrasy hypothesis maintains that if a worker is disabled, with no other variable considered, he is more likely to be underutilized. Redundant disadvantage would result if disabled workers are even more likely to be underutilized because of other characteristics—for example, race, sex, or age. Redundant disadvantage may result from differing disability incidence among race-sex-age groups. Or, disabilities may have different consequences for different population groups. For example, among partially disabled workers, whites are more likely to be employed than Negroes. This means that not only are Negroes more likely to report disability, but the disabled among them are more likely to be unemployed. The persistence of higher rates among blacks may indicate redundant disadvantage, directly or indirectly.

The higher incidence of disability among Negroes could be made consistent with the idiosyncrasy hypothesis, without recourse to the redundant disability hypothesis, if it could be shown that Negroes' disabilities would disqualify them from their occupations. Negroes are disproportionately employed in manual occupations, and these are occupations in which physical disability could be a bar to employment. Similarly, the high unemployment rate among disabled Negro women may be related to the requirements of household and service jobs. These jobs do not usually require strength but may require agility and stamina. The lack of data on the type of work disability prevents testing these suppositions.

One way to examine the redundancy hypothesis is to examine the correlations among percent disabled, percent underutilized, and percent Negroes. Geographic divisions of the United States were used as analytic units, and underutilization was calculated as percent of the full-time labor force over 16 years of age. Percent Negro is positively correlated both with percent underutilized (0.12) and with percent disabled (0.16). The idiosyncrasy hypothesis suggests that underutilization and disability are positively related, but they have a weak negative relation (−0.02). The redundancy hypothesis suggests that Negroes may be more likely to be underutilized because they are more likely to be disabled: that is, disability may be an intervening variable. However, the negative relationship between disability and underutilization becomes even stronger, although only slightly, when percent Negro is controlled. It seems more likely to argue that percent Negro is positively associated with both disability and underutilization, but not in a way that would confirm the redundancy hypothesis. Nor does the idiosyncrasy hypothesis receive support.

Cognitive and Affective Disabilities

Census data do not provide any information about workers with mental illnesses, emotional disturbances, mental retardation, and other limiting conditions. Most data about mental illness deal with the institutionalized population, which by definition is not subject to labor force participation. If they are not institutionalized, persons with limiting conditions are potential workers, but little is known about their labor force behavior. Many cases go undiagnosed. Persons being treated are difficult to identify. Some are treated by private physicians, some by counselors, some by clergy. Others attend clinics or live in halfway houses. If reported, conditions such as alcoholism or drug addiction, which are defined as disabilities in current legislation, may be described as physical conditions by some authorities (or respondents) and as behavioral conditions by others.

The idiosyncrasy hypothesis implies that persons with mental or emotional disturbances would be more likely to be underutilized. Mental, behavioral, or emotional disturbances probably affect employment in a different way from physical disorders. Chronic physical problems may be visible or discovered during a preemployment physical examination, but many emotional and mental disorders may be hidden. An emotional disorder may contribute to unstable, intermittent employment, with no single employer aware of the condition. Chronic conditions may erode work efficiency over a period of time, making a previously capable worker less desirable. Although there have been studies of the work experience of mentally and emotionally disabled workers, no quantitative estimate of their labor underutilization is possible.

A sample of former mental patients were interviewed about their work history after treatment. About one-third felt that their history of illness had hurt their job chances. The posthospital experience of lower-class patients seems particularly dismal: many of them never achieve full-time, stable employment. They hold a series of temporary jobs at irregular intervals, or they find only part-time work. Untreated individuals, if their symptoms are obvious, are unlikely to be hired. A group of employers were given personality profiles of a number of potential "employees." In reality, they were given casebook descriptions of various disorders. Only 29% of those "workers" would have been hired, and they were the ones whose symptoms were least severe or least obvious to the lay person.[7]

Involuntary part-time work seems to be a particular problem of former mental patients, often because they cannot find full-time work. However, ex-psychiatric patients who are full-time workers are more likely to report that they "know what is expected of them" and "have the ability to do what is expected of them" than are such former patients who are part-time workers. Similar feelings of competence are reported not only at work, but also at home and for the self in general.[8]

However, the direction of causality is difficult to determine. Physical disability may be the *result* of a job and lead later to underutilization. Emotional disability may be the *result* of underutilization as well as a cause of subsequent underutilization. There is evidence that chronically unemployed men have low self-esteem and faulty interpersonal relations.[9] Even short-term unemployment, if it recurs frequently, may lead to mental disorders.[10] Uncertainty about being able to find and hold a job, aside from financial worries, diminishes a worker's sense of potence and mastery of his or her environment. Nor is unemployment the only influence on mental stability. Underemployment, to the extent that it involves irregular hours of work and inadequate pay, is likely to occur in some lower-level jobs that have close supervision with low personal autonomy. Over time, such jobs may tend to reduce the worker's competence and sense of mastery.[11]

The idiosyncrasy hypothesis implies a priori disability. These studies suggest that psychological disabilities may interact with underutilization in a causal circle. This evidence does not discredit the idiosyncrasy hypothesis, but it does suggest a subtle, complex reinforcement phenomenon that cannot be adequately analyzed with the data in hand.

Summary and Conclusions

On balance, there is limited evidence in favor of the idiosyncrasy hypothesis. The idiosyncrasy hypothesis receives support if one analyzes unemployment and level of income for physically disabled workers in 1961–62 and 1970. There is little difference in overall rates of underutilization for the disabled and able-bodied. The comparison of 1970 data with 1961–62 data supports the notion that economic conditions (or other extraneous variables) may influence the disabled labor force and the civilian labor force in the same direction.

The idiosyncrasy hypothesis examines disability with all other variables held constant. An alternative hypothesis, the redundancy hypothesis, suggests that other characteristics may amplify the effect of disability. The alternative hypothesis received little support, but data about type and severity of disability were not available. Chapters 6 through 8 deal with the discrimination hypothesis, which considers the effect of age, race, and sex, and this will permit a different perspective on the redundancy hypothesis. Age, which is related both to disability and to underutilization, will be considered in the next chapter. The converse of the idiosyncrasy hypothesis implies that the magnitude of underutilization can be accounted for by the magnitude of disabled workers. This hypothesis received almost no support, unless one could explain a large residual.

Mental and emotional disabilities were considered even though no quantitative estimates were available. Studies of former mental patients and unemployed workers suggest that mental disorders and underutilization may reinforce each other. Consequently, the idiosyncrasy hypothesis, while not necessarily false, may well be simplistic.

The level of operationalization possible with census data is fairly crude. For "idiosyncrasy" to be interpreted in its broadest sense, a variety of subtle distinctions would be required. Further work in this area would benefit from measures of mental health and emotional stability. Theoretically, the idiosyncrasy hypothesis could also include persons whose behavior is perceived deviant—for example, exconvicts, dishonorably discharged veterans, and political dissidents. The relationship of work to deviant behavior in particular deserves more research.

CHAPTER 6

The Discrimination Hypothesis: Age

Everett Hughes described age, sex, and race as "master social positions," ascribed positions that significantly affect achievement within the stratification system.[1] Achievement is frequently described in terms of work, and so it is likely that master social positions affect adequacy of employment. The discrimination hypothesis says that less-preferred workers, judged by age, sex, and race, are more likely to be underutilized. However, age must be treated somewhat differently. Attitudes toward race and sex may change over time, but race and sex are fixed positions. Age, on the other hand, is constantly changing. As with the idiosyncrasy hypothesis, the discrimination hypothesis does not specify a mechanism; despite the label, overt employer discrimination is not the only mechanism. Tacit enculturation, the age-sex division of labor, and legal restrictions on employing the young or old may also be important factors.

Greater underutilization of the young is expected because of their inexperience and because their commitment to the labor force may be limited. Many students are available only for part-time work during the school year or for summer work. Limited commitment to a specific job shows up in high frictional unemployment for young graduates. New workers "shop around" and try out different jobs, and during this period they are likely to report being unemployed. Where the "last hired, first fired" policy is used, young workers are more likely than others to be terminated or laid off, and this may increase their unemployment. As for underemployment, many entry-level jobs are unstable and low paying. Persons holding these jobs are likely to be underutilized by hours of work, level of income, or mismatch. For all of these reasons, we would expect underutilization to be higher among young persons than among workers in the intermediate years.

At the other end of the work career, underutilization is expected to be higher among the elderly. Despite the Age Discrimination Act of 1967, it seems likely that many older workers, once disemployed or retired, have difficulty finding new jobs. Despite their experience, they are less likely to be highly educated, and the skills they do have may be obsolete. In the United States, "exit-level" jobs, which would require some downward mobility, are not so numerous nor so institutionalized as entry-level jobs. Consequently, underemployment is not expected to be the problem for the elderly that unemployment is.

Intermediate-aged workers, defined here as those aged 25 to 55, are expected to have fairly low underutilization (except perhaps for women returning to the labor force). Men in this age group tend to have fairly stable work lives. The underutilization that does occur is expected to result from variables other than age.

In summary, the discrimination hypothesis predicts that if you are young or old, you are more likely to be underutilized. More specifically, rates of underutilization should be highest among the young and lowest among the intermediate-aged. The primary form of underutilization among the elderly should be unemployment, but underemployment should be greater among the young.

The logic of the discrimination hypothesis requires that the master social positions be considered independently. Education, occupation, wage rates, and many other variables may intervene between age, sex, and race and underutilization, but age, sex, and race are logically prior and should be tested with other things considered equal. This chapter is concerned with the relation of age to underutilization. First, we examine age-specific participation rates, for these give us an approximation of the "risk" to underemployment among young and old Americans. This is followed by presentation of the data on underutilization for 1970, with a discussion of the forms of underutilization and how they vary by age. A limited comparison to 1960 data is made. These data permit an assessment of the adequacy of the discrimination hypothesis, at least as it applies to age. However, because age could be taken as a proxy for other variables (such as experience, education, and marriage), the findings are examined further to see if an alternate explanation works equally well.

Age-Specific Participation

The labor force is related to the overall population by the age-specific labor force participation rates. Age-specific labor force participation rates in 1970 ranged from 16.3% for persons aged 65 and over to 73% for persons aged 40–44. The young and the old had the lowest participation rates: 42.1% for ages 16–19, 68.1% for ages 20–24, 53.7% for ages 60–64, and 16.3% for ages 65 and over. For ages under 50, there is a weak negative correlation between age-specific labor force participation rates and percent underutilization in the age group ($r = -0.04$). (A curvilinear relation is predicted, so ages over 50 were omitted in the correlation.)

Despite relatively low participation rates at the younger ages, the 1970 labor force was a young one. One-fifth of the labor force in 1970 was below the age of 25; 32% were below the age of 30. This is not really paradoxical, for workers under the age of 25 came from the large postwar birth cohorts. They accounted for a large proportion of the population, so that even with low participation rates, they could account for a large proportion of the labor force. By contrast, only 10% of the labor force were over the age of 60, with only 4% over the age of 65.

Underutilization and Age

UNDERUTILIZATION IN 1970

Table 6.1 cross-classifies the civilian labor force for 1970 by age and type of utilization. The expected curvilinear relationship shows up in the inadequately utilized category, but the underutilization of the over-65 increases only slightly. Peak underutilization occurs among workers aged 20–24, although the rate for teens is also high.

Underutilization may be related to the total population by partitioning the age-specific labor force participation rates into adequately utilized participation rates and inadequately utilized participation rates. This is done in table 6.2. One prediction from the hypothesis is that adequate participation will rise with age until the intermediate years, and then decline. As column 2 shows, this is indeed the case. Inadequate participation is expected to be higher for the young and the old. This is not the case, as column 3 shows. Inadequate participation rises from ages 16–19 to ages 20–24, then drops. The inadequate participation rate of the old is the lowest of all. At older ages, there may be a trade-off of nonparticipation for inadequate participation.

FORMS OF UNDERUTILIZATION

The expected curvilinear relationship is found in unemployment. Unemployment rates are highest from ages 16 to 24: more than one of every nine teenagers in the labor force is unemployed. Then the rates drop below the overall 4.4% rate until age 65. At age 65 and older, unemployment rises to 5.3%, about 80% of what it is from 20 to 24, when it is 6.7%.

The pattern for hours of work is less clear, because the range of variation is only one percentage point. Again, teenagers have the highest rate, 2.4%, and persons aged 65 and over are next with 2.3%. Other rates are exactly 1.7%, the national rate, or somewhat lower.

Level of income shows a mixed pattern. The highest underutilization by level of income occurs in the age group 20–24; however, a rate well above the national rate occurs among ages 35–39. Older workers have a rate of 6.0% compared with the national rate of 6.6%. This change from the expected pattern is probably due to the design of the poverty index. Persons in their intermediate years are most likely to be supporting dependents, and so their cutoff level is higher. For elderly heads of households, even those with dependents, the cutoff figure is lower because of reduced food allowances. On the other hand, the design of the poverty index would seem to make it less likely that such a large number of young people would show up among the working poor. Remember that students are not included in this category, and that the cutoff used here is much lower for non–heads of households. Persons aged 20–24, who are 12.6% of the labor force, are 18.2% of the underutilized by level of income.

Table 6.1. *Civilian labor force by age and type of utilization, 1970 (Thousands o*

Type of utilization	Total, all ages (1)	16–19 years (2)	20–24 years (3)	25–29 years (4)	30–: years (5)
Total, all types	79899 (100.0%)	5918 (100.0%)	10105 (100.0%)	8928 (100.0%)	7639 (100
Adequately utilized	61256 (76.7%)	4248 (71.8%)	6521 (64.5%)	6746 (75.6%)	5901 (77.2
Inadequately utilized	18643 (23.3%)	1670 (28.2%)	3584 (35.5%)	2182 (24.4%)	1738 (22.8
By unemployment	3519 (4.4%)	681 (11.5%)	676 (6.7%)	360 (4.0%)	248 (3.3%
By hours of work[a]	1455 (1.9%)	143 (2.4%)	187 (1.9%)	134 (1.5%)	119 (1.6%
By level of income	5432 (6.6%)	548 (9.3%)	993 (9.8%)	537 (6.0%)	504 (6.6%
By mismatch[b]	8237 (10.4%)	298 (5.0%)	1728 (17.1%)	1151 (12.9%)	867 (11.4

[a] Adjusted with Current Population Survey, March, 1970. See appendix B.
[b] Adjusted with Current Population Survey, March, 1970. See appendix D.

Source: U.S. Bureau of the Census, *1970 Public Use Samples.*

·kers, with percentages)

35–39 years (6)	40–44 years (7)	45–49 years (8)	50–54 years (9)	55–59 years (10)	60–64 years (11)	65 years and older (12)
7551 (100.0%)	8666 (100.0%)	8647 (100.0%)	7918 (100.0%)	6651 (100.0%)	4574 (100.0%)	3302 (100.0%)
5836 (77.3%)	6845 (79.0%)	6947 (80.3%)	6471 (81.7%)	5399 (81.2%)	3758 (82.2%)	2584 (78.3%)
1715 (22.7%)	1821 (21.0%)	1700 (19.7%)	1447 (18.3%)	1252 (18.8%)	816 (17.8%)	718 (21.7%)
247 (3.3%)	277 (3.2%)	245 (2.8%)	225 (2.8%)	213 (3.2%)	173 (3.8%)	174 (5.1%)
142 (1.9%)	149 (1.7%)	166 (1.9%)	126 (1.6%)	126 (1.9%)	88 (1.9%)	75 (2.3%)
539 (7.1%)	538 (6.2%)	500 (5.8%)	427 (5.4%)	412 (6.2%)	233 (5.1%)	201 (6.0%)
787 (10.4%)	857 (9.9%)	789 (9.2%)	669 (8.5%)	501 (7.5%)	322 (7.0%)	268 (8.1%)

Table 6.2. *Decomposition of age-specific labor force participation rates, 1970*

	Labor force partici- pation rate (1)	Ade- quately utilized partici- pation rate (2)	Inade- quately utilized partici- pation rate (3)	Ratio of (3) to (2) (4)
Total, aged 16 and over	55.0	42.2	12.8	0.30
16–19 years	39.2	28.1	11.1	0.40
20–24 years	62.4	40.3	22.1	0.55
25–34 years	66.6	50.8	15.8	0.31
35–44 years	70.2	54.9	15.3	0.28
45–54 years	76.6	62.0	14.6	0.24
55–64 years	62.2	50.7	11.5	0.23
65 years and older	13.6	10.6	3.0	0.28

Source: U.S. Bureau of the Census, *1970 Public Use Samples.*

Mismatch shows the greatest variation by age. Teenagers have not yet received enough education to be mismatched. Most mismatch cutoffs begin beyond the high school diploma. College age students and nonstudents in the 20–24 age bracket show an extremely high incidence of mismatch. This is especially disturbing given the large size of the age group. On the other hand, the number of well-educated persons in this cohort who work should increase. As these young adults grow older, the median age of the labor force will shift and the mismatch cutoffs might rise as well. This "hump" of mismatched young persons may be smoothed out. (The education composition of persons aged 20–24 and the education-specific mismatch rates for the population are considered later.)

For ages 20–65, the curvilinear relationship holds. Mismatch declines with age until age 65. The slight increase in mismatched persons at age 65 and older was a bit of a surprise, for the curvilinear relationship was expected to hold for unemployment more than for the categories of underemployment. Older persons are less educated, but the most educated among them may continue to participate in the labor force, and perhaps their "exit jobs" require fewer skills. (The average retirement age tends to rise with more skilled occupations, but presumably this would not account for higher mismatch.)

The case for the discrimination hypothesis would be stronger were unemployment the only criterion. The situation becomes much more complex in the other categories. Teenagers are overrepresented in unemployment, hours of work, and income. Although persons aged 20–24 account for 12.6% of the labor force, they account for only 10.7% of the adequately utilized and they are overrepresented in every component of underutilization. Persons aged 35–39 are slightly overrepresented in every category except unemployment, but the extent of overrepresentation tends to be small. Persons aged 50–59 are overrepresented among the adequately utilized and underrepresented among all the categories of underutilization. Persons aged 65 and over are slightly overrepresented among the adequately utilized, but they are also overrepresented in two underutilization categories. The amount of scatter in the pattern is summarized by this fact: although the young and old are relatively more likely to be underutilized, they account for only 30% of all underutilized persons.

UNDERUTILIZATION BY AGE, 1960

Additional support for the discrimination hypothesis could be found if 1960 data showed a similar trend. Only unemployment data are used because hours of work and mismatch data could not be adjusted for age in 1960. The 1970 data fit the hypothesis better because of higher unemployment rates for teenagers and those aged 70 and over. In 1960, unemployment rates for the young were high, but the curvilinear relationship is weakened by the declining unemployment rates after ages 64–69.

Having data for two points in time permits limited cohort analysis. If the discrimination hypothesis were true, young cohorts with high unemployment in 1960 should have lower unemployment in 1970 when they are ten years older. Intermediate age groups in 1960 should have higher unemployment in 1970. Chart 1 shows this to be the case. Teenagers in 1960 had lower unemployment rates as adults, and unemployment rates rose for the older cohorts.

It might be objected that most unemployment rates were lower in 1970. The overall unemployment in 1970 was 4.4%, compared with 4.9% in 1960. Consequently, it is possible that decreased unemployment in the younger age cohorts is an artifact of improved economic conditions and not a result of age. The most dramatic way of refuting this is to reverse the rates. This is done in chart 2. Suppose that better economic conditions had prevailed in 1960 and worse conditions in 1970. Would young cohorts still have shown a decline in unemployment? Chart 2 shows that they would have. In the intermediate cohorts, unemployment rates tended to rise due to the "artificial recession." But the rate of increase accelerated until the usual retirement age. Only the comparison of ages 65–74 in 1960 with ages 75 and over in 1970 shows a different result.

This look at 1960 unemployment data supports the discrimination hypothesis and suggests that the relative disadvantage of age may be increasing. Despite better overall economic conditions in 1970, the unemployment among the young and elderly increased.

ADEQUACY OF THE HYPOTHESIS

Inspection of the data tends to support the hypothesis that age is associated with underutilization. Chi-square for the data in table 6.1 is highly significant, but this is not surprising, given the large sample size. Measures of association based on chi-square provide weak support; the contingency coefficient C is 0.17, and Cramer's V is 0.09; phi-square is 0.03. Values of 1 would indicate strong association. The closer to zero the value calculated, the more likely it is that the two variables are independent.

The measures of association might be affected by the number of five-year age categories. The statement of the discrimination hypothesis used three broad age classifications: young, intermediate, and old. It seems useful to test the data using these categories. The Kruskal-Wallis one-way analysis of variance by rank was computed for young age groups (16–29), intermediate age groups (30–54), and old age groups (55+), using overall rates of underutilization. The resulting H was significant at $P = .02$. The null hypothesis rejected by this test is that the means of the three categories are equal, against the alternative hypothesis that they are unequal.

The hypothesis posed in this chapter, that the young are more underutilized than the old, and the old are more underutilized than the intermediate-aged, poses ordered alternatives. The Jonckheere-Terpstra distribution-free test for ordered alternatives was used, and the test statistic J was significant at $P = .01$.[2] This supports the hypothesis that younger, older, and intermediate-aged

Chart 1. *Unemployment rates for five-year birth cohorts, 1960 and 1970*

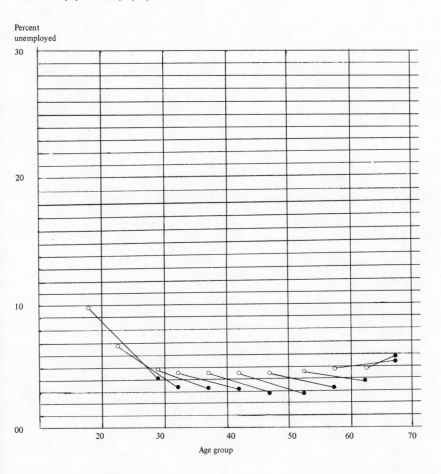

Legend: ○ 1960 unemployment rate
          ● 1970 unemployment rate

Chart 2. *Aging versus recession: five-year age cohorts with 1970 unemployment rates reported for 1960, and 1960 unemployment rates reported for 1970*

Percent
unemployed

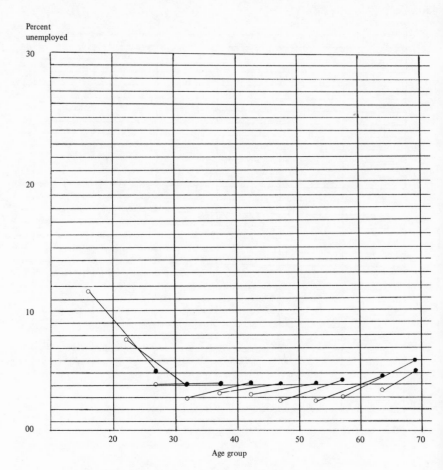

Age group

Legend: ○ 1970 unemployment rate reported for age group in 1960
            • 1960 unemployment rate reported for age group in 1970

workers are relatively more underutilized in that order. However, these measures deal with aggregate underutilization and not with underutilization by components.

Alternative Explanations

The discrimination hypothesis treats age as an independent variable. This hypothesis is supported by the age-specific rates, both in 1960 and 1970, and by nonparametric tests of differences among rates in broad age groups. On the other hand, when five-year groups are used, measures of association show a weak relationship between age and utilization. It is appropriate to consider alternative interpretations of the findings. Perhaps there is a spurious relation between age and utilization. Three alternative explanations are considered here: the age composition of the labor force, educational differences by age, and marital status.

AGE COMPOSITION OF THE LABOR FORCE

If the young and elderly are a relatively small fraction of the labor force, even a high age-specific rate of underutilization would affect relatively few persons. Measures of association are corrected for total sample size, and not the size of subgroups within the sample. Where subgroups are small, statistical independence would be more likely. (As it turns out, the young were a relatively large proportion of the 1970 labor force. The reasoning, however, deserves consideration as an alternative explanation for the elderly.)

To turn the argument around, suppose you look at the discrimination hypothesis as predicting lower rates of underutilization among intermediate-aged workers. In absolute numbers, there are more persons underutilized in the intermediate ages than at either end of the age range. Then lower underutilization rates are partly a function of labor force composition; with fewer intermediate-aged workers, there would be higher rates of underutilization.

Standardization is a technique that permits an assessment of what value a rate *would have*, if the population had a specific composition. Table 6.3 shows actual and standardized rates of underutilization and unemployment. Column 2 shows 1970 age-specific underutilization rates standardized by the 1960 age composition of the labor force. Among the young and old, labor force participation rates declined between 1960 and 1970. The number of underutilized persons in 1970 is presented as a percent of the 1960 age group. When this is done, rates of underutilization for teenagers drop over 6 percentage points. Persons aged 20–24 have the highest standardized rates, but then the rates decline steadily, reaching their lowest point with the elderly. The rates drop 7.5 points for persons 65 and over.

The 1960 unemployment data could not be age-adjusted, but it was possible to standardize with unemployment data alone. Columns 3 and 5 are the actual

Table 6.3. *Underutilization and unemployment rates, standardized for labor for* (*Rates per hundred persons aged [*x − x + n*])*

Age (x − x + n)	1970 underutili- zation rate— actual (1)	1970 underutili- zation rate— standardized[a] (2)	1970 1970 unemp ment rate— actual (3)
Total, 16 and over	23.3%	21.3%	4.4%
16–19 years	28.2	22.0	11.5
20–24 years	35.5	32.6	6.7
25–34 years	23.7	23.8	3.7
35–44 years	21.8	21.9	3.2
45–54 years	19.0	18.8	2.8
55–64 years	18.4	18.1	3.4
65 years and over	21.7	14.2	5.3

[a] Standardized by 1960 age composition of labor force.
[b] Standardized by 1970 age composition of labor force.

Sources: U.S. Bureau of Labor Statistics, *Handbook of Labor Statistics, 1973,* tab *Experience,* table 6.1.

icipation rates and labor force age structure

	1960	
1970 unemploy-ment rate—standardized[a] (4)	1960 unemploy-ment rate—actual (5)	1960 unemploy-ment rate—standardized[b] (6)
4.0%	4.9%	5.0%
9.0	9.8	13.0
6.0	6.9	7.0
4.0	4.6	4.0
3.0	4.1	4.0
3.0	4.0	4.0
3.0	4.6	5.0
3.0	5.0	8.0

. Bureau of the Census, *Employment Status and Work*

age-specific unemployment rates in 1970 and 1960. Column 6 is 1960 unemployment rates applied to the 1970 age composition; column 4 is 1970 unemployment applied to the 1960 age composition. The lowest overall unemployment rate results from using 1970 unemployment and the 1960 age composition (column 4). With this standardization, the relative disadvantage of older workers disappears. The disadvantage of younger workers remains, but is smaller.

Table 6.3 indicates that although both 1960 and 1970 data support the hypothesis, the 1970 age composition influenced the excess unemployment of the elderly. The two overall rates of unemployment were decomposed as follows:[3]

$$t. - T. = \text{Gross } I + \text{Residual } I$$

where:　　　　$t.$ = overall unemployment rate in 1960

　　　　　　$T.$ = overall unemployment rate in 1970

　　　　Gross I = difference in unemployment rates due to age composition

　　　　Residual I = difference in unemployment rates due to age-specific
　　　　rates and the interaction of rates and composition

$$0.56 = -0.15 + 0.71$$

The negative Gross I indicates that based on composition alone, 1970 overall rates would be higher, and not lower, than 1960 overall rates. That is, the 1970 age composition of the labor force was conducive to higher levels of unemployment. This means that reduction in age-specific unemployment rates accounts for the overall decline in unemployment. ("Accounts for" should be understood as a statistical explanation within the context of the technique. Chart 2 indicated that improved economic conditions could also "account for" lower unemployment.) Thus, changes in age-specific unemployment rates seem to be more important than age composition in explaining declines.

EDUCATION COMPOSITION

Mismatch and unemployment are the two categories in which underutilization of the young is most evident. Mismatch hits young adults aged 20–24 the hardest; they account for only 12.6% of the labor force but for 21% of the mismatched. Persons aged 25–29, although not so likely to be underutilized by unemployment, account for 14% of the mismatched. An explanation that is consistent with the discrimination hypothesis is that entry jobs start at the bottom, where young workers may appear in statistical terms to be overskilled.

A second explanation is the higher educational attainment of the young compared with the old. The young are mismatched, the argument runs, as an artifact of the instrument. It does not indicate any "real" underutilization. As older, less-skilled workers retire, the average educational attainment within occupations will rise. Mismatch cutoffs will also rise. Thus, the apparent underutilization of the young is due to education composition, for which age is a proxy. Over time, mismatch rates for these cohorts would decline, even if they stayed in their 1970 occupations. If true, this argument would weaken the discrimination hypothesis and cast doubt on the value of the Labor Utilization Framework.

This second argument does not explain high mismatch among the old. Aside from this, and concentrating only on the young, the argument can be evaluated by inspecting table 6.4. The table uses the education distribution of persons aged 20–29 as its composition standard. The discrimination hypothesis normally includes ages 16–24, but teenagers have often not completed their education. Besides, the mismatch rates for those aged 25–29 are high, and so the age group 20–29 is used to test the education composition argument. When young workers' education distribution is used as a standard, the overall mismatch rate rises from 10.4% to 12.5%. If the whole population were educated as well as persons in their twenties, mismatch cutoffs remaining the same, mismatch would increase by about 2%.[4] On the other hand, if workers in their twenties had the same mismatch rates as the whole population for each education level, their overall mismatch rate would also rise. (The rate for workers aged 20–29 would rise about .5% to 15.6%).

Young workers are well educated. Persons aged 20–29 account for 34% of all four-year college graduates; college graduates account for 27% of all mismatches. But composition alone does not explain all of the differences in mismatch. The higher education profile of the young is offset by marginally lower mismatch rates for given levels of education. But their *age-specific* rates for mismatch are high. To put it differently, the young are underutilized partly because they are young and not just because they are overeducated.

A brief digression is in order. There may be two sorts of mismatch, a "real" mismatch corresponding to an actual underuse of skills, and a "statistical" mismatch which results from using the standard score. In a relatively well utilized subpopulation (e.g., the intermediate-aged), a large mismatch percentage may represent freedom from unemployment, short hours, and low income as well as the limits of the first standard deviation. Ironically, subpopulations that have inferior educations may have "mismatch insurance." This idea will be explored in more depth in chapter 11.

MARRIAGE

Age is associated with both marriage and underutilization. In fact, one might argue that the discrimination hypothesis is mistaken in arguing that age is related to underutilization. Married persons are more likely to participate in the labor force. There is a strong positive relation between the percent of an age cohort "married, spouse present" and the age-specific labor force participation rate ($r = 0.93$). Further the married person is less likely to be underutilized

Table 6.4. *Mismatch rates standardized by education distribution, 1970*

Completed years of school (i)	Number of workers aged 20–29 (N_i)	All workers[a]	
		Number mismatched[b] (m_i)	Rate (percent) (c_i)
Less than 8 years	698	0	0.0
8 years	599	0	0.0
9–11 years	2772	15	0.1
12 years	7989	502	1.8
College 1	1688	698	16.1
College 2	1608	1942	44.9
College 3	837	669	34.4
College 4	1880	1942	34.7
College 5	542	474	26.4
College 6+	420	974	35.1
Total	19033	7216	10.4

| Tabulated mismatch percentage | 15.1% | | |

Mismatch rates for all workers standardized by education composition of young workers = $(\Sigma N_i c_i / N.) \times 100 = 12.5\%$.

[a] Aged 16 and over.
[b] Unadjusted. See appendix D.

Source: U.S. Bureau of the Census, *1970 Public Use Samples.*

($r = -$o.66). Perhaps married persons are more persistent in locating a job, or are more "settled down," or feel the economic pressure of providing for dependents. From this notion, we would expect the correlation between percent underutilized and participation rate, when controlled for percent married, to become positive. It does in fact change to a simple correlation of $r =$ o.82.

This evidence, while interesting, is inconclusive. It implies that, having married, the young person's labor market activity becomes more diligent. What may happen instead is that people postpone marriage until they have a good job. Both sequences would produce these results. The large, positive correlation between marriage and participation is probably due to the fact that both of these are statuses descriptive of the majority of intermediate-aged males. It is reasonable to argue that age is related to marriage, labor force participation, and underutilization; this supports both the discrimination hypothesis and the postulated importance of age as a "master social position."

Conclusions

The discrimination hypothesis contends that age affects underutilization; specifically, the young and the old are more likely to be underutilized than the middle-aged. It is a phenomenon of age and not of current economic conditions, as the utilization of birth cohorts from 1960 to 1970 showed.

If we limit the analysis to inadequate participation, the data tend to support the hypothesis. The results are not explained equally well by relying on any other single-variable explanation. Four alternatives were examined: temporal fluctuations, age composition, education composition, and percent of the cohort married. The predicted curvilinear pattern persisted from 1960 to 1970, although the 1970 pattern was more obvious. During the decade, although underutilization declined, the relative underutilization of the young and old increased. In part, this was due to a change in age composition, but age-specific rates also worsened. The data indicated that the young are more likely to be underutilized than the elderly, and the elderly are more likely to be underutilized than the intermediate-aged.

The relative disadvantage of both young and old workers is most obvious in unemployment, but the young and old are also more likely to be mismatched. From 1960 to 1970, while overall unemployment improved, it deteriorated for both the young and the old (those aged sixty-five and older). For both groups labor force participation was simultaneously declining. Education composition helps to explain the high mismatch of the young. Young workers' lower education-specific mismatch rates are countered by their high age-specific mismatch rates.

Events since 1970 tend to support the hypothesis as well, although public discussion of these trends has tended to blur two facts: the number of young workers has increased dramatically, and the overall rate of unemployment has also gone up. The first fact is true because today's young workers are still coming from the large postwar birth cohorts. Even without any change in participation rates, they would account for a larger percentage of the labor force. By parallel reasoning, we would expect the *number* of unemployed young persons to rise. What has happened is that the *rate* of unemployment among young persons has also gone up. Among minority teenagers, the rate approaches 40%. Larger numbers of young workers with higher rates might be expected to "account for" the higher unemployment, but they do not. The general increase in unemployment outstripped even the rise in teenage unemployment. Teenagers, who accounted for 27% of unemployment in 1970, accounted for only 22.4% of it in 1975. Further, the increase in teenage unemployment could not be dismissed as a sudden, large influx of youngsters looking for their first jobs. It is true that a larger *number* of young unemployed workers in 1975 were entrants—628,000 compared with 401,000 in 1970—but this was a slightly smaller *percentage* of the young 1975 unemployed workers.[5] Other underutilization components are not available for 1975, but unemployment still continues to fall more heavily upon the young.

Age is not the only master social position which may affect underutilization. Chapter 7 takes up race and sex as master social positions. Chapter 8 considers the possible redundant effects of master social positions: how much of an advantage does the middle-aged white male have over the teenaged female or the elderly Negro?

The Discrimination Hypothesis: Race and Sex

Young workers can take some comfort in knowing that their utilization is likely to improve, for the "disadvantage" of youth disappears (all too rapidly, as a rule). But if workers are underutilized because of the other master social positions, race and sex, they can expect relief only if attitudes change, labor demand soars, or corrective legislation is enforced. Are race and sex barriers to adequate utilization? This chapter begins with the hypothesis that they are. Other things being equal, nonwhites are expected to be more underutilized than whites, and women more than men.

Race and sex are considered separately in this chapter. As in the two preceding chapters, the analysis proceeds by looking first at labor force participation rates. Overall underutilization for 1970 is compared with that in 1960, and each component of underutilization is discussed. Support for the hypothesis and alternative explanations are compared. Education and occupation are the two principal alternative explanations examined. In chapter 8, race and sex are considered jointly.

Race and Labor Market Discrimination

Unemployment, the only indicator of underutilization now available, has always been more severe for blacks than for whites. Since 1960, the ratio of nonwhite to white unemployment has fluctuated in a narrow band from 1.8 to 2.1. Those blacks who are employed are more likely to be stuck in "dead-end," low-paying jobs, where the work is irregular. Not only blacks, but other nonwhite racial groups, as well as white immigrants, found themselves used as a reserve of cheap labor.[1] Descendants of the white immigrants, and some Asian Americans, have escaped the cheap labor pool. Blacks have had more difficulty. The Negro population was disproportionately rural, and this might have aggravated their underutilization. But even in cities, and even for skilled nonwhite workers, discriminatory practices limited employment.

Many labor market disadvantages are redundant: the victims of racial discrimination are also likely to be poorly educated and to have inferior occupational attainments. Where discrimination exists, even college degrees may not guarantee good-paying jobs. In this chapter, utilization will be considered with preliminary controls for occupation and education. In later chapters the effects of education, occupation, and industry will be considered in more depth.

For most of the analysis in this chapter, *color* is a more appropriate term than *race*. "Nonwhite" is the category used to designate Negroes, American Indians, Japanese, Chinese, Filipinos, Hawaiians, Aleuts, Koreans, and Eskimos. About 90% of this category are Negroes (the term used in the 1970 census). It could be argued that the underutilization of Negroes differs from that of other racial groups, particularly the Chinese and Japanese. The more affluent Asian groups might have lower underutilization rates. However, because Asian Americans constitute a very small percentage of the population, separate reports on each group would be unreliable, and their effect on nonwhite underutilization rates is likely to be small.

NONWHITES IN THE LABOR FORCE

In 1970, nonwhites accounted for about 11% of the United States population aged 16 and over. Their proportion in the labor force is similar. Table 7.1 shows labor force participation rates for whites and nonwhites in census years 1940–70. White participation rates increased from 51.8 in 1940 to 56.6 in 1970. Most of this increase is due to the increased participation of white women, which has more than compensated for the lower participation rates of white males. During the thirty-year period, the nonwhite participation rate declined from 58.4 to 56.1. Most of the nonwhite decline occurred among males. Nonwhite female participation increased only marginally, compared with the large increase among white females. The rising white female participation increased the contrast between white and nonwhite participation rates.

The reasons for the decline in participation are not entirely understood. Some of the decline may be an artifact of the data collection. For example, the net census undercount of blacks affects participation rates. The government adjusts the participation rates for undercount. However, a different adjustment procedure can be shown to yield slower declines in participation among young nonblack workers, and a steeper decline among prime-aged nonwhite males. It would also show a greater increase among nonwhite females than the official statistics show.[2] Another source of apparent declines in participation is changes in the labor force definition. One of these occurred in 1965. Before that date, enrollees in manpower programs were counted as "unemployed." After that date, the enrollees—many of them from minority groups—were counted as "employed" or "not in the labor force."[3] Of course, not all of the decline is due to statistical manipulation. Some substantive reasons for the 1960–70 decline in nonwhite participation include higher school enrollment among black males and higher reported illness and disability.[4] The decline in nonwhite participation rates is difficult to interpret because it may also include discouraged workers or those who prefer street life-styles and "hustling" to regular employment. Table 7.1 decomposes the labor force participation rates into adequate and inadequate participation. Nonagricultural rates are shown for 1960 and 1970 to control for differences in farm employment between the two racial groups.

From 1960 to 1970, nonwhite workers became more homogeneous in their employment, and they narrowed the gap between themselves and white workers. Farm employment declined for both groups, but it declined more among nonwhites. Nonagricultural participation between the two groups became more similar. The industrial composition of the nonwhite labor force now differs very little from that of whites. This is important, for the adequacy of participation improved more rapidly outside agriculture. Judging only from industrial composition, we would expect the utilization of nonwhites to be improving.

When we examine nonagricultural workers, columns 6 and 7 do show an improvement in nonwhite adequate participation. The 1960–70 increase, 2.8 points, combines a 6.8-point increase in adequate participation and a 4-point decline in inadequate participation. (White participation increased 2.6%, a 1.9% increase in adequate participation and a 0.7% increase in inadequate participation.) Nonwhite workers substantially improved their adequate participation by 1970, but this reflects how much further behind they were in 1960. In 1960, 41% of whites but only 31% of nonwhites were adequately participating. By 1970, nonwhites had not yet arrived at the point that whites had passed in 1960.

UTILIZATION AND COLOR, 1960–70

Table 7.2 compares utilization for nonagricultural workers in 1960 and 1970. During the decade, there was a 28% increase in the nonwhite labor force, and an 8.2% increase in adequate utilization. This represents a substantial growth both in employment and in adequate employment. The white labor force increased by 21.4%, although adequate participation declined marginally by 0.3%. As we will see below, this decline is due solely to an increase in mismatch.

Unemployment diminished for both groups, possibly because of economic conditions, and the decline was steeper for nonwhites. Nevertheless, the nonwhite 1970 rate is even higher than the white 1960 rate, and is 1.5 times as high as the white 1970 rate. Involuntary part-time employment increased slightly among nonwhites from 1960 to 1970. The nonwhite rate in 1970 was 161% of the white rate in 1960 and 227% of the white rate in 1970. It is possible that for nonwhites there is a trade-off between full-time unemployment and part-time unemployment.

The most remarkable decline in underutilization for both color groups occurred among the working poor. The nonwhite rate was cut almost in half, and the white rate dropped by 40%. Still, color differentials remained large. It is difficult to pinpoint all the reasons for decline in the working poor. A general

Table 7.1. *Labor force participation rates by color, 1940–70, with decomposition*

Year	Total Labor force participation rate (LFPR) (1)	LFPR (2)	White Adequate LFPR (3)	Inadequa LFPR (4)
1970[a]	55.5	56.6	44.0	12.6
Nonagricultural workers	55.0	55.1	43.1	12.0
1960	55.3	55.2	....	....
Nonagricultural workers[b]	52.7	52.5	41.2	11.3
1950	53.4	53.1	....	....
1940	52.4	51.8	....	....

[a] All 1970 figures presented for workers aged 16 and over. Other years are presente
[b] For workers aged 16 and over.

Sources: Column 1 and all denominators used in columns 2–7 from U.S. Bureau
U.S. Summary, table 78; other data from idem, *1960* and *1970 Public Use Sample*

es for adequacy of utilization in 1960–70

Nonwhite

LFPR (5)	Adequate LFPR (6)	Inadequate LFPR (7)
56.1	38.4	17.7
54.7	37.9	16.8
56.3	....	....
51.9	31.1	20.8
56.1	....	....
58.4	....	....

or workers aged 14 and over except as in note b.

ne Census, *General Social and Economic Characteristics,*

Table 7.2. *Civilian nonagricultural labor force by color and type of utilizatic (Thousands of workers aged 16 and over, with percentages)*

| | 1970 | | |
Type of utilization	All colors (1)	White (2)	Non-white (3)
Total, nonagricultural workers	77606 (100.0%)	69012 (100.0%)	8594 (100.0%)
Adequately utilized	59949 (77.2%)	53997 (78.2%)	5952 (69.3%)
Inadequately utilized	17657 (22.8%)	15015 (21.8%)	2642 (30.7%)
By unemployment[a]	3440 (4.4%)	2883 (4.2%)	557 (6.5%)
By hours of work[b]	1294 (1.7%)	1000 (1.5%)	294 (3.4%)
By level of income	4940 (6.4%)	3853 (5.6%)	1087 (12.6%)
By mismatch[c]	7983 (10.3%)	7279 (10.5%)	704 (8.2%)

[a] Includes those unemployed workers with no industrial category.
[b] Adjusted. See appendix B.
[c] Adjusted. See appendix D.

Source: U.S. Bureau of the Census, *1970 Public Use Samples.*

60 and 1970

	1960	
All colors (4)	White (5)	Non-white (6)
63558 (100.0%)	56841 (100.0%)	6717 (100.0%)
48666 (76.6%)	44631 (78.5%)	4035 (60.1%)
14892 (23.4%)	12210 (21.5%)	2682 (39.9%)
3226 (5.1%)	2642 (4.7%)	584 (8.7%)
1405 (2.2%)	1181 (2.1%)	224 (3.3%)
6844 (10.8%)	5220 (9.2%)	1624 (24.2%)
3417 (5.4%)	3167 (5.6%)	250 (3.7%)

rise in wages, federal manpower and poverty programs, and the change in the business cycle are all possible parts of the reason for nonwhites in the labor force at both points. Alternative nonwork sources of income might have been more available in 1970. Besides these factors, a large proportion of the working poor in 1960 had probably left the labor force by 1970, and new workers were less likely to be poor.

Mismatch increased both for nonwhites and for whites, but the white mismatch rate was higher than the nonwhite rate. In 1960, white mismatch was 1.9 points higher than nonwhite; by 1970, the gap was 2.3 points. However, nonwhite mismatch was accelerating at a faster rate than for whites. White mismatch in 1970 was 188% of its 1960 value, but nonwhite mismatch was 222% of its 1960 value. Mismatch differs from the other components because its incidence among whites is higher. Possible reasons for this are discussed below.

The 1960 data provide stronger evidence for the discrimination hypothesis, although 1970 data also lend support. The trend, on the other hand, does *not* support the hypothesis, for it points to greater equality of utilization. While nonwhites are more likely to be underutilized, they still account for a small proportion of the underutilized. Eighty-five percent of the underutilized are white.

EDUCATION AND NONWHITE UTILIZATION

Economists of education have speculated that it is economically irrational for Negroes to seek advanced education because of their difficulty in translating added years of education into added income. In terms of our framework, lower education would be "mismatch insurance," and it would help explain the lower rates of mismatch among nonwhites. Economists of the "structural unemployment" school, on the other hand, feel that the lower educational attainment of Negroes is responsible for their higher unemployment and their concentration in unskilled, unstable, and low-paying jobs.

In other words, educational attainment may be a better explanation of the results in table 7.2 than the discrimination hypothesis, for it could explain both the higher nonwhite rates of unemployment, involuntary part-time work, and low wages, and the lower rate in mismatch. Education differentials may be due to discrimination, but in terms of this discussion, education and not discrimination would become the independent variable.

Columns 2 and 5 of table 7.3 show the difference in educational levels between the nonwhite and white labor forces. One-fifth of nonwhites have less than an eighth grade education compared with 8% of whites. Over 62% of whites, but only 43% of nonwhites, have achieved at least twelve years of schooling, the median attainment of the population. Only 16% of nonwhites have gone beyond high school education, but 27% of whites have.

Education-specific underutilization rates are given in columns 3 and 6. ($\Delta =$

39.6.) These rates are the number of full-time workers expressed as a percent of all workers with the same level of education. Adjustments were not possible for involuntary part-time work or for part-time mismatch. The rates document the extent of nonwhite disadvantage. Not only are more nonwhites poorly educated, but at most levels of education their underutilization rates are higher. Among persons with an elementary education or less, 24.3% of nonwhites but only 17.3% of whites are full-time underutilized. Only when five or more years of college have been completed do the white rates outstrip the nonwhite rates. Rates become higher at higher levels of education because mismatch comes into play. The gap between nonwhites and whites becomes wider at four years of college.

When the difference between the rates is decomposed, there is a large, positive component representing the difference in education-specific rates. Higher education-specific rates of underutilization explain the difference in white and nonwhite rates. The component for education composition is negative and reduces the effect of the rates by about one-fifth. The inferior education composition of nonwhites helped offset their higher education-specific rates.

Thus, education alone cannot explain the differences in utilization by color. It appears that discrimination, or something which produces a discriminatory effect, accounts for the difference in utilization. Education composition alone is not an adequate explanation.

How can these data be reconciled with other studies that show a strong "new market" for black college graduates?[5] Actually, the data are not contradictory. Today's black college graduates are showing a relatively higher rate of return on their college investment, compared with either the previous experience of young blacks or their experience vis-à-vis whites. Certainly the income of black college graduates is adequate; the incidence of underutilization by income drops substantially for blacks with every education increment. Where well-educated blacks are underutilized, it is by mismatch. Over one-third of blacks with some college are substantially better educated than others in their occupations. It may be the case that young blacks are more able to convert their education into income than into occupational attainment or prestige.

A further note on table 7.3 is in order. Orientals, American Indians, and other nonblack racial minorities help account for the high rates of underutilization among well-educated workers. For those with some college, 40% are mismatched, although other forms of underutilization are negligible.

OCCUPATION AND COLOR, 1970

Lower mismatch among nonwhites could be explained if their occupational attainment were lower. This would mean a lower mismatch cutoff, one that might be statistically "suitable" given their lower educational attainment. In addition, low occupational attainment might help explain the higher prev-

Table 7.3. *Labor force by color, education level, and education-specific* *(Thousands of workers aged 16 and over)*

		Nonwhite labor force	
Education level[a] (i)	Number (n_i) (1)	Proportion (n_i/n) (2)	Under-utilizat rate[b] (t_i) (3)
Less than 8 years	1843	.209	24.3
8 years	792	.090	23.1
9–11 years	2338	.265	22.7
12 years	2429	.275	23.2
College 1–3	775	.088	50.1
College 4	358	.040	56.9
College 5–6+	287	.033	34.8
Total	8822	1.000	26.5

Difference between rates = 7.1 (due to education composition = −2.1; due

[a] Years of school completed.
[b] Number of underutilized full-time workers as a percent of all workers.

Source: U.S. Bureau of the Census, *1970 Public Use Samples.*

erutilization of full-time workers, 1970

White labor force

Number (N_i) (4)	Pro- portion (N_i/N) (5)	Under- utilization rate[b] (T_i) (6)
5428	.076	17.3
6154	.087	12.5
14715	.207	12.4
25414	.358	11.2
9846	.138	38.2
5234	.074	40.8
4286	.060	35.9
71077	1.000	19.4

ication-specific rates = 9.2; due to interaction = 0.1).

rt-time workers could not be adjusted.

alence of unemployment, short hours, and low incomes. In short, occupation distribution competes with discrimination as an explanation for table 7.2.

Nonwhite occupational attainment was considerably below that of whites both in 1960 and in 1970. The index of dissimilarity in 1960 was 39.4; in 1970 it was 29.6. Despite a more equal distribution in 1970, substantial differences remained. Nonwhites were overrepresented among service workers, private household workers, and labor except farm labor. They were underrepresented in every white-collar category and among skilled blue-collar workers. Between 1960 and 1970, nonwhites increased their representation among professional and clerical workers. Labor, private household workers, and farm labor showed the largest declines. The white distribution shifted away from farm and blue-collar occupations toward white-collar occupations, but the shift was much less dramatic than that of nonwhite workers.

As previous comparisons of 1960 and 1970 data suggest, the underutilization rates in 1970 tended to be lower. The exceptions were the rates for professionals and sales workers, which rose through mismatch. The largest decreases were among service and farm workers; these were likely to have been decreases in underutilization by level of income. Table 7.4 presents the underutilization rates for major occupational groups in 1960 and 1970. As in table 7.3, full-time rates are given because hours of work could not be adjusted. Unlike table 7.3, the rates have been computed as a percent of full-time workers only. This is because part-time work is more prevalent in some occupational groups and would have the effect of diluting the underutilization rate for those groups.

The most interesting part of table 7.4 is the direct standardizations by nonwhite occupational distributions. The rate for the 1970 white labor force worsens with the successive application of the 1970 and 1960 nonwhite occupational distributions. Even worse is the unstandardized rate for the nonwhite labor force (i.e., 1970 nonwhite distribution with 1970 nonwhite rates). The progressive deterioration of underutilization rates may be repeated with the 1960 rates. The rate rises using the 1970 nonwhite distribution and climbs still higher using the 1960 nonwhite distribution. The highest rate of all is that for nonwhites in 1960.

From this analysis we can draw two conclusions:

1. The nonwhite occupational distribution contributed to higher underutilization in both 1960 and 1970;

2. However, not all of the difference was due to composition; underutilization rates were higher for nonwhites, even holding composition constant.

This first look at color differences in utilization supports the view that nonwhites are more likely to be underutilized even when education and occupation are controlled. We have labeled this residual effect "discrimination." Nevertheless, researchers should not content themselves with an overly simplistic label. For example, the large number of young nonwhites with some college may be underutilized only while they gain experience and a work record.

Women in the Labor Force

One issue of the feminist movement, "equal pay for equal work," reflects a widespread assumption that women are victimized in the labor market. This assumption is a variant of the discrimination hypothesis. This survey of women's utilization tends to support it, for women seem to be somewhat less well utilized than men. However, women participate less often in the labor force. In 1970, 73.2% of all men were labor force participants; 16% of all men were inadequate participants. Among women, 41.6% participated, but 10.3% were inadequate participants. While 161 males participated adequately for every 100 women adequately participating, among the inadequately participating the ratio was 134 to 100. It may be that nonparticipation is an acceptable alternative to inadequate participation for women.

Table 7.5 presents utilization categories by sex for 1960 and 1970. The pattern observed is similar to that in table 7.2; women are higher than men in every category of inadequate utilization except mismatch. Between 1960 and 1970, there was a decline in underutilization by hours of work and level of income shared by both sexes; mismatch increased for both sexes, but more for men than for women. The overall decline in unemployment, however, was not shared by women. This is partly explained by the fact that 42% of the unemployed women in 1970, but only 22% of the men, were entrants or reentrants to the labor force.[6]

Underutilization by level of income was the single largest source of women's underutilization in both 1960 and 1970. This is true despite the fact that the operational definition "loads the dice" against them. The poverty level assigns male heads of households a higher cutoff than females. In this study, a lower poverty level was assigned to secondary workers, many of whom are women. (For a description of the operational definition, see appendix C.)

How can we explain the higher underutilization among women? The same two variables are introduced here as for nonwhites earlier in the chapter: education and occupation. Does either account for the greater underutilization of women, or must we look for a residual explanation, such as "discrimination"?

WOMEN AND EDUCATION, 1970

Table 7.6 presents education level and underutilization by sex. Larger proportions of males than of females report very low and very high educations. Female rates of underutilization tend to be higher than male rates at those education levels where their proportions are lower, and vice versa. Thus, we might expect that the effects of composition and rates have different signs. In fact, they do. As among nonwhites, higher underutilization among women is due to their higher *rates* of underutilization. Composition alone tends to be favorable to adequate utilization. Thus, education composition is not a sufficient explanation of higher female underutilization.

Table 7.4. Occupational distribution by color, with underutilization rates for full-time labor force, 1960 and 1970 (Based on workers aged 16 and over, except as noted)

Major occupational group	1960			1970		
	Non-white (1)	White (2)	Under-utilization rate[a] (3)	Non-white (4)	White (5)	Under-utilization rate[b] (6)
Total	100.0%	100.0%	25.5%	100.0%	100.0%	25.1%
Professional, technical, and kindred	4.8	12.1	11.2	9.1	14.8	15.2
Managers, officers, and proprietors	2.6	11.7	25.0	3.5	11.4	27.2
Clerical	7.3	15.7	26.2	13.2	18.0	29.3
Sales	1.5	7.0	17.7	2.1	6.7	24.3
Craftsmen and foremen	6.0	13.8	28.4	8.2	13.5	17.2
Operatives	20.4	17.9	25.0	23.7	17.0	20.3
Labor, excluding farm	13.7	4.4	35.3	10.3	4.1	27.8
Service workers, excluding private						

workers	14.2	1.7	59.2	7.7	1.3	56.4
Farm managers and farmers	3.2	4.3	51.0	1.0	2.4	28.5
Farm laborers and foremen	9.0	3.0	56.4	2.9	1.6	64.6
Comparison by color, within year	$\Delta_{14} = 18.1$		$\Delta_{12} = 39.4$			$\Delta_{45} = 29.6$
Comparison by year, within color				$\Delta_{25} = 6.0$		

1970 full-time rate of underutilization = 25.1.
1970 full-time rate of underutilization, standardized by 1970 nonwhite occupation distribution = 27.6.
1970 full-time rate of underutilization, standardized by 1960 nonwhite occupation distribution = 33.0.
1970 full-time rate of underutilization, nonwhite labor force = 36.4.
1960 full-time rate of underutilization = 25.5.
1960 full-time rate of underutilization, standardized by 1970 nonwhite occupation distribution = 31.0.
1960 full-time rate of underutilization, standardized by 1960 nonwhite occupation distribution = 36.1.
1960 full-time rate of underutilization, nonwhite labor force = 46.9.

[a]Based on persons aged 14 and over. Number of underutilized full-time workers expressed as a percent of all full-time workers. Part-time workers could not be adjusted.
[b]Based on persons aged 16 and over. Rate computed as in column 3.

Sources: Columns 3 and 6, U.S. Bureau of the Census, *1960* and *1970 Public Use Samples*; other columns, idem, *Statistical Abstract of the United States: 1976*, table 601.

Table 7.5. *Nonagricultural labor force by sex and utilization, 1960 and 1970*

		1960	
Utilization	Total, both sexes (1)	Male (2)	Fema (3)
Total civilian labor force	63558 (100.0%)	41664 (100.0%)	2189 (100.
Adequately utilized	48666 (76.6%)	32452 (77.9%)	1621 (74.1
Inadequately utilized	14892 (23.4%)	9212 (22.1%)	5680 (25.9
By unemployment[a]	3226 (5.1%)	2075 (5.0%)	1151 (5.3%
By hours of work[b]	1405 (2.2%)	706 (1.7%)	699 (3.2%
By level of income	6844 (10.7%)	3727 (8.9%)	3117 (14.2
By mismatch[c]	3417 (5.4%)	2704 (6.5%)	713 (3.2%

Difference between sexes
within years $\Delta_{23} = 7.1$

Difference between years
within sexes $\Delta_{25} = 5.8$

Difference between years

[a] Includes those not reporting industrial classification.
[b] Adjusted. See appendix B.
[c] Adjusted. See appendix D.

Source: U.S. Bureau of the Census, *1960* and *1970 Public Use Samples.*

ousands of workers aged 16 and over, with percentages)

Total, both sexes (4)	1970 Male (5)	Female (6)
77606 (100.0%)	47143 (100.0%)	30463 (100.0%)
59949 (77.2%)	37023 (78.5%)	22926 (75.3%)
17657 (22.8%)	10120 (21.5%)	7537 (24.7%)
3440 (4.4%)	1823 (3.9%)	1617 (5.3%)
1294 (1.7%)	635 (1.3%)	659 (2.1%)
4940 (6.4%)	2166 (4.6%)	2774 (9.1%)
7983 (10.3%)	5496 (11.7%)	2487 (8.2%)

$$\Delta_{56} = 6.7$$

$_{36} = 6.2$

$$\Delta_{14} = 5.5$$

Table 7.6. *Labor force by sex, education level, and education-specific underutiliza*
(Thousands of workers aged 16 and over)

Female

Education level[a] (i)	Number (n_i) (1)	Proportion (n_i/n) (2)	Underutili zation rat (t_i) (3)
Less than 8 years	2074	.066	24.0%
8 years	2230	.073	18.4
9–11 years	6488	.211	18.1
12 years	12355	.402	14.9
College 1–3	4202	.137	35.6
College 4	2135	.071	27.0
College 5+	1214	.040	32.9
Total	30698	1.000	20.8

Difference between rates = 0.9% (due to education composition = −1.0; due to

[a] Years of school completed.
[b] Number of underutilized full-time workers as a percent of all workers. Part-time

Source: U.S. Bureau of the Census, *1970 Public Use Samples.*

full-time workers, 1970

	Male	
Number (N_i) (4)	Proportion (N_i/N) (5)	Underutili- zation rate[b] (T_i) (6)
5197	.106	17.1%
4716	.096	11.5
10565	.215	11.2
15488	.315	10.2
6419	.130	41.3
3457	.070	48.9
3359	.068	36.8
49201	1.000	19.9

cation-specific rates = +1.8; due to interaction = +0.1).

rkers could not be adjusted.

The most significant group in table 7.6 is women who have completed twelve years of school. They are the modal class—40% of female workers are in this category—but their underutilization rate is almost five points higher than men in the same category. This is the exception to the generalization that women have higher rates where their proportions are lower. A larger proportion of women than of men is found in this class, and their rates are higher. Only 1% of these women are mismatched; underutilization by level of income is the most important component of their underutilization.

The lower rates of underutilization among women with some college reflect their lower mismatch. Why is mismatch more of a problem for men than for women? Appendix C notes that the median education for women is somewhat higher than that for men, and this increases the sense of paradox. If we consider mismatch alone, without taking account of hours of work or income (for more women than men are already tabulated as underutilized in these categories), the difference persists. Over 12.6% of men are mismatched if we do not examine hours or income; 9.1% of women are. We might hypothesize that more of women's training is relegated to the school system. On-the-job training is less available for women, and so formal credentials become more important.[7] Professional and technical fields in which many women are employed, including nursing, librarianship, social work, and teaching, require certification as a prerequisite for employment. The proportion of the female labor force employed in such occupations is 11%, but only 6% of men are employed in such occupations.[8] The responsibility of schools in training women may mean that there is a better "match" between women's education and their jobs. Such an explanation is plainly a posteriori and deserves attention by researchers.

WOMEN'S OCCUPATIONS AND UTILIZATION

The last section implied the extent to which women's jobs are separate from men's jobs. If women's occupational distribution differs sharply from men's, and if women are exploited as marginal labor, then standardizing underutilization rates for women's occupations should raise the rates. Table 7.7 shows the extent of occupational segregation.[9] In 1960 and 1970, at least 40 women out of every 100 would have had to change occupations to have the same distribution as men. Women are concentrated in service and clerical occupations, although high proportions are also professional workers or operatives.

When 1970 underutilization rates are applied to the 1970 female occupational distribution, the rate rises as predicted. The 1960 female occupational distribution raises the rate still higher. The unstandardized female rate is even higher than the standardized rates. The entire process repeated for 1960 rates shows higher rates at each step. It appears that female occupation-specific underutilization rates declined faster than the rates for the labor force as a whole. This happened through complex shifts. Women increased their proportions in five groups, of which three had lower rates in 1970 than in 1960.

They decreased their proportion in six groups, of which three had higher rates in 1970. The result was still higher underutilization for women than for men, but at a rate that had been improved by the pattern of occupational shifts.

Occupation composition alone does not explain higher rates of female underutilization, but shifts in composition have helped improve female utilization.

Conclusions

The discrimination hypothesis predicts that both nonwhites and females will be relatively more underutilized. Nonwhites were more underutilized than whites both in 1960 and in 1970, but the trend is toward equal utilization. Nonwhites led whites in every category of underutilization except mismatch. Whites had higher percentages mismatched, but the rate of acceleration in mismatch is higher for nonwhites. In this sense, the trend is also toward equal *underutilization*.

Low education may provide nonwhites with "mismatch insurance," but it does not guarantee lower underutilization. At most levels of education, nonwhites are more likely to be underutilized than whites. Further, nonwhites tend to be concentrated in the occupations with high underutilization rates. Even when occupation is the same, the nonwhite rate of underutilization is higher. The discrimination hypothesis receives strong support among nonwhites, although there is a trend toward more equal utilization.

Women were also more underutilized than men, both in 1960 and in 1970, although the sex differential was less than the color differential. Education composition did not explain the difference; indeed, women's education was somewhat more favorable to adequate utilization. Occupation shifts helped to account for some of the decline in women's underutilization between 1960 and 1970.

Neither education nor occupation composition seems to be a satisfactory alternative to the discrimination hypothesis. However, the evidence of unequal rates of underutilization in similar occupations provides only ambiguous support for the hypothesis. The occupational groups used here are gross. Occupational distributions may approach each other without affecting underutilization if women and nonwhites hold the least-skilled, lowest-paid jobs in the group.[10] That is, their occupations may not really be equal. For example, the professional, technical, and kindred group includes college professors, who are more likely to be male, and kindergarten teachers, who are more likely to be female. We have treated differences in rates as manifestations of discrimination, but differences in composition may reflect discrimination too. This idea is taken up again in chapters 9 and 10. In the next chapter, we analyze the cumulative effects of age, color, and sex on utilization.

Table 7.7. *Occupational distribution by sex, with underutilization rates for full-time labor force, 1960 and 1970 (Based on workers aged 14 and over, except as noted)*

Major occupational group	1960			1970		
	Male (1)	Female (2)	Underutilization rate[a] (3)	Male (4)	Female (5)	Underutilization rate[a] (6)
Total	100.0%	100.0%	25.5%	100.0%	100.0%	25.1%
Professionals, technical, and kindred	10.4	13.4	11.2	14.4	15.9	15.2
Managers, officers, and proprietors	11.6	4.2	25.0	11.3	3.7	27.2
Clerical	7.0	31.0	26.2	7.6	35.2	29.3
Sales	7.2	8.3	17.7	7.2	7.4	24.3
Craftsmen and foremen	20.9	1.4	28.4	21.0	1.8	17.2
Operatives	19.7	15.9	25.0	19.3	14.1	20.3
Labor, excluding farm	7.6	0.9	35.3	6.6	1.0	27.8

Service workers, excluding private households	6.7	14.8	34.4	8.0	16.3	32.2
Private household workers	0.1	8.3	59.2	0.2	3.9	56.4
Farm managers and farmers	5.8	0.6	51.0	2.8	0.2	28.5
Farm laborers and foremen	3.0	1.2	56.4	1.7	0.5	64.6
Comparison by sex within year	$\Delta_{12} = 44.4$			$\Delta_{45} = 41.4$		
Comparison by year, within sex		$\Delta_{14} = 6.1$			$\Delta_{25} = 8.7$	

1970 Full-time rate of underutilization = 25.1.
1970 Full-time rate of underutilization, standardized by 1970 female occupation distribution = 25.4.
1970 Full-time rate of underutilization, standardized by 1960 female occupation distribution = 25.7.
1970 Full-time rate, female labor force = 27.1.
1960 Full-time rate of underutilization = 25.5.
1960 Full-time rate of underutilization, standardized by 1970 female occupation distribution = 25.9.
1960 Full-time rate of underutilization, standardized by 1960 female occupation distribution = 27.8.
1960 Full-time rate, female labor force = 29.2.

ᵃNumber of underutilized full-time workers expressed as a percent of all full-time workers. Part-time workers could not be adjusted. Rates in 1970 for workers aged 16 and over.

Sources: Columns 3 and 6: U.S. Bureau of the Census, 1960 and 1970 Public Use Samples; other columns: idem, General Social and Economic Characteristics, U.S. Summary, table 81.

CHAPTER 8

The Discrimination Hypothesis: Interactions

In chapter 2 it was hypothesized that marginal statuses would have a cumulative or even multiplicative effect on underutilization. To put it differently, "more marginality," or more categories of marginality, should intensify underutilization. By this reasoning, one would expect black women to be more underutilized than white women, and young or old black women to be even more underutilized. By the same token, young white men should be more underutilized than older white men, but less so than young black men. In a more formal sense I will be looking for significant interactions among marginal statuses and underutilization. Goodman's hierarchical log-linear models are used for this.

There are two principal parts to this chapter. The first analyzes the combination of race and sex. Because of the data available for adjusting involuntary part-time work, it is possible to include a time variable in this analysis as well, and to compare 1960 data with 1970. In the second part of the chapter, age is added to the analysis, and the interactions among age, race, and sex in 1970 are analyzed.

Race and Sex

Data in chapter 7 supported the hypothesis that nonwhites are more underutilized than whites, and that women are more underutilized than men. To extend the hypothesis, we would expect that nonwhite women are even worse off than either nonwhites alone or women alone. This is by no means an obvious hypothesis, judging from the literature. When 1960 census data were available for analysis, it was possible for one commentator to say, "It is in the perspective of the Negro father that we must regard the Negro mother as being overemployed."[1] The argument was that relative to nonwhite men, nonwhite women were well off. When 1970 data became available, the argument was made that relative to white women, nonwhite women were better off. In the 1970's, nonwhite female median earnings approached and in some groups, slightly exceeded, that of white women.[2] But the discrimination hypothesis implies that white men are the standard of comparison. Implicit in the LUF is the notion that work is multidimensional, and that earnings alone are not an adequate indicator. Depending on the *distribution* of earnings and occupations, black women could be more underutilized than white women even though the median earnings for the two groups were the same. Because of its multidimensional character, the LUF offers a succinct summary of the market position of nonwhite females. In this chapter, the concept "inadequate utilization" is used to summarize several dimensions of work. (For the use of the LUF as a dichotomous variable, see appendix A.)

Table 8.1 is the cross-classification of utilization categories by year, race, and sex. Inspection of the table reveals few surprises given the findings about time effects in chapter 4 and the conclusions of chapter 7. Overall utilization improved between 1960 and 1970, but it improved because of a 9-point increase in adequate utilization among nonwhites. For whites, there was a slight decrease in adequate utilization that is explained by higher mismatch. Nonwhite males improved their utilization by over 11 points, nonwhite females by 7 points, and white females by only half a point. Nevertheless, there remained a sizable gap in adequate utilization between white and nonwhite males and between white and nonwhite females. The overall male-female gap declined from 3.8 points in 1960 to 3.2 points in 1970.

Of greater interest are the interactions that are not apparent. In the discussion that follows, Y refers to the variable year, which takes on values 1970 and 1960. R refers to race—more properly, color, because it is dichotomized as white and nonwhite. S refers to sex, and U refers to utilization, dichotomized as adequate or inadequate.

Table 8.1 may be modeled as

$$G_{ijkl} = 8.46 + .11\lambda^{Y} + .97\lambda^{R} + .19\lambda^{S} + .47\lambda^{U} + .01\lambda^{YR}$$
$$- .05\lambda^{YS} + .05\lambda^{YU} + .08\lambda^{RS} + .17\lambda^{RU} + .05\lambda^{SU}$$
$$- .001\lambda^{YRS} - .05\lambda^{YRU} - .01\lambda^{RSU} \quad (1)$$

If the null hypothesis of "no effect" were true, a standardized lambda parameter would have a normal distribution with zero mean and unit variance. Model (1) presents unstandardized lambdas; they may be standardized by dividing by the standard error (0.005). The discussion of table 8.2 will help establish that model (1) does indeed fit the data. λ^{YRS} and λ^{YR} are not statistically significant, but λ^{YRS} must be retained, and in the hierarchical model scheme λ^{YR} is included whenever λ^{YRS} is.

Single variable effects reflect marginal distributions, and so the relatively large λ^{R} shows what a large proportion of the labor force whites constitute. λ^{Y} shows the larger labor force size in 1970. λ^{S} shows that males predominate in the labor force. But the small negative value of λ^{YS} reflects the slightly higher proportion of females in the 1970 labor force. The positive value of λ^{YU}, though small, shows improved utilization in 1970. The positive associations λ^{RU} and λ^{SU} show that whites and men, respectively, are better utilized.

Three-variable effects show an interaction among variables. The negative value of λ^{YRS} reflects the composition changes of the labor force. To put it differently, the estimated effect of being white or male in 1970 is less positive than the main effects for year and race or sex indicate. This is an indication

Table 8.1. *Nonagricultural civilian labor force by color, sex, and type of utilization, 1960 and 1970*
(Thousands of workers aged 16 and over, with percentages)

	1970			1960		
	All colors (1)	White (2)	Nonwhite (3)	All colors (4)	White (5)	Nonwhite (6)
Both sexes:						
Nonagricultural workers	77606 (100.0%)	69012 (100.0%)	8594 (100.0%)	63558 (100.0%)	56841 (100.0%)	6717 (100.0%)
Adequately utilized	59449 (77.2%)	53997 (78.2%)	5952 (69.3%)	48666 (76.6%)	44631 (78.5%)	4035 (60.1%)
Inadequately utilized	17657 (22.8%)	15015 (21.8%)	2642 (30.7%)	14892 (23.4%)	12210 (21.5%)	2682 (39.9%)
By unemployment	3440 (4.4%)	2883 (4.2%)	557 (6.5%)	3226 (5.1%)	2642 (4.6%)	584 (8.7%)
By hours of work[a]	1294 (1.7%)	1000 (1.5%)	294 (3.4%)	1405 (2.2%)	1181 (2.1%)	224 (3.3%)
By level of income	4940 (6.4%)	3853 (5.6%)	1087 (12.6%)	6844 (10.7%)	5220 (9.2%)	1624 (24.2%)
By mismatch[b]	7983	7279	704	3417	3167	250

Nonagricultural workers	47143 (100.0%)	4670 (100.0%)	42473 (100.0%)	41664 (100.0%)	37720 (100.0%)	3944 (100.0%)
Adequately utilized	37023 (78.5%)	3397 (72.7%)	33626 (79.2%)	32452 (77.9%)	30027 (79.6%)	2425 (61.5%)
Inadequately utilized	10120 (21.5%)	1273 (27.8%)	8847 (20.8%)	9212 (22.1%)	7693 (20.4%)	1519 (38.5%)
By unemployment	1823 (3.9%)	263 (5.6%)	1560 (3.7%)	2075 (5.0%)	1722 (4.6%)	353 (8.9%)
By hours of work[a]	635 (1.3%)	124 (2.7%)	511 (1.2%)	706 (1.7%)	601 (1.6%)	105 (2.7%)
By level of income	2166 (4.6%)	504 (10.8%)	1662 (3.9%)	3727 (8.9%)	2819 (7.5%)	908 (23.0%)
By mismatch[b]	5496 (11.7%)	382 (8.2%)	5114 (12.0%)	2704 (6.5%)	2551 (6.7%)	153 (3.9%)

(continued)

Table 8.1. *Nonagricultural civilian labor force (continued)*

	1970			1960		
	All colors (1)	White (2)	Nonwhite (3)	All colors (4)	White (5)	Nonwhite (6)
Females:						
Nonagricultural workers	30463 (100.0%)	26539 (100.0%)	3924 (100.0%)	21894 (100.0%)	19121 (100.0%)	2773 (100.0%)
Adequately utilized	22926 (75.3%)	20371 (76.8%)	2555 (65.1%)	16214 (74.1%)	14604 (76.4%)	1610 (58.1%)
Inadequately utilized	7537 (24.7%)	6168 (23.2%)	1369 (34.9%)	5680 (25.9%)	4517 (23.6%)	1163 (41.9%)
By unemployment	1617 (5.3%)	1323 (5.0%)	294 (7.5%)	1151 (5.2%)	920 (4.8%)	231 (8.3%)
By hours of work[a]	659 (2.1%)	489 (1.8%)	170 (4.3%)	699 (3.2%)	580 (3.0%)	119 (4.3%)
By level of income	2774 (9.1%)	2191 (8.2%)	583 (14.9%)	3117 (14.2%)	2401 (12.6%)	716 (25.8%)
By mismatch[b]	2487 (8.2%)	2165 (8.2%)	322 (8.2%)	713 (3.3%)	616 (3.2%)	97 (3.5%)

[a] Adjusted. See appendix B.
[b] Adjusted. See appendix D.

Source: U.S. Bureau of the Census, *1960* and *1970 Public Use Samples.*

that being white and male does not unambiguously improve utilization. λ^{YRU} shows how the race-utilization relation has changed with time. The association of whites with adequate utilization in 1960 had weakened by 1970.

Table 8.2 is analogous to an analysis of variance table. The "total variation" in row one is indicated by the chi-square statistic obtained from an independence model. In this case, the independence model stated that utilization is independent of the joint variable year-race-sex. Two-factor associations account for 90% of the variation. Race is extremely important in explaining utilization. Sex is important, but plays a much smaller role. Year is least important, although it just misses being significant.[3] (The criterion level for χ^2 on one degree of freedom is 10.825.) Among the three-factor interactions, it is a surprise to find that λ^{YRU} explains nearly all of the residual. λ^{RSU}, though small, is significant at the .01 level. Because it is of major interest in this section, it will be analyzed further.

Three-factor interactions, say *RSU*, may be interpreted as meaning that the association between utilization and race varies according to sex, or that the association between sex and utilization varies according to race. (Presumably, it also says that the association between race and sex varies according to utilization, but this interpretation makes no sense because utilization is treated here as a dependent variable.) Table 8.3 explores these interpretations.

The odds-ratio indicates the strength of an interaction. The odds-ratios for year and utilization, given sex and race, were previously analyzed in table 4.2. Table 8.3 presents the odds-ratios for race, sex, and utilization. The entries in table 8.3 may be interpreted as "the odds (given the control condition) that a nonwhite (or woman) will be adequately utilized." Entries less than one show a negative relationship.

The first entry in the table may be interpreted as a moderately strong negative association between adequate utilization and being nonwhite, when males in 1970 are considered. The second entry shows that the association is even more negative when females in 1970 are considered. If this is compared with the third panel of the table, it can be seen that all nonwhites, male and female, were worse off in 1960, but their relative positions were reversed. The association with adequate utilization was more negative for nonwhite males than for females in 1960.

There are three principal conclusions to be drawn from table 8.3. First, as the zero-order entries show, being nonwhite and being female are both associated with underutilization, but race is the greater handicap. The race and sex disadvantages persist in every comparison. Second, although the negative associations are found in every comparison, there are important improvements between 1960 and 1970. That is, the negative associations become weaker. White females improve relative to white males (0.83 to 0.87), nonwhite males improve relative to white males (0.41 to 0.70), and nonwhite females improve relative to white females (0.43 to 0.57). Third, there is an interesting reversal in the relative position of nonwhite females. Among nonwhites, the position of nonwhite females relative to nonwhite males deteriorated (0.87 to 0.70). Between the races, nonwhite women were slightly better off than nonwhite men

Table 8.2. *Analysis of variation in odds pertaining to variable U in four-way contingency table*

Source of variation	Degrees of freedom	Likelihood-ratio χ^2
1. Total variation due to the main effects of variables *Y*, *R*, *S* and "interaction" effects among them.	7	1561.73
1a. Due to (*RU*)	1	1221.48
1b. Due to (*YU*)/(*RU*)	1	10.85
1c. Due to (*SU*)/(*RU*), (*YU*)	1	180.15
1d. Due to residual interaction effects of 2 or more factors on *U* by forward selection	4	149.25
1d1. Due to (*YRU*)/(*RU*), (*YU*), (*SU*)	1	130.00
1d2. Due to (*RSU*)/(*YRU*), (*RU*), (*YU*), (*SU*)	1	6.71
1d3. Due to (*YSU*)/(*RSU*), (*YRU*), (*RU*), (*YU*), (*SU*)	1	0.07
1d4. Due to residual interaction effects	1	12.47

in 1960 (0.43 to 0.41). This had reversed itself in 1970 (0.57 to 0.70). Thus, while there was considerable improvement across the board between 1960 and 1970, nonwhite women did not share in it to the same extent as nonwhite men. (The 1970 odds-ratio for nonwhite women to white men was even more negative, 0.49.)

Is one worse off being both nonwhite and female? Every comparison in table 8.3 suggests that the answer is yes—and while in 1970 the nonwhite female was better off than in 1960, her position relative to the nonwhite male had deteriorated. On the other hand, the interaction term for race, sex, and utilization is not nearly so important as that for year, race, and utilization in explaining table 8.1. The next section permits further analysis of the 1970 data, with age added as a variable.

Race, Sex, Age, and Utilization

Table 8.4 cross-classifies age, race, and sex for 1970. The age variable was trichotomized into young workers, workers in the prime working ages, and old workers. Young workers were defined as those aged 16 to 24, and old workers as those aged 50 and over. In the analysis of this table, R indicates race (color); S, sex; A, age; and U, utilization. The hypothesis predicts that being young or old will increase the disadvantage of being black or female. The worst utilization should be among young or old black females.

The most parsimonious model that fits the data in table 8.4 consists of the interactions ASR and RSU and all two-factor associations. Equations 2, 3, and 4 present the coefficients for the model at each age level.

For young workers,

$$G_{ijkl} = 7.40 + .17\lambda^A + .99\lambda^R + .15\lambda^S + .50\lambda^U - .06\lambda^{AR} - .06\lambda^{AS} - .18\lambda^{AU}$$
$$+ .09\lambda^{RS} + .12\lambda^{RU} + .06\lambda^{SU} - .01\lambda^{ASR*} - .04\lambda^{RSU} \quad (2)$$

For prime-aged workers,

$$G_{ijkl} = 7.40 + .49\lambda^A + .97\lambda^R + .15\lambda^S + .50\lambda^U - .03\lambda^{AR} + .01\lambda^{AS*} + .07\lambda^{RU}$$
$$+ .09\lambda^{RS} + .12\lambda^{RU} + .06\lambda^{SU} + .03\lambda^{ASR} - .04\lambda^{RSU} \quad (3)$$

For old workers,

$$G_{ijkl} = 7.40 - .67\lambda^A + .99\lambda^R + .15\lambda^S + .50\lambda^U + .09\lambda^{AR} + .05\lambda^{AS} + .11\lambda^{AU}$$
$$+ .09\lambda^{RS} + .12\lambda^{RU} + .06\lambda^{SU} - .02\lambda^{ASR*} - .04\lambda^{RSU} \quad (4)$$

As in Model (1), the coefficients are unstandardized; starred effects (*) are not significant at $P = .01$ level. With such large data sets, the reduction in chi-square, to be discussed below, is probably of greater interest.

Several things about these equations are worth noting. First, the main effect for race is overwhelming. Parameters λ^{RS} and λ^{RU} confirm previous observa-

Table 8.3. Odds-ratios for race, sex, and utilization (N in thousands of workers)

Control variables	Odds-ratio (adequate:inadequate)	N
1970, race (nonwhite:white)		
Male	0.70	47143
Female	0.57	30463
Weighted average	0.65	....
1970, sex (female:male)		
White	0.87	69012
Nonwhite	0.70	8594
Weighted average	0.85	....

1960, race (nonwhite:white)			
Male	0.41		41664
Female	0.43		21894
Weighted average	0.42		...
1960, sex (female:male)			
White	0.83		56841
Nonwhite	0.87		6717
Weighted average	0.83		...
Zero order, race	0.52		...
Zero order, sex	0.82		...

Source: Table 8.1.

Table 8.4. *Civilian labor force by age, race, sex, and utilization, 1970*

	All ages (1)	16–19 (2)	20–24 (3)	25–29 (4)	30–34 (5)
Total	79899	5918	10105	8928	7639
White, both sexes	71077	5289	8896	7771	6690
Male total	44350 (100.0%)	3023 (100.0%)	4757 (100.0%)	5169 (100.0%)	4480 (100.0%)
Adequately utilized	34765 (78.4%)	2184 (72.2%)	3050 (64.1%)	3998 (77.3%)	3538 (79.0%)
Inadequately utilized	9585 (21.6%)	839 (27.8%)	1707 (35.9%)	1171 (22.7%)	942 (21.0%)
By unemployment	1609 (3.6%)	337 (11.1%)	301 (6.3%)	140 (2.7%)	115 (2.6%)
By hours of work[a]	613 (1.4%)	71 (2.4%)	76 (1.6%)	54 (1.1%)	43 (0.9%)
By level of income	2017 (4.6%)	235 (7.8%)	356 (7.5%)	196 (3.8%)	176 (3.9%)
By mismatch[b]	5346 (12.0%)	196 (6.5%)	974 (20.5%)	781 (15.1%)	608 (13.6%)
Female total	26727 (100.0%)	2266 (100.0%)	4139 (100.0%)	2602 (100.0%)	2210 (100.0%)
Adequately utilized	20448 (76.6%)	1674 (73.9%)	2761 (66.7%)	1958 (75.3%)	1707 (77.2%)
Inadequately utilized	6279 (23.4%)	592 (26.1%)	1378 (33.3%)	644 (24.7%)	503 (22.8%)
By unemployment	1335 (5.0%)	230 (10.1%)	250 (6.0%)	134 (5.1%)	86 (3.9%)

(continued)

35–39 (6)	40–44 (7)	45–49 (8)	50–54 (9)	55–59 (10)	60–64 (11)	65+ (12)
7551	8666	8647	7918	6651	4574	3302
6600	7695	7745	7183	6013	4188	3007
4336 (100.0%)	4894 (100.0%)	4838 (100.0%)	4438 (100.0%)	3789 (100.0%)	2675 (100.0%)	1951 (100.0%)
3434 (79.2%)	3916 (80.0%)	3969 (82.0%)	3705 (83.5%)	3151 (83.1%)	2248 (84.0%)	1572 (80.6%)
902 (20.8%)	978 (20.0%)	869 (18.0%)	733 (16.5%)	638 (16.9%)	427 (16.0%)	379 (19.4%)
101 (2.3%)	110 (2.2%)	118 (2.4%)	106 (2.4%)	98 (2.6%)	103 (3.9%)	80 (4.1%)
57 (1.4%)	59 (1.3%)	55 (1.2%)	56 (1.2%)	59 (1.6%)	41 (1.5%)	42 (2.1%)
187 (4.3%)	211 (4.3%)	175 (3.6%)	123 (2.8%)	167 (4.4%)	97 (3.6%)	94 (4.8%)
557 (12.8%)	598 (12.2%)	521 (10.8%)	448 (10.1%)	314 (8.3%)	186 (7.0%)	163 (8.4%)
2264 (100.0%)	2801 (100.0%)	2907 (100.0%)	2745 (100.0%)	2224 (100.0%)	1513 (100.0%)	1056 (100.0%)
1733 (76.5%)	2240 (80.0%)	2344 (80.6%)	2216 (80.7%)	1772 (79.7%)	1244 (82.2%)	799 (75.6%)
531 (23.5%)	561 (20.0%)	563 (19.4%)	529 (19.3%)	452 (20.3%)	269 (17.8%)	257 (24.4%)
97 (4.3%)	120 (4.3%)	88 (3.0%)	105 (3.8%)	90 (4.0%)	55 (3.6%)	80 (7.6%)

Table 8.4. *Civilian labor force (continued)*

	All ages (1)	16–19 (2)	20–24 (3)	25–29 (4)	30–34 (5)
By hours of work[a]	515 (1.9%)	42 (1.9%)	73 (1.8%)	48 (1.8%)	39 (1.8%)
By level of income	2251 (8.4%)	233 (10.3%)	431 (10.4%)	228 (8.8%)	203 (9.2%)
By mismatch[b]	2178 (8.1%)	87 (3.8%)	624 (15.1%)	234 (9.0%)	175 (7.9%)
Nonwhite, both sexes	8822	629	1209	1157	949
Male total	4851 (100.0%)	376 (100.0%)	598 (100.0%)	634 (100.0%)	511 (100.0%
Adequately utilized	3470 (71.5%)	233 (62.0%)	362 (60.5%)	443 (69.9%)	370 (72.4%
Inadequately utilized	1381 (28.5%)	143 (38.0%)	236 (39.5%)	191 (30.1%)	141 (27.6%
By unemployment	273 (5.6%)	63 (16.7%)	53 (8.9%)	40 (6.3%)	19 (3.7%)
By hours of work[a]	152 (3.1%)	20 (5.3%)	16 (2.7%)	14 (2.2%)	17 (3.3%)
By level of income	565 (11.7%)	48 (12.8%)	100 (16.7%)	58 (9.1%)	56 (11.0%
By mismatch[b]	391 (8.1%)	12 (3.2%)	67 (11.2%)	79 (12.5%)	49 (9.6%)

(continued

35–39 (6)	40–44 (7)	45–49 (8)	50–54 (9)	55–59 (10)	60–64 (11)	65+ (12)
55 (2.4%)	57 (2.0%)	67 (2.3%)	45 (1.6%)	46 (2.1%)	24 (1.6%)	19 (1.8%)
221 (9.8%)	204 (7.3%)	199 (6.9%)	207 (7.6%)	164 (7.4%)	83 (5.5%)	78 (7.4%)
158 (7.0%)	180 (6.4%)	209 (7.2%)	172 (6.3%)	152 (6.8%)	107 (7.1%)	80 (7.6%)
951	971	902	735	638	386	295
506 (100.0%)	537 (100.0%)	502 (100.0%)	407 (100.0%)	367 (100.0%)	237 (100.0%)	176 (100.0%)
380 (75.1%)	401 (74.7%)	382 (76.1%)	319 (78.4%)	289 (78.7%)	171 (72.2%)	120 (68.2%)
126 (24.9%)	136 (25.3%)	120 (23.9%)	88 (21.6%)	78 (21.3%)	66 (27.8%)	56 (31.8%)
17 (3.3%)	22 (4.1%)	18 (3.6%)	4 (1.0%)	16 (4.4%)	11 (4.6%)	10 (5.7%)
13 (2.6%)	14 (2.6%)	21 (4.2%)	11 (2.7%)	10 (2.8%)	8 (3.4%)	8 (4.5%)
56 (11.1%)	57 (10.6%)	55 (10.9%)	48 (11.8%)	35 (9.5%)	31 (13.0%)	21 (11.9%)
40 (7.9%)	43 (8.0%)	26 (5.2%)	25 (6.1%)	17 (4.6%)	16 (6.8%)	17 (9.7%)

Table 8.4. *Civilian labor force (continued)*

	All ages (1)	16–19 (2)	20–24 (3)	25–29 (4)	30–34 (5)
Female total	3971 (100.0%)	253 (100.0%)	611 (100.0%)	523 (100.0%)	438 (100.0%
Adequately utilized	2573 (64.8%)	157 (62.1%)	348 (57.0%)	347 (66.4%)	286 (65.3%)
Inadequately utilized	1398 (35.2%)	96 (37.9%)	263 (43.0%)	176 (33.6%)	152 (34.7%
By unemployment	302 (7.6%)	51 (20.2%)	72 (11.8%)	46 (8.8%)	28 (6.4%)
By hours of work[a]	175 (4.4%)	10 (3.9%)	22 (3.6%)	18 (3.4%)	20 (4.5%)
By level of income	599 (15.1%)	32 (12.6%)	106 (17.3%)	55 (10.5%)	69 (15.8%)
By mismatch[b]	322 (8.1%)	3 (1.2%)	63 (10.3%)	57 (10.9%)	35 (8.0%)

[a] Adjusted. See appendix A.
[b] Adjusted. See appendix C.

Source: U.S. Bureau of the Census, *1970 Public Use Samples.*

35–39 (6)	40–44 (7)	45–49 (8)	50–54 (9)	55–59 (10)	60–64 (11)	65+ (12)
445 (100.0%)	434 (100.0%)	400 (100.0%)	328 (100.0%)	271 (100.0%)	149 (100.0%)	119 (100.0%)
289 (64.9%)	288 (66.4%)	252 (63.0%)	232 (70.7%)	188 (69.4%)	93 (62.4%)	93 (78.2%)
156 (35.1%)	146 (33.6%)	148 (37.0%)	96 (29.3%)	83 (30.6%)	56 (37.6%)	26 (21.8%)
32 (7.2%)	25 (5.8%)	21 (5.2%)	10 (3.1%)	9 (3.3%)	4 (2.7%)	4 (3.4%)
17 (3.8%)	19 (4.4%)	23 (5.8%)	13 (4.0%)	10 (3.7%)	17 (11.4%)	6 (5.0%)
75 (16.9%)	66 (15.2%)	71 (17.8%)	49 (14.9%)	46 (17.0%)	22 (14.8%)	8 (6.7%)
32 (7.2%)	36 (8.2%)	33 (8.2%)	24 (7.3%)	18 (6.6%)	13 (8.7%)	8 (6.7%)

tions about the proportion of white males in the labor force and the association of whites with adequate utilization.

Some differences among these equations are also worth noting. The marginal distribution is indicated by the main effect for age. The association of age and race (AR) shows the higher proportion of nonwhites among young workers, and to a lesser extent among prime-aged workers. Similarly, the associations of AS and AU show higher proportions of women and of underutilized workers among young workers. The interaction for RSA is insignificant for the young and the old. The interaction RSU will be discussed in more detail below.

Although equations (2), (3), and (4) are estimated for the most parsimonious model, other models also fit the data well. That is, there was no significant difference between the model and a fitted chi-square at the .001 level.

	Fitted marginals	Degrees of freedom	L.R.χ^2
H_1	$(RSA)(RSU)(RAU)(SAU)$	2	5.21
H_2	$(RSA)(RSU)(RAU)$	4	15.99
H_3	$(RSA)(RSU)(SAU)$	4	5.91
H_4	$(RSA)(RSU)(AU)$	6	16.99

A comparison of these models shows that RAU contributes little to the explanation (H_4 compared with H_2, or H_1 compared with H_3). A better way to see this is by examining table 8.5.

Over 95% of the total variation due to the main effects of R, S, A and the interaction effects among them is explained by two-factor association. The remaining chi-square is partitioned in table 8.5. The significance of RSU may be interpreted as meaning that the interaction of race, sex, and utilization is the same at every age level, or it may be interpreted as it was done for table 8.1. Table 8.6 analyzes the odds-ratios for the interaction.

Table 8.6 shows again that the association between being nonwhite and being adequately utilized is negative at every age and sex level. There is a negative association between being female and adequately utilized at every age. For young and prime-aged white women, it is only slightly negative. Old women and nonwhite women show a moderately negative association with adequate utilization. At every age level, the pattern of odds-ratios looks similar. This may explain why interactions that included age were less significant: race and sex already accounted for much of the variation.

There are some interesting features of the table that deserve closer attention. Generally, the younger the nonwhite male age group, the closer the utilization approaches that of white males. For nonwhite females, the pattern is different: older nonwhite women approach white women more closely than young nonwhite women, and prime-aged white women are worst off. Because of this difference in patterns, there is a considerable gap in relative utilization between nonwhite males and females below the age of 55. After that age the gap between sexes is closed, although the gap between races is widest.

When we compare females to males, young white women do relatively better

Table 8.5. *Analysis of three-factor and four-factor interactions by backward elimination*

Source of variation	Degrees of freedom	χ^2
1. Total due to residual three-factor and four-factor interactions	9	61.58*
1a. Due to residual four-factor interactions	2	5.21
1b. Due to three-factor interactions (assuming that four-factor interactions are nil)	7	56.37*
Partition of (1b) by backward elimination:		
1b1. Due to *RSU/RSA, RAU, SAU*	1	36.75*
1b2. Due to *SAU/RSA, RAU*	2	10.12
1b3. Due to *RAU/RSA*	2	10.62
1b4. Due to *RSA*	2	8.88

*Significant at $\alpha = .001$.

Table 8.6. *Odds-ratios for race, sex, age, and utilization (N in thousands of workers)*

Control variables	Odds-ratio (adequate: inadequate)	N	Control variables	Odds-ratio (adequate: inadequate)	N
Young, race (nonwhite: white)			*Young, sex* (female: male)		
Male	0.73	8754	White	0.98	12675
Female	0.53	7269	Nonwhite	0.71	1838
Weighted average	0.64	....	Weighted average	0.95	....
Prime years, race			*Prime years, sex*		
Male	0.72	26407	White	0.91	36501
Female	0.51	12784	Nonwhite	0.63	4930
Weighted average	0.65	....	Weighted average	0.88	....
Old, race			*Old, sex*		
Male	0.60	14040	White	0.81	20391
Female	0.59	8405	Nonwhite	0.79	2054
Weighted average	0.60	....	Weighted average	0.81	....

Source: Table 8.4.

than prime-aged white women and older women. Nonwhite women, compared to nonwhite men, show the same U-shaped pattern we saw in comparison to white women. Old nonwhite women are closest to nonwhite men, young nonwhite women are next, and prime-aged nonwhite women are relatively worst off. The gap between races is similar until the old age group.

Discussion

It is now time to review the findings from these tables and models in terms of the discrimination hypothesis. The discrimination hypothesis predicts that every marginal status diminishes adequate utilization, and persons with more than one marginal status are even less likely to be adequately utilized.

Race is the most important marginal status in underutilization. The square of Goodman's analogue to the partial correlation coefficient (r^2) for race and year is .79. For race and sex, it is .51. This means the relative decrease in U's unexplained variation when year or sex alone is used, compared with the case when race is also used. The association between race and adequate utilization is always negative (see tables 8.3 and 8.6). That is, even being male or being in the prime working ages is not enough to overcome the disadvantage of being nonwhite.

There is a secular decline in the disadvantage. Being nonwhite in 1970 is not so negatively correlated with adequate utilization as it was in 1960. This may be demonstrated by comparing the weighted averages in table 8.3.

The next question is whether being female increases the disadvantage of being nonwhite. Sex is as important a factor in underutilization as race, if you compare the explanation of utilization with sex included to the case in which sex is not included ($R^4 = 0.55$). Using both race and sex compared with using neither yields an R^2 of .90. In 1960 being female was a slightly greater disadvantage. The secular decline is also reflected in table 8.3's weighted average for 1970 (0.85) compared with the weighted average for 1960 (0.83). Using both sex and year improved the prediction of utilization very little because the time effect was slight.

To return to the earlier question, does being female increase the disadvantage of being nonwhite? The answer seems to be yes. The association between nonwhite females and adequate utilization is negative regardless of control variables (see tables 8.3 and 8.6). The secular improvement affected nonwhite women less than nonwhite men and less than white women. Despite the improved utilization of nonwhite women, their position relative to nonwhite men and white women declined.

The third element of the discrimination hypothesis is age. All other things being equal, are the young most likely to be underutilized? This was the conclusion of chapter 6, and there is evidence that the main effect of age is important. The association of age with utilization is in the expected direction for young and prime-aged workers, but not for old workers. The ordering hypothesized in chapter 6 was not supported. Age is relatively unimportant in three-factor or higher interactions.

This leads us into the next issue, the cumulative effect of youth or old age with other marginal statuses. First, is it worse to be young and nonwhite? Young nonwhite teenagers are believed to have the worst employment problems. Admittedly our measure does not include discouraged workers, who perhaps are a significant number of nonwhite teenagers. The data confirm that the association between youth and adequacy is more negative for nonwhites than for whites. But it is more negative for nonwhites at every age, and the weighted average for young workers by race in table 8.6 is only marginally worse than that for prime-aged workers.

Youth does not increase the disadvantage of sex—relative to men, young women are somewhat better utilized than older women. Young white women are nearly at parity with young white men.

Being old appears to deteriorate the position of nonwhite men, though not of nonwhite women. Old age also deteriorates the position of women relative to men, although this generalization does not apply to nonwhite women.

Finally we come to the question of the nonwhite female who is either young or old. Is there a cumulative disadvantage for her? If one contrasts nonwhites with whites, the young female is worse off than the young male, although—ironically—the prime-aged female is even worse off. If one contrasts women with men, prime-aged nonwhites are again worst off, with old nonwhites nearly as well utilized as whites. It seems fair to conclude that youth and old age are not so disadvantageous for nonwhite females as for other workers, but only by comparison to the greatly disadvantaged position of nonwhite females in the prime years.

Young nonwhite women may be somewhat better off because of their education and access to better jobs. Older nonwhite women may do well in comparison to other older workers because of their longer experience. The comparison by age groups, although it has not confirmed every combination of the discrimination hypothesis, has underscored the relatively worse position of nonwhite females.

Summary

The predictions of the discrimination hypothesis have not all been borne out. Nonwhite women have a double disadvantage that has not been affected proportionately by the secular decline. Age does not worsen this situation; in fact, the position of the younger workers is relatively better than in other age-sex groups. So even though the economic improvements have short-changed nonwhite women, cohort changes may improve their utilization. Nonwhite men are disadvantaged because of their race; age does not increase the disadvantage significantly. Among white workers, youth is a disadvantage and so is the combination of being old and female.

CHAPTER 9

The Achievement Hypothesis: Effects of Training

Perhaps the achievement hypothesis should be called the "underachievement hypothesis." It suggests that persons who have not invested in their education are more likely to be underutilized than those who have. In general, persons with inadequate formal education or vocational training, and those who refuse to migrate for job-related reasons, are expected to be more underutilized. The argument is similar to that found in human-capital approaches to underutilization and sociological approaches to achievement.[1]

The difference in this analysis lies primarily in the time frame. The LUF includes unemployment, and so the independent variables for achievement must exist prior to the employment contract because, presumably, they affect hiring decisions. Thus, this study does not include on-the-job training, which is not a useful achievement criterion for the unemployed.[2] Nor is occupation used, as Duncan and his colleagues did, because the unemployed may not have an occupation to report. (However, occupation is used in chapter 10 as an indicator of marginal job structure.)

This chapter begins with some theoretical and practical problems in analyzing underutilization and achievement. The first analytic section considers formal schooling, in terms of completed years of school, and its relation to underutilization in 1960 and 1970. The second section considers some data about vocational education and underutilization.

Schooling

DATA

In many ways, the data and analysis in this chapter are less satisfying than those of previous chapters. Some of the difficulties are theoretical and others are practical.

Mismatch as Overachievement
The theoretical background for this hypothesis draws from structural unemployment theory (see chapter 2). The structuralists did not have underemployment data to test their theory, but they did note that unemployment was higher among persons with little education, and that less-educated persons

had lower rates of labor force participation. They hypothesized that the rising education of the labor force would push those at the bottom of the education ladder from the labor force. Thus, while 3.8% of the adult population in 1970 had a sixth grade education or less, the figure for the labor force was 5.8%.[3]

This thesis also has implications for those at the top of the education ladder. Unless high-level skilled jobs are growing at the same rate as highly trained personnel, more and more educated people will assume less-skilled jobs. In terms of the LUF, the mismatch rate will rise. The achievement hypothesis predicts that unemployment, short hours, and low income are inversely related to education—and, willy-nilly, mismatch must be directly related to education. As a consequence, the *overall* rate of adequate utilization must bear a curvilinear relationship to education. Each of these predictions is borne out in table 9.1.

The structuralists have not explicitly dealt with mismatch, although they imply a temporal sequence: *first* the employers downgrade the uneducated, and *then* the jobs are filled with educated people, creating mismatch. This suggests that the first three types of underutilization, in historical terms, are earlier indicators of labor market maladjustment. With rising education, mismatch becomes more important. Table 9.1 bears out the historical trend to greater mismatch. Because mismatch involves relatively well-educated people entering less-skilled jobs, it may be that we see in mismatch the *process* that leads to structural unemployment among displaced workers.

The achievement hypothesis is concerned primarily with underachievement. However, mismatch is a phenomenon of *overachievement* relative to the labor market. For this reason, although mismatch is included in the tables in this chapter, it is discussed very little in the analysis.

Practical Difficulties

A second difficulty in this chapter is practical: the tables are limited to full-time members of the labor force. In this chapter, "full-time workers" includes all of the unemployed, even those who might be seeking part-time work, and no part-time workers, not even those who are normally full-time workers. This means that the underutilized by hours of work are not included. There are two justifications for omitting this category. First, there were no data available for adjusting the 1960 part-time work statistics. Data from 1960 could not be omitted from the chapter because of the change in educational level of the labor force. Second, the use of full-time workers omits the students who are part-time workers, an important part of the part-time labor force. All students could have been omitted, but it seems more sound to distinguish the cases.

For the part-time student worker, completed years of schooling do not represent completed education. He is not being judged solely on his prior achievement, for allowance is usually made for his student status. The full-time worker, however, even though he may also be a student, has offered his prior credentials on an equal footing with workers who have completed their educations. The distinction between these two cases is not based on commitment to the labor force, but on the extent of reliance on prior achievement.

For these reasons, the tables in this section should be regarded with caution. The summary category "inadequately utilized" is not comparable to that used in chapters 6, 7, or 8, and so a dichotomous treatment of utilization, such as that used in the Goodman analysis, would be misleading. One final point: because comparability with the 1960 data was important in this chapter, workers aged 14 and over are included in the tables. Both in 1960 and in 1970, however, the number of full-time workers aged 14 and 15 is very small, and so the loss in comparability is minimal.

Trends

Table 9.1 presents an overview of utilization by completed years of schooling. The first trend to note is the secular decline in underutilization that applied both overall and at every level of schooling except for junior college and graduate education. The exceptions are due to the rise in mismatch. The second trend is the shift in education composition from 1960 to 1970. Almost 37% of the 1960 labor force had a ninth grade education or less, compared with 26% of the 1970 labor force. At the other end of the spectrum, only 20% had at least one year of college in 1960 compared with 25% in 1970. The median education in 1970 was 12.1 years, but 52% of the 1960 labor force had less than a high school education. Much of this shift was due to the retirement of the older, less-educated workers, but some of it is also due to the decreased propensity of the uneducated to be in the labor force.

In both 1960 and 1970, the percent adequately utilized follows the predicted inverted-U pattern, except for a recovery among the most educated. Utilization seems to improve until 12 years of school are completed, when mismatch rises and utilization deteriorates. Because mismatch is logically inconsistent with the achievement hypothesis, we turn to an analysis of two other components, unemployment and level of income.

In 1960, unemployment falls below the overall average of 5.8% only for people with high school diplomas or more. This relationship is repeated in 1970, but the relative disadvantage of the least educated declines somewhat. Only 7% of those with six grades or less in 1970 are unemployed, compared with 9.5% in 1960. If you decompose the difference between the unemployment rates in 1960 and 1970, the identity is:

$$0.53\% = 0.51 - 0.06 + 0.08$$

This means that about 96% of the difference may be attributed to the change in education composition. Interestingly, the effect of rates is negative, and there is a small positive interaction effect.

High rates of underutilization by level of income occur among those with a junior high school education or less. For both 1960 and 1970, the rates continue to decline with every increment in education. A three-component decomposition of underutilization rates by level of income gave these results:

$$6.2\% = 0.6 + 4.5 + 1.1$$

Table 9.1. Completed years of schooling by utilization categories, full-time civilian labor force, 1960 and 1970 (Thousands of workers aged 14 and over, with percentages)

1970

	Total, all levels (1)	6th grade or less (2)	7th–9th grade (3)	10–11th grade (4)	12th grade (5)	College 1–2 (6)	College 3–4 (7)	College 5+ (8)
Total full-time CLF	59199 (100.0%)	4061 (100.0%)	12285 (100.0%)	10794 (100.0%)	23903 (100.0%)	7608 (100.0%)	6529 (100.0%)	4019 (100.0%)
Adequately utilized	52892 (76.4%)	3081 (75.9%)	10112 (82.3%)	9115 (84.5%)	20495 (85.7%)	4270 (56.2%)	3451 (52.9%)	2382 (59.3%)
Inadequately utilized	16307 (23.6%)	980 (24.1%)	2173 (17.7%)	1679 (15.5%)	3410 (14.3%)	3338 (43.8%)	3078 (47.1%)	1637 (40.7%)
By unemployment	3618 (5.2%)	283 (7.0%)	959 (7.8%)	791 (7.3%)	1068 (4.5%)	291 (3.8%)	172 (2.6%)	54 (1.3%)
By level of income	5461 (7.9%)	697 (17.1%)	1212 (9.9%)	875 (8.1%)	1840 (7.7%)	407 (5.3%)	295 (4.5%)	135 (3.4%)
By mismatch	7228 (10.5%)	0 (0.0%)	2 (0.0%)	13 (0.1%)	502 (2.1%)	2640 (34.7%)	2611 (40.0%)	1448 (36.0%)

Total full-time CLF	59900 (100.0%)	5951 (100.0%)	16012 (100.0%)	9352 (100.0%)	16574 (100.0%)	5080 (100.0%)	4529 (100.0%)	2402 (100.0%)
Adequately utilized	44564 (74.4%)	3600 (60.5%)	12021 (75.1%)	7544 (80.7%)	13791 (83.2%)	3764 (74.1%)	2317 (51.2%)	1527 (63.5%)
Inadequately utilized	15336 (25.6%)	2351 (39.5%)	3991 (24.9%)	1808 (19.3%)	2783 (16.8%)	1316 (25.9%)	2212 (48.8%)	875 (36.4%)
By unemployment	3452 (5.8%)	568 (9.5%)	1184 (7.4%)	692 (7.4%)	664 (4.0%)	165 (3.3%)	88 (1.9%)	91 (3.8%)
By level of income	8438 (14.1%)	1783 (30.0%)	2807 (17.5%)	1116 (11.9%)	1993 (12.0%)	402 (7.9%)	242 (5.3%)	95 (4.0%)
By mismatch	3446 (5.7%)	0 (0.0%)	0 (0.0%)	0 (0.0%)	126 (0.8%)	749 (14.7%)	1882 (41.6%)	689 (28.6%)

Source: U.S. Bureau of the Census, *1960* and *1970 Public Use Samples*.

Education composition accounted for less than 10% of the change; the lion's share was due to the change in rates.

To summarize, there is support for the structuralists' emphasis on low achievement as an important factor in unemployment. For underemployment, at least as measured by level of income, there is an inverse relationship between education and underutilization, but the changes over time are not due to improved education as much as to other factors. A preliminary case has been made for the achievement hypothesis.

UNDERACHIEVEMENT—OR DISCRIMINATION?

Chapters 6 through 8 presented data that discrimination affects utilization directly, but it may also affect utilization indirectly through schooling. This could happen in two ways. The groups most affected by discrimination may have such low schooling that one could argue that cross-classifications by education or by race and sex are merely two aspects of the same phenomenon. This is the congruence pattern.

The other pattern, the incongruence pattern, asserts that the relationship between achievement and race-sex background is not perfect. Thus, race will have an independent effect even on high achievers in minority groups, and low achievement will affect majority groups.

Distribution of Education
Table 9.2 shows the distribution of education by race and sex for 1960 and 1970. Nonwhites lagged behind whites in 1970, but they lagged even farther behind in 1960. In 1960, only 17.6% of nonwhites, but 65.8% of whites, had gone beyond junior high school. In 1970 the figures had jumped to 43.2% for nonwhites and 72.3% for whites. The position of nonwhite women relative to nonwhite men improved. In 1960, 22.1% of nonwhite women had gone beyond junior high, but 37.1% of nonwhite men had. In 1970, the respective figures were 69% and 56.9%, a rather dramatic improvement for nonwhite women and a reversal of their 1960 position. In 1960, 5.4% of nonwhite women and 8.6% of nonwhite men went beyond high school. In 1970, there was another reversal: 17.8% of women but 14.5% of men went on. Nonwhite women in 1960 had less education than nonwhite men except at the very bottom of the educational scale. By 1970, nonwhite women had a substantially higher education distribution until the senior college level, where there is an insignificant difference.

The congruence pattern, because it hypothesizes that low achievement and underutilization are twin effects of a single cause, implies a relationship of the form, "The lower the achievement the higher the underutilization." But there is more than this relationship reflected in the data. Nonwhite women, although more underutilized, are not lower in education. Indeed, although they are somewhat higher in education than nonwhite men by 1970, they are relatively less able to convert their achievement into adequate utilization than they were in 1960. Achievement appears to be more than an intervening variable.

The Incongruence Pattern

The incongruence pattern suggests that an independent effect for achievement may be established by taking the data for white males as a standard. A series of standardizations is given in table 9.3. The extent to which nonwhite rates are lowered by the white male education composition may be taken as an "achievement effect." For example, if nonwhite males had the same education as white males, their underutilization rate would be lowered from 17.3% to 10.1%—but if nonwhites also had the white male schedule of specific rates, the rate would be lowered to 8.2%. Or, to go in the other direction, the lower education of nonwhite males would raise white males' rates from 8.6% to 10.1%, and that may be taken as the "achievement effect." The "discrimination effect" arises in using nonwhites' specific rate schedule, and that brings the rate to 17.3%.

	Achievement effect compared with white male education	Discrimination effect given equal education
Nonwhite males	1.9%	0.7%
Nonwhite females	1.0%	12.5%
White females	−0.2%	5.5%

As the figures show, nonwhite females are in an incongruent position, for their education is closer to that of white males, but their education-specific rates are seriously higher. For nonwhite males, the "discrimination effect," or the difference in rates given standard education, is smaller than the achievement effect. The anomalous case is that of white females. They have somewhat higher achievement than white males. Table 9.2 shows this to be mostly in the lower ranges of schooling. But even if they had white males' education, their specific rates would still be higher by five percentage points.

Summary

The sketchy data do not permit a multivariate analysis of the achievement effect of education, but a few tentative conclusions are possible. First, underachievement affects unemployment for those without a high school diploma; low level of income strikes hardest at those without any high school education at all. Second, underachievement alone is not sufficient to explain underutilization among nonwhites, especially nonwhite females. Their achievement is offset by higher education-specific rates of underutilization.

Table 9.2. *Cumulative percent distribution of completed years of schooling by color and sex, full-time civilian labor force, 1960 and 1970 (N in thousands of workers aged 14 and over)*

	White			Nonwhite		
	Both sexes	Male	Female	Both sexes	Male	Female
			1970			
6th grade or less	4.9	5.7	3.5	15.7	19.4	11.2
7–9th grade	22.7	25.3	18.3	37.7	43.1	31.0
10–11th grade	37.7	40.2	33.4	56.8	61.3	51.2
12th grade	73.1	72.1	74.6	84.0	85.5	82.2
College 1–2 years	84.2	83.1	86.0	91.4	92.1	90.7
College 3–4 years	94.0	92.9	95.9	96.7	96.7	96.8
College 5–6 years	100.0	100.0	99.9[a]	99.9[a]	100.0	100.0
Total	71857	44882	26975	3912	4917	3995

6th grade or less	7.8	8.8	5.7	19.9	34.1	10.3
7–9th grade	34.2	36.5	29.4	72.4	62.9	78.9
10–11th grade	50.9	53.5	45.4	82.3	76.9	86.1
12th grade	79.9	79.1	81.5	93.2	91.4	94.6
College 1–2 years	88.7	87.5	91.0	96.3	95.5	97.0
College 3–4 years	95.9	95.4	96.9	98.9	98.5	99.4
College 5–6 years	100.0	99.9[a]	100.0	99.9[a]	100.0	100.0
Total	58228	39089	19139	11082	4483	6599

[a]Total may not add to 100 because of rounding.

Source: U.S. Bureau of the Census, *1960* and *1970 Public Use Samples.*

Table 9.3. *Actual and standardized partial full-time utilization rates, 1970*

Education composition used	Rate schedule used			
	Male		Female	
	White	Nonwhite	White	Nonwhite
White males	8.2%	8.9%	13.7%	20.7%
Nonwhite males	10.1	17.3	....	....
White females	8.0	....	13.4	....
Nonwhite females	9.2	....	....	22.9

Note: Partial full-time underutilization rate = [(number unemployed) + (number underutilized by level of income)] /(number of full-time workers).

Vocational Training

The 1970 census contained for the first time a vocational training question, asked of respondents aged 14 to 64. For some workers, vocational training represents achievement beyond that reflected in completed years of schooling. Unfortunately, the question was worded to include high school vocational courses, so the distinction is not sharp. Vocational training also includes apprenticeship, schools of nursing, business, or trades, and Armed Forces schools, but not correspondence, on-the-job training, or combat training in the Armed Forces.

Vocational training represents an additional sort of "achievement," and so the achievement hypothesis predicts that those who have vocational training will have better utilization than those who do not. In 1970, 28.3% of the labor force reported vocational training; 11.5% of all nonwhites and 36.6% of all women received training. The proportions of nonwhites and women in the labor force are similar. Among the full-time workers aged 14 and over, the trained workers show somewhat better utilization:

	Vocational training	Civilian labor force
% unemployed	3.7	4.5
% level of income	5.8	6.8
% mismatch	9.1	8.9

Again, mismatch is an exception. CPS data do not include vocational training questions, so the adjustment for hours of work could not be made, but the gross numbers of part-time workers can be compared. About 14% of trained workers and 14.3% of the labor force are part-time workers.

Another way of assessing the impact of training is to look at the severity of utilization. A person was considered "severely underutilized" by level of income if his income were less than 75% of the appropriate poverty cutoff. If we look at *gross* private underutilization, 13.0% of the civilian labor force but only 8.8% of the trained workers were severely underutilized by level of income. This is income considered without reference to other LUF components. Severe mismatch (1.5 standard deviations beyond mean education) affects 4.2% of the civilian labor force but 3.9% of the trained personnel.

A cautious conclusion is that achievement measured in terms of vocational training is associated with reduced utilization and reduced severity of utilization.

Conclusions

Compared with other hypotheses, the achievement hypothesis must be tested with rather weak data and proxy indications. Two components of underutilization, hours of work and mismatch, are largely ignored. Nevertheless, some tentative conclusions are possible. Underachievement, in terms of few years of schooling completed or little training, is associated with higher underutilization. High achievement, measured by vocational training or formal education, improves utilization, except that mismatch (by definition) is more prevalent among the highly educated.

But the explanatory power of the achievement variables is limited. The education-specific rates of utilization differ by race and sex groups, so that even high achievement by nonwhites is not always rewarded. The achievement hypothesis is most useful in explaining the underutilization of whites in the prime working years and older.

CHAPTER 10

The Structural Hypothesis: Marginal Jobs

Studies by Miller and others, which eliminated whole categories of "marginal workers," showed substantial unemployment and underemployment remaining among nonstudent male heads of household. Aside from discrimination and low educational attainment, how does one account for this underutilization? The structural hypothesis contends that some jobs are so located as to be "marginal" to the economy.

Marginal workers are likely to be underutilized in any setting. Although culture determines in part what personal characteristics are marginal, and to what extent being female or aged is a handicap, we would expect less country-to-country variation in identifying marginal workers than we would in identifying marginal jobs. What job is marginal depends on the economy. The peripheral industry in one country is central to another's economy, and technologies that are outmoded in an advanced country may be highly competitive in a developing one. In particular, trade-offs between labor-intensity and capital-intensity will affect utilization levels. Thus, although it is difficult to quantify, the structural hypothesis is potentially important both to account for residual underutilization and to analyze international differences in utilization.

Ideally, one would like to examine a number of variables to find marginal jobs. Variables such as technology, land tenure systems, foreign trade and competition, and the quirks of the local labor market will help determine what jobs are marginal. Obsolete occupations, uncompetitive firms, and declining industries are all expected to be marginal job sites.

The data used in this chapter are far from ideal because of the limited information on economic structure available in census data. The principal areas investigated here are sector, occupational group, and class of worker. Agriculture is taken as representative of the primary sector, and also as a declining industry. The analysis undertaken here could easily be applied to other industries and to more detailed occupational groups.

As used in this chapter, the structural antecedents of underutilization are attributed to relatively impersonal forces. A few dual-labor market theorists hypothesize that some jobs are marginal by *intention*—that is, employers deliberately package the least essential tasks into unstable, poorly compensated jobs, so that even high turnover will not disrupt production. The least-preferred workers are hired for these jobs. This is a provocative idea, but one impossible to test with census data. Further, it does not explain residual underutilization among preferred workers. For that, we turn to a more impersonal variant of the structural hypothesis.

Agriculture as a Declining Industry

Agricultural production is climbing and its product is never obsolete, but relative to the labor force, agriculture is a declining industry for several reasons. First, the emphasis has shifted from labor-intensive to capital-intensive cultivation. The proportion of the labor force employed in agriculture declined by half from 1960 to 1970. Second, the shift to capital-intensive cultivation has made the small farm noncompetitive. Agriculture was once the prototype of perfect competition, but the shift to machinery, as in so many other industries, has discouraged the entry of new producers. The old-style family farm was once the typical farm, but now it is likely to be obsolete. At a time when unionization was improving the job security, hours, and wages in manufacturing, farm labor became, by comparison, a "marginal" job. For these reasons, we expect agricultural workers to be inadequately utilized relative to the rest of the labor force.

Table 10.1 compares the agricultural sector with nonagricultural workers in 1970. If you look at the unemployment figure alone, agricultural workers appear to be better off than their counterparts in industry and services. But relying on published unemployment data would give a misleading picture of the agricultural labor force, for their "inadequately utilized" percentage is twenty points higher than the nonagricultural workers' percentage. The principal difference is in level of income. Remember that the poverty index is already adjusted to account for farm-nonfarm residence. Even so, farm workers have over three times the level of underutilization by level of income as the nonagricultural labor force.

For females, the difference between agricultural and nonagricultural employment is even more startling. The summary figure shows farm women 2½ times more likely to be underutilized than women not in agriculture. The figures for underutilization components are so small that their reliability is suspect, but they indicate again a high level of underutilization by income. Women in agriculture appear to be more underutilized than their nonagricultural counterparts on every component except mismatch. However, women are a much smaller proportion of the agricultural labor force than of the nonagricultural.

Table 10.2 partitions the variation in table 10.1. No model fits the data; the residual chi-square for three-factor interaction was 19.73 on one degree of freedom. The association of sector and sex (AS) accounted for 60% of the variation. Another 30% was accounted for by the association of sector and utilization (AU). The association of sex and utilization (SU), which may be interpreted as the "marginal worker" aspect of this table, accounts for less than 10%. Even with this incomplete fit, the relative importance of sector or industry—specifically, agriculture—is clear.

A final perspective on underutilization in agriculture is the time effect (see table 4.1). Agriculture employed 6.2% of the 1960 labor force, but only 2.8% of the 1970 labor force. The trend to better utilization in 1970 was obvious for agriculture. Nonagriculture remained about the same because of a rise in mismatch, although other categories declined. Utilization improved disproportionately in agriculture, although a large gap still exists. This improvement occurred while the agricultural labor force shrank, relatively and absolutely. Perhaps the most marginal jobs are being eliminated from agriculture while the industry as a whole adjusts to increased mechanization. But marginal workers in agriculture may be doubly marginal, as the data for women indicate.

Agriculture has been used as an example of an industry and also as the representative industry of the primary sector. A similar analysis could be undertaken for other types of industry. For example, higher underutilization by level of income would be expected in traditionally low-wage industries. Industries with seasonal production or with large numbers of part-time workers are likely to show underutilization by hours of work. These data could not be interpreted unambiguously as supporting the structural hypothesis, however. To the extent that these industries provide jobs of the last resort, there is likely to be an interaction of personal marginal characteristics and structural marginality.

Occupation Group and Marginality

Certain jobs, once acquired, are relatively stable and well paid. In manufacturing, union contracts protect many jobs and provide ceilings for hours and wages. For this reason, the structural hypothesis predicts that underutilization will be low among craftsmen, foremen, and operatives. Unstable job situations include that of unskilled independent contractors, especially day laborers and some household workers who have several different employers in the course of a week. Migrant farm laborers are in a similar situation. For somewhat different reasons, many service jobs offer unstable, often part-time, employment in firms highly vulnerable to fluctuating demand. In some cases, as with fast-food outlets, demand may fluctuate in a regular daily pattern.

Major occupation groups are a crude measure of these organizational influences. Table 10.3 shows that the predictions of the structural hypothesis are largely borne out. The proportion of adequately utilized craftsmen and operatives is somewhat greater than their proportion of the labor force. Given the rate of unionization in these groups, it is not surprising to see that unemployment is a greater problem than hours or wages. Operatives are even more vulnerable than craftsmen and foremen to industrial layoffs. Notice their unusually large share of unemployment. Operatives account for over one-fifth of the unemployed. The lower blue-collar categories show disproportionately high underutilization, as expected. The underutilization share of private household workers is 2½ times larger than their share of the labor force.

Table 10.1. *Civilian labor force by sector, sex, and type of utilization,* ▮

| Type of utilization | Both sexes | |
	Agriculture (1)	Nonagriculture (2)
Total	2293 (100.0%)	77606 (100.0%)
Adequately utilized	1307 (57.0%)	59949 (77.2%)
Inadequately utilized	986 (43.0%)	17657 (22.8%)
By unemployment	79 (3.4%)	3440[a] (4.4%)
By hours of work[b]	161 (7.0%)	1294 (1.7%)
By level of income	492 (21.5%)	4940 (6.4%)
By mismatch[c]	254 (11.1%)	7983 (10.3%)

[a] Includes those unemployed workers not reporting an industry.
[b] Adjusted. See appendix B.
[c] Adjusted. See appendix D.

Source: U.S. Bureau of the Census, *1970 Public Use Samples.*

housands of workers aged 16 and over, with percentages)

	Males		Females	
iculture	Nonagriculture (4)	Agriculture (5)	Nonagriculture (6)	
58 0.0%)	47143 (100.0%)	235 (100.0%)	30463 (100.0%)	
5 .0%)	37023 (78.5%)	92 (39.1%)	22926 (75.3%)	
3 .0%)	10120 (21.5%)	143 (60.9%)	7537 (24.7%)	
9%)	1823[a] (3.9%)	20 (8.5%)	1617[a] (5.3%)	
8 2%)	635 (1.3%)	33 (14.1%)	659 (2.1%)	
6 .2%)	2166 (4.6%)	76 (32.3%)	2774 (9.1%)	
0 .7%)	5496 (11.7%)	14 (6.0%)	2487 (8.2%)	

Table 10.2. *Analysis of the variations in table 10.1 by backward elimination*

Source of variation	DF	χ^2
1. Total due to the mutual dependence among A, S, and U	4	1543.43
1a. Due to AS	1	952.15
1b. Due to AU/AS	1	445.43
1c. Due to $SU/AS, AU$	1	126.10
1d. Due to residual 3-factor interaction	1	19.73

Note: A = sector; S = sex; U = utilization.

Table 10.4 is useful for comparing the percentage underutilized in 1970 and 1960. (Because of the difficulty in adjusting 1960 hours of work data, that component is omitted.) The pattern of unemployment by occupation group changed very little between the two dates, although the magnitude declined. Labor and farm labor show persistently high unemployment, even higher in 1970 than in 1960. Farmers, farm labor, and private household workers led the rates for low income in both years. Two white-collar groups, managers and clerical workers, substantially improved in the income category, and improvements were made in the lower blue-collar occupations.

Mismatch increased in every occupational group, but the largest relative increases were among service workers, sales workers, labor and farm laborers. This mismatch more than doubled; for service workers it more than tripled. Managers and proprietors and sales workers had the highest rates of mismatch. Operatives were relatively unaffected. Higher rates of mismatch indicate a greater heterogeneity in education within occupation groups. To the extent that service workers and sales workers are young and relatively inexperienced, their mismatch may be temporary and may disappear after a promotion to a different occupational group (e.g., a supervisory position).

The results of table 10.4 largely support those of 10.3 and they underline the well-utilized positions in professional, craft, and semiskilled jobs. Unskilled blue-collar work and service jobs, as predicted, have higher rates of underutilization.

Class of Worker and Firm

One sort of marginality is found in highly competitive industries in which every firm is small and vulnerable. A different situation occurs in industries tending to oligopoly, where the smaller firm is likely to be squeezed out. In general, size of firm is likely to affect utilization, simply because large firms affect the market more and control sufficient resources to ensure steady production. A corollary of this buffering effect is that jobs in large firms should be more stable. By contrast, small enterprises should have higher underutilization.

Census data do not provide a direct test of this notion, but a proxy variable can be constructed from class of worker data. Government workers, except for elected politicians and some patronage appointments, are afforded considerable job security through civil service legislation. Their utilization is expected to be adequate. Self-employed workers and unpaid workers, on the other hand, are more likely to be in a small enterprise, and so their utilization should be lower. (It would have been useful to eliminate solo professional practices; as we have seen, professionals in general are well utilized.) Unfortunately, private employees form such a heterogeneous category that it is difficult to analyze their utilization. They are used here as a baseline group.

Data for 1960 (table 10.5) partly confirms the hypothesis. Of course, unemployment among the self-employed is difficult to define.

Table 10.3. *Civilian labor force by utilization type and major occupational group, 1970*
(Thousands of workers aged 16 and over)

Major occupational group	Total (1)	Adequately utilized (2)	Inadequately utilized				
			Total (3)	Unemployed (4)	Hours of work[a] (5)	Level of income (6)	Mismatch[b] (7)
Total, all groups[c]	79899 (99.9%)	61256 (100.0%)	18643 (100.0%)	3519 (99.9%)	1455 (100.0%)	5432 (100.0%)	8237 (100.0%)
Professional, technical, and kindred	11106 (13.9%)	9416 (15.4%)	1640 (9.1%)	198 (5.6%)	45 (3.1%)	350 (6.4%)	1097 (13.3%)
Managers and proprietors, except farmers	6127 (7.7%)	4582 (7.5%)	1545 (8.3%)	75 (2.1%)	56 (3.8%)	242 (4.5%)	1172 (14.2%)
Clerical	13441 (16.8%)	10355 (16.9%)	3086 (16.6%)	433 (12.3%)	119 (8.2%)	789 (14.5%)	1745 (21.2%)
Sales	5130 (6.4%)	3779 (6.2%)	1351 (7.3%)	172 (5.0%)	55 (3.8%)	273 (5.0%)	851 (10.3%)
Craftsmen and foremen	10307 (12.9%)	8517 (13.9%)	1790 (9.6%)	411 (11.7%)	147 (10.1%)	412 (7.6%)	820 (10.0%)

Operatives, including transport	13375 (16.7%)	10461 (17.0%)	2914 (15.6%)	803 (22.8%)	458 (31.5%)	937 (17.3%)	716 (8.7%)
Labor, excluding farm	3398 (4.3%)	2384 (3.9%)	1014 (5.4%)	307 (8.7%)	133 (9.1%)	297 (5.5%)	277 (3.4%)
Farmers and farm managers	1307 (1.6%)	856 (1.4%)	451 (2.4%)	8 (0.2%)	93 (6.4%)	254 (4.7%)	96 (1.2%)
Farm labor and foremen	986 (1.2%)	450 (0.7%)	536 (2.9%)	71 (2.0%)	68 (4.7%)	238 (4.4%)	159 (1.9%)
Services, excluding private households	8334 (10.4%)	5765 (9.4%)	2569 (13.8%)	364 (10.3%)	154 (10.6%)	907 (16.7%)	1144 (13.9%)
Private household workers	1063 (1.3%)	475 (0.8%)	588 (3.1%)	43 (1.2%)	127 (8.7%)	258 (4.7%)	160 (1.9%)
Not classified	5325 (6.7%)	4216 (6.9%)	1109 (5.9%)	634 (18.0%)	[d]	475 (8.7%)	[d] ....

[a] Adjusted. See appendix B.
[b] Adjusted. See appendix D.
[c] May not add to 100% because of rounding.
[d] Could not be determined.

Source: U.S. Bureau of the Census, *1970 Public Use Samples.*

Table 10.4. *Full-time underutilized workers in major occupational groups, 1960 and 1970 (percentages)*

Major occupational group	1970[a]			1960[b]		
	Unemployed (1)	Level of income (2)	Mismatch[c] (3)	Unemployed (4)	Level of income (5)	Mismatch[c] (6)
Professional, technical, and kindred	1.8	3.2	8.0	1.4	4.4	3.3
Managers and proprietors, excluding farm	1.2	4.0	18.5	1.1	9.0	13.6
Clerical	3.2	5.9	11.4	3.6	11.1	7.6
Sales	3.4	5.3	15.3	3.0	7.5	5.2
Craftsmen and foremen	4.0	4.0	7.7	5.5	7.2	4.4
Operatives	6.0	7.0	4.9	7.4	11.8	3.1
Labor, except farm	9.0	8.7	6.6	11.3	16.6	2.6
Farmers and farm managers	0.6	19.4	7.0	0.5	37.9	4.5

Farm laborers and foremen	7.2	24.1	14.0	6.5	35.3	5.5
Services, except private households	4.4	10.9	11.0	5.5	19.1	3.3
Private household workers	4.1	24.3	6.3	4.9	23.8	4.2
Not classified by occupation	11.9	8.9	. . . [d]	10.7	13.1	. . . [d]

[a] Workers aged 16 and over.
[b] Workers aged 14 and over.
[c] Unadjusted.
[d] Could not be determined.

Source: U.S. Bureau of the Census, *1960 and 1970 Public Use Samples.*

Table 10.5. *Underutilization categories by class of worker, 1960 and 1970*
(Full-time workers only; thousands of workers aged 14 and over, with percentages)

	1970				1960			
	Total, all categories (1)	Unemployed (2)	Level of income (3)	Mismatch[a] (4)	Total, all categories (5)	Unemployed (6)	Level of income (7)	Mismatch[a] (8)
Total, all classes	69188 (100.0%)	3618 (100.0%)	5461 (100.0%)	7216 (100.0%)	49743 (100.0%)	3333 (100.0%)	8438 (100.0%)	3446 (100.0%)
Private employees	52061 (75.3%)	3181 (87.9%)	3913 (71.7%)	5179 (71.8%)	33683 (57.7%)	2896 (86.9%)	5750 (68.1%)	2519 (73.1%)
Government workers	10950 (15.8%)	320 (8.9%)	614 (11.2%)	1376 (19.1%)	7210 (14.5%)	176 (5.3%)	605 (7.2%)	471 (13.7%)
Federal	3015 (4.4%)	137 (3.8%)	131 (2.4%)	413 (5.7%)	...	...	...	...
State	2820 (4.1%)	70 (1.9%)	153 (2.8%)	413 (5.7%)	...	...	...	...
Local	5115 (7.3%)	113 (3.2%)	330 (6.0%)	550 (7.7%)	...	...	...	...

Self-employed workers	5840 (8.4%)	102 (2.8%)	732 (13.4%)	643 (8.9%)	8226 (16.5%)	131 (3.9%)	1756 (20.8%)	449 (13.0%)
Own business, included	4862 (7.0%)	91 (2.5%)	696 (12.7%)	441 (6.1%)	⋯ ⋯	⋯ ⋯	⋯ ⋯	⋯ ⋯
Own business, not included	978 (1.4%)	11 (0.3%)	36 (0.7%)	202 (2.8%)	⋯ ⋯	⋯ ⋯	⋯ ⋯	⋯ ⋯
Unpaid workers[b]	334 (0.5%)	12 (0.3%)	202 (3.7%)	18 (0.2%)	498 (1.0%)	4 (0.1%)	327 (3.9%)	7 (0.2%)
Other	3 (0.0%)	3 (0.1%)	0 (0.0%)	0 (0.0%)	126 (0.3%)	126 (3.8%)	⋯ ⋯	⋯ ⋯

[a] Unadjusted.
[b] See appendix C.

Source: U.S. Bureau of the Census, *1960* and *1970 Public Use Samples*.

More categories for class of worker were used in 1970, and this permits refinement of the prediction. For example, distinguishing among types of government workers shows that local government workers are better utilized, although more vulnerable to low income. Both federal and state employees bear disproportionate shares of mismatch. All government workers are relatively secure from unemployment.

We might suppose incorporated firms to be better "job buffers" than unincorporated ones, and so we predict that self-employed persons in incorporated firms are better utilized than those who are not. Table 10.5 refutes that idea, for the self-employed in incorporated businesses have somewhat worse utilization than other self-employed workers. Self-employed workers are relatively worse off on level of income; perhaps this helps account for the 50% decrease in self-employed workers between 1960 and 1970.

In summary, class of worker data offer evidence in the hypothesized direction. The size-of-firm argument may deserve further consideration if better data are made available.

Conclusions

The structural hypothesis contends that some underutilization can be attributed to marginal jobs. How is this hypothesis related to the three previous ones dealing with marginal workers? Some theorists argue that both workers and jobs may be stratified from top to bottom. Jobs at the top are filled by people at the top. Eventually, one comes to the marginal jobs, the leftovers, which are filled with the least-preferred workers. What are the determinants of the number of marginal jobs? Are low-paying, unstable jobs found in the highly competitive industries, the small firms, the obsolete occupations? There is some evidence here to indicate that is the case. If so, oligopoly, firm size, and rate of technological change may affect the number of marginal jobs.

On the other hand, the interaction between population structure and economic structure is more subtle than this chapter suggests. "Jobs" as identifiable bundles of regular activities in preexisting structures may not be there. Instead, a person's activity is called his or her "job." Redundant labor is likely to drift to the "jobs you take when you can't find a job"—cab driving, waiting on tables, and so forth. The supply of unused labor may create its own limited demand structure. Or, an alternative, parallel, and subterranean economic structure, centering on illegal goods and services, may recruit some of the redundant labor.

So far as the data in this chapter permit conclusion, it seems likely that economic structure, or at least industry and occupation, affect utilization in regular and predicted ways. Census data are simply insufficient to investigate the structural hypothesis in great detail. There is fertile ground here for innovative research linking organizational studies and labor force studies.

Conclusions and Recommendations

Two themes are interwoven throughout this study, and in this chapter it is appropriate to separate them for analysis. The first might be called the technical-conceptual theme, for it deals with the feasibility and practicality of approaches to underutilization. It touches on the epistemology of underemployment and the policy implications of underutilization data. The second theme is the significance of underutilization to sociology, which includes the links to classical and contemporary theory and the salience of the empirical findings.

Concepts and Findings

Of all the improvements in labor statistics that might be useful, only the measurement of underemployment has been mandated by Congress.[1] But Congress did not specify any conceptual or theoretical framework, and unfortunately, there is a fair amount of confusion in academic circles as to what "underemployment" is. In its loosest sense, it is an umbrella concept covering most of the ills to which workers (and employers) are heir—worker dissatisfaction, poor job design, even long coffee breaks. The popular press occasionally uses the term "underemployed" to describe women in predominately female, low-status jobs, so the usage may extend even to perceived inequality. At the other extreme, such concepts as "disguised unemployment," defined through marginal productivity analysis, have not been applied to employment patterns in industrial countries. Between the extremes of fuzzy thought and irrelevant precision, there has been little synthesis. The problems of synthesis and a conceptual framework were attacked together. The general model of underutilization was presented primarily to supply the conceptual framework Congress could not provide.

CONCEPTUAL FRAMEWORK

The term "underutilization" includes both unemployment and three forms of inadequate employment. Inadequate employment is measured along three dimensions—hours of work, level of income, and skills. Unemployment is the limiting case: no hours of work, no earnings, no use of skills.

All jobs may be classified along the three dimensions, but each dimension has a distinctive distribution of jobs. Adequate hours are more widespread than adequate income, and an adequate income is more widespread than use of high-level skills.

This conceptual scheme implies the measurement system. The three dimensions should be treated separately. A technique such as the rate of return to education would be inappropriate, using this model, because it tries to measure the skills continuum in terms of income. As the data in chapters 7 and 8 show, it is easier for young blacks to convert their education into income than to convert it into occupational attainment. The approach used here treats time, money, and occupational attainment (which is closely related both to skills and to prestige) as scarce resources allocated in labor markets. An underutilized worker is one who, despite his will, has minimal job resources on at least one of these dimensions.

Hours, income, and skills are probably sufficient for classifying the labor force in most advanced countries.[2] But underutilization, speaking more generally, results from the friction caused in fitting a population into the social organization of work. So three elaborations are in order. First, in some developing countries, different dimensions may be used, or they may be defined differently. For example, "income" might be defined to include farm produce consumed by the farm workers in lieu of cash income. Second, "inadequacy" along one of these dimensions may have a different definition than that used here. For example, one could work for so long or at so skilled a level that efficiency drops. Third, the unit of analysis used could be different. For example, household or other consumption units might be used.

The use of individual workers as the unit of analysis implied the use of a hierarchy of forms of underutilization. The terms "private" and "social" underutilization were introduced to distinguish underutilization's effects on individuals from those on society.[3] The distinction of net from gross private underutilization recognizes that a hierarchy of underutilization is implicit in various conceptual treatments. The forms of underutilization are not necessarily mutually exclusive, although a mutually exclusive categorization may be developed. The advantage of mutually exclusive categories is that the worker is the unit of analysis. Then indices of gross private underutilization would count some workers two or three times, and so they would need a set of weights.

CONCEPTS AND MEASUREMENTS

Once these concepts were clarified, the second task was outlining criteria for choosing among measurement schemes: how do we measure? I have read into the national legislation two requirements for underemployment measurement. The first is the need for a single, national statistic giving the overall magnitude of underemployment. The second is the need for compositional detail showing who is underemployed. The measures widely used in developing countries do not meet these criteria. The Labor Utilization Framework and the indices designed by a few economists do meet these needs. The LUF is technically superior to the other measures because it is comparable to current labor force measures, it is a refined measure, and it does not confound labor commitment with underemployment.

Labor market realities are too complex to be fit neatly into the taxonomy of forms of underutilization. Between the concept and its measure lies a lot of slippage. First, the concept itself may be controversial, like the labor force concept. The concept needs to be expressed in a way that the instrument can measure. An operational definition is a measurable way of tapping the content of the concept. The first slippage occurs here, as in our operational definition of "idiosyncrasy" as physical disability. The data used then offer another opportunity for error. For example, our data on physical disability were flawed by response error. Finally, even with sound operational definitions and excellent data, there is likely to be measurement error.

To illustrate the complexities of labor utilization measurement, consider the following cases. A young housewife with a college degree chooses to work three afternoons a week at a part-time job. A part-time chef at a fast-food chain is laid off for three afternoons a week; now he will work only on weekend afternoons. A high school dropout, after looking for work for three months, quits looking, although he would still like a job. An older woman works as a housekeeper five days a week, but her cash income is below the poverty level. She receives her room and board during the week. An older worker, although he has had very little formal schooling, has had years of on-the-job training and has just been promoted to supervisor. Are they underutilized?

Let's examine these cases in terms of private underutilization first. The housewife wants part-time work, so she is not underutilized. The fast-food chef is underutilized, because he wants more work but was laid off. The dropout is a discouraged worker. He is not in the labor force, so he is not inadequately utilized. The housekeeper probably shows up as inadequately utilized, because her room and board are not priced and added to her earnings. The older worker is not underutilized. He certainly is not mismatched, for that would mean having too much education for the position. (If his on-the-job training had been excellent, he might be mismatched if he were qualified for an even better job than supervisor.)

In each case, we have some slippage: in the labor force concept, for the dropout; in the operational definition of income, for the housekeeper; in the sensitivity of the measurement instrument, for detecting mismatch of the supervisor.

SOCIAL UNDERUTILIZATION

Now consider the same cases in terms of the loss to society. Are the housewife and short-order cook both underutilized in the sense that they could be working longer hours? Is the housekeeper underutilized because she could contribute more to GNP in a higher-paying job? How much does society lose from the idleness of the dropout? One way to deal with social underutilization would be to set a standard of average labor input and measure deviations from it. At any rate, subtle value judgments would be needed.

Private underutilization also requires a standard, but in this case it is a standard of minimum labor input, assuming the voluntary nature of labor input. Even the most skilled American, if he or she does not work or look for work, is not underutilized in terms of the private measure. But if he actively seeks work or works at least one hour for pay or profit, then his job activity can be compared with the minimal labor yardstick. Plainly, the setting of the minimum also requires subtle value judgments. Otherwise, the most ambitious worker will always be, by definition, underutilized—his working hours will never be long enough, his income never high enough, his job never challenging enough. The yardstick must be relatively stable and "objective." Otherwise, relative effort, relative rewards, and relative deprivation become closely tied to underutilization. Just as the poor "ye have always with ye" so the underutilized may persist at the lower end of the distribution of jobs. It is for this reason that measurement cutoffs must be set so carefully and operational definitions must be treated with care.

With measures of social underutilization, a societal assessment of the worker's potential must replace the voluntary assumption of the labor force approach, and an "average" yardstick must replace a "minimal" yardstick. Measures of social underutilization, if viewed another way, can also be seen as measures of labor *potential*. This may justify their development, but I think their use will be quite different from uses of private underutilization measures.

The cost of private utilization may be reckoned, however, without considering the broader issues of social underutilization. Such measures as labor force time lost and foregone income can be readily computed.

FURTHER WORD ON MISMATCH

Part of the neglect of underemployment comes from social scientists' tendency to study what they can measure. In overcoming this inertia, the congressional mandate may accentuate another tendency, that of assuming that underutilization is what the underutilization index measures. This sort of nominalism overlooks the slippage between concepts and their operational definition. The content of the concepts "underutilization" and particularly "social underutilization" can probably never be completely measured, so a warning against premature closure is appropriate. In particular, new forms of work organization may make new forms of underutilization salient. A more serious source of slippage in this study is the measurement of mismatch: specifically, the problem of setting the mismatch cutoff. The need to study mismatch comes up frequently in the literature, but the difficulty in measuring it is also mentioned.[4]

The best conclusion that can be made about mismatch at this point is that it is an objective and subjective phenomenon whose measurement is obscured by cohort and period effects. Our knowledge of the objective problem is mostly anecdotal: there are Ph.D.'s driving taxis for want of better jobs. The subjective problem can be documented by the many survey respondents who report themselves "significantly overeducated" for their jobs, but it is difficult to discern whether their problem is one of underemployment or of alienation. For this reason it seemed better to use a purely statistical cutoff as a proxy for objective criteria and to assume that well-educated persons want the sort of jobs usually held by the well-educated, in lieu of subjective data.

The problem with the statistical cutoff is that roughly 16% of every occupation will exceed the education cutoff for mismatch, by definition. (Actually, the percentage is likely to be somewhat smaller because of the rounding procedures described in appendix D.) When the preliminary tabulations for hours of work and level of income have been made, the 16% will be reduced somewhat. But take a relatively privileged group, say white males, whose utilization is relatively good. As their unemployment declines and their wages and hours improve, their mismatch figure begins to approach 16% as an upper limit. Is this still a "real" problem, or an artifact of the measuring instrument? The statistical measure has the advantage of being "objective," but that does not guarantee that it is meaningful. "Statistical mismatch" also includes the related difficulties of cohort and period effects.

The cohort effect comes about because young workers have more education than older workers. With the baby boom reaching employment age, this becomes a relatively greater problem in the labor force as a whole. For any given occupation, the effect on the mismatch cutoff depends upon the age distribution and the education of its recruits. The college graduate with a bachelor's degree in agriculture might earn an equivalent salary either as a county extension agent or as the manager of a corporation's ranch, but the variability in education among ranchers is likely to be greater and therefore his chances of appearing mismatched are greater as a rancher. By contrast, simple jobs with high turnover may provide entry opportunities for young graduates. The graduates may feel mismatched and may quit as soon as possible, but the occupation's mismatch cutoff will be high because of the graduates' relatively large proportion of the occupation. Thus they will not appear to be mismatched.

The period effect represents the labor market's adjustment to the increased supply of highly educated manpower. Educational attainment may become the employer's screening variable, or the proxy for docility, reliability, and intelligence. Credentialism may be involved, for a degree or diploma may be required of current entrants even though this represents more than the statistical mismatch level of education. Presumably, these cohort and period effects would complicate any measure of mismatch simply because of the dynamic interchange between schools and labor markets.

Two other possible methods of setting mismatch cutoffs deserve comment. The first uses the functional requirements of the occupation as found in the *Dictionary of Occupational Titles*. The functional requirements can be translated into years of schooling needed to do the job, but they are not necessarily equal to the level of education socially defined as sufficient. The major disadvantage of this approach—and one which would make the cohort distortions even stronger—is that the functional requirements for most jobs are so low.[5] A preliminary investigation indicates that the volume of mismatch would be increased dramatically. In one sense, functional mismatch cutoffs are more "real" than statistical cutoffs; in another sense, they ignore an important dimension of reality.

A second alternative is to use the employer's minimum requirements for jobs. Everyone who exceeded the minimum would be mismatched. The great advantage of this measure is that it incorporates credentialism and other period effects, although it does not solve cohort problems. Its greatest disadvantage is technical. Many employers have no set requirements; they hire the best-qualified comers. Cutoffs for many occupations might be set through a content analysis of employment notices in, for example, classified ads and professional bulletins. However, it is unlikely that cutoffs could be established for the entire range of occupations.

There is a variant of this approach worthy of investigation. Low mismatch among women may result from higher underutilization in other categories, but it may also indicate that women's educations are better fitted to their jobs. Oppenheimer, as noted in chapter 7, suggests that training for "women's work" is often relegated to formal schooling. By the same token, mismatch is rather low in the crafts, where the percentage of men is high but where apprentice and trade-school programs are specific and narrowly focused. In general, mismatch may be low where licensing is required or where occupational groups are strong. It may be that high mismatch represents the attempts of men to overqualify themselves to be competitive for jobs without set requirements. A general, diffuse, liberal arts diploma may not prepare one for a job in any narrow vocational sense, but it may give a competitive edge. Knowledge of actual employment requirements would facilitate testing these ideas.

(A quite different objection to mismatch does not deal with cutoffs at all, but with the use of formal education as a proxy for skills. This objection is discussed in great detail in appendix D.)

It may sound as if the statistical measure of mismatch should be kept only by default. Certainly the two alternatives discussed above are not unqualified improvements. Actually, the statistical measure may yet prove itself to be useful in time-series analysis. Time-series data would permit a more sensitive cohort analysis than that in chapter 6. As for period effects, an analysis of mismatch cutoffs over time should tell us something about the extent of credentialism and its rate of diffusion through major occupation groups and population groups.

As an immediate recommendation, I suggest that no cutoffs lower than twelfth grade be set. A high school diploma has become the expected educational attainment in the United States, so it is misleading to count a worker as mismatched for being a high school graduate. Mismatch is a complementary phenomenon to structural unemployment and one that affects far more people.

It is an area that deserves much more research and that promises considerable payoff. Education has been the vehicle of upward mobility for many Americans, but its efficacy may be waning. If college graduates from working-class families are more often mismatched than graduates from middle-class families, then other variables than educational attainment may give the competitive edge. This is a qualitative dimension not explored in the current literature of the economics of education, which is primarily interested with monetary returns to education. Certainly it is too early for the verdict of *ignorabimus* upon mismatch.

FINDINGS

The central problem of this work was to determine the extent to which underutilization overlaps labor force marginality. We can conceive of several categories of workers who, for one reason or another, are less likely to hold good jobs—they are targets of discrimination, or they have little schooling, or they are disabled. These are the marginal workers. Are they the workers actually underutilized? This study showed considerable overlap between marginal workers and underutilization. Yet there is a large residual of workers who appear to be preferred workers, at least from census data, but who may hold "marginal jobs."

Overall underutilization declined from 25.1% in 1960 to 23.3% in 1970. This estimate of one in four workers underutilized is similar to that found elsewhere in the literature. However, although the overall decline was fairly small, there was a shift in the distribution of underutilization among the component forms (Δ = 6.8). The declines were greatest in unemployment and underutilization by level of income. Mismatch increased in 1970. There were also substantial shifts in the composition of the underutilized. A sizable decline in underutilization occurred among nonwhites, and a lesser decline among women. The overall decline correlated with the evidence from leading economic indicators for 1960 and 1970.

Three hypotheses predicted greater underutilization among certain population groups: the idiosyncrasy hypothesis for the disabled; the discrimination hypothesis for nonwhites, women, teenagers, and the elderly; and the achievement hypothesis for the less educated. A fourth hypothesis linked underutilization to declining industries, small firms, and obsolete occupations.

The idiosyncrasy hypothesis received little support if one compared overall rates of underutilization for disabled and able-bodied workers in 1961–62 and 1970. Physically disabled workers were somewhat more likely to be unemployed and poorly compensated than the labor force as a whole. They constitute a relatively small proportion of all workers, and their slightly greater underutilization does not help explain the national rates. The idiosyncrasy hypothesis treats disability *ceteris paribus*. An alternative hypothesis, the redundant disadvantage hypothesis, would suggest that other characteristics may amplify the effect of disability. The alternative hypothesis was not supported when percent Negro in the labor force was controlled.

Disabled workers are much less likely to participate in the labor force at all, but a comparison of evidence of 1961–62 and 1970 showed that for those working, national economic trends influenced both disabled and able-bodied workers in the same direction. Variant idiosyncrasies that could not be tested include the underutilization of the mentally or behaviorally "stigmatized," such as the retarded, exconvicts, mental patients, and dishonorably discharged veterans.

Everett Hughes proposed age, sex, and race as "master social positions" that significantly affect achievement within the stratification system. Age is the changing master social position and was hypothesized to affect the utilization of young and old workers. There was indeed greater underutilization of the young and old. Analysis of birth cohorts in 1960 and 1970 showed that this was not a function of economic conditions alone. As younger cohorts aged, their utilization improved beyond what economic conditions suggested. As older cohorts aged, their utilization deteriorated. In fact, the age-specific underutilization rates of the young and old worsened between 1960 and 1970. Four alternatives to age—temporal fluctuations, age compositions, education compositions, and percent of the cohort married—did not explain the findings as well.

The Jonckheere-Terpstra distribution-free test for ordered alternatives showed that the young are significantly more likely to be underutilized than the elderly, who in turn are significantly more likely to be underutilized than those in the prime working years. The relative disadvantage of both young and old workers was most obvious in unemployment, but they were also more likely to be mismatched. The young have higher age-specific mismatch rates.

The discrimination hypothesis predicted that nonwhites would be more underutilized than whites. This was true to a highly significant degree in both 1960 and 1970, but the trend is toward equal utilization. Whites had higher percentages mismatched in both years, but the rate of acceleration in mismatch is higher for nonwhites. In this sense, the trend is also toward equal underutilization.

Low education may provide nonwhites with "mismatch insurance," but it does not guarantee lower underutilization. At every level of education below four years of college, nonwhites are more likely to be underutilized than whites. Nonwhites are concentrated in occupations with higher underutilization rates, but even when occupation is controlled the nonwhite rate of underutilization is higher.

The discrimination hypothesis for sex was supported in 1970, though it received stronger support in 1960. By 1970, women were slightly less utilized than men in overall rates; women were more likely to be unemployed and involuntary part-time workers. Women's education-specific underutilization rates tended to be similar to or somewhat lower than men's, but their occupation composition made their expected underutilization higher than men's.

Their mismatch, however, is lower. One possibility is that the rather narrow demand for women's labor channels both training and utilization. This would tend to lower mismatch rates and offset the slightly higher unemployment rates. Women may also find nonparticipation a feasible alternative to underutilization more often than men do.

The final part of the discrimination hypothesis predicts interactions among marginal statuses. Goodman's modified regression technique was used to analyze the data. Race is clearly the strongest influence on underutilization, and nonwhite women suffer a double disadvantage that has not been affected proportionately by the secular decline in underutilization. Age does not worsen this situation; in fact the position of young nonwhite female cohorts is relatively better than that of older nonwhite females. Even though recent economic improvements have short-changed nonwhite women, cohort changes may improve their utilization. Nonwhite men are disadvantaged because of their color; age does not affect the disadvantage significantly. Among white workers, youth is a disadvantage and so is the combination of being old and female.

The achievement hypothesis predicted that low education would be associated with underutilization. Underachievement, in terms of few years of schooling or job instability, was associated with higher unemployment and underutilization by level of income. Higher educational attainment or specialized training (i.e., vocational education) improved utilization except that mismatch, by definition, was more prevalent among the highly educated. The explanatory power of the achievement variables is limited. The education-specific rates of utilization differ by race and sex groups, so that even high achievement by nonwhites is not always rewarded. The achievement hypothesis is most useful in explaining the underutilization of whites in the prime working years and older.

To summarize the results of the first three hypotheses, two sorts of labor marginality are associated with underutilization. Race has a pervasive effect on underutilization, one that even overrides other sorts of marginality. Among whites, low achievement, sex, and age affect utilization. Physical disability is not significantly associated with underutilization.

The fourth hypothesis differs from the others in its concern with marginal jobs—jobs in industries, firms, or occupations that result in underutilization of their incumbents. Census data provide only rough-and-ready operational measures of job marginality. Sector, major occupational group, and class of worker variables were used in lieu of such variables as level of technology, competitive position, and size of firm. There was limited support for the hypothesis.

Agriculture has more underutilization than nonagricultural enterprise, despite the fact that unemployment rates are lower than in nonagriculture. In agriculture, even more than in the labor force as a whole, women are more likely than men to be underutilized. Interestingly, between 1960 and 1970 utilization improved more in agriculture than in the labor force as a whole, although the number of agricultural employees declined both absolutely and relatively to the rest of the labor force. This decline occurred during a decade of increased production and capital-intensity and declining competitiveness— indication, according to the hypothesis, that marginal jobs are being eliminated.

Major occupational groups are a crude measure of such organizational influences as employee associations and stability of work. The hypothesis predicted relatively good utilization among professionals, craftsmen, and operatives, the groups most likely to be protected by worker associations. Unstable job situations, especially those of unskilled independent contractors, are most prevalent in farm and nonfarm labor, private household work, and service jobs. These were expected to be the groups with the highest underutilization. Those predictions were largely borne out in terms of overall rates, although lower white-collar workers had very high mismatch rates. Class of worker data were an inconclusive proxy variable for size of firm.

Manpower Policy and Labor Utilization

The LUF is a relatively economical measurement scheme that requires few changes in current data collection. The major addition is including the reason for part-time work in all labor force surveys. An alternative approach, somewhat less desirable because of its subjective nature, would be to ask part-time workers if they would like more work or if they would accept a full-time job. Some such question should probably be added to the long questionnaire for the 1980 United States Census, and further experimentation with the wording of the question would be useful.

Even while experimental work continues, it should be possible to begin publishing a series of underemployment indicators. They need to be made available on a seasonally adjusted basis with sufficient geographic detail for use by local governments. For planning purposes, it would also be useful to prepare tables of gross private underutilization. For example, it would be useful to know how many involuntary part-time workers are also mismatched. Eventually, time-series data should be used to correlate underutilization with trends in labor force size, economic growth, and welfare expenditures. When the unemployment rate jumps from 5% to 8%, does underemployment decline, increase, or remain the same?

Other innovations that should be undertaken are the regular reporting of the number and composition of discouraged workers, and a cross-tabulation of underemployment data by degree of labor force commitment. Combining the LUF with degrees of commitment would probably yield the following categories:

> Unemployed
> > Seeking full-time work
> > Seeking part-time work

Underutilized by hours of work
Usually full-time worker
Usually part-time worker*

Underutilized by level of income

Mismatched
Full-time
Part-time

Adequately utilized
Full-time
Part-time

These recommendations deal primarily with regular government data collection, and one of the advantages of the LUF is the ease and economy with which it can be adapted to current labor force statistics. The LUF could also be useful in other sorts of social surveys. For example, the relationship of work satisfaction and status discrepancy to underemployment could be a useful contribution to the sociology of work.

A final area of needed research is partly conceptual and partly judgmental, but amenable to creative empirical analysis. The nature of the hierarchical arrangement of the LUF requires discussion and interpretation. If the unemployed and involuntary part-time workers are really "worse off" in a welfare sense than the mismatched, a system of weights would need to be worked out before any policies (e.g., revenue sharing) were based on the data.

It will take several years of monitoring the data before any policy initiatives can be based on LUF. In particular, the mismatch indicator in its current form is probably not sufficiently well developed to suggest policy action. On the other hand, the monitoring itself can be useful in the enforcement of current policies. For example, selected industry groups could be monitored for the adequacy of their affirmative action program. Higher mismatch rates for minorities and women in the same industry, compared with those for white men, would be a warning that further investigation might be warranted.

The hours of work and income criteria might be linked to unemployment to allocate CETA funds. For funds already allocated, analysis of local underemployment data should certainly help pinpoint the population groups and job areas needing programs. If underemployment data were included in the 1980 census, it would be relatively inexpensive for local employment offices to prepare their own detailed files of employment adequacy.

With these data available, a number of studies on important current labor topics could be undertaken. What are the effects of rapid immigration on labor adequacy? Does it make a difference if the migrants are illegal aliens? What

---

* That is, a voluntary part-time worker whose hours have been cut even further.

would be the effect for young earners of the repeal of mandatory retirement from adequate jobs? What job areas upgrade most rapidly when college graduates are in abundant supply? The measurement of underemployment does not so much suggest a direction for government policy as provide a tool for evaluating the effects of policy, or offer evidence of the need for policy changes. In the long run, however, the data may point to a need for greater emphasis on labor-intensive technology.[6]

Sociological Significance

Early sociologists saw the quality of labor as an important area of investigation. Despite its recent neglect in sociology, underutilization promises to be a useful variable in measuring full participation in society. It is important to recognize that inadequate work is a function of economic and social organization. The special model of underutilization grounds the forms of underutilization in the typical economic differentiation of industrial societies.

The most important sociological outcome of utilization studies lies in analyzing the links between economic organization and social organization. In the language of the dual-labor market theorists, what is the relative importance and overlap of marginal workers and marginal jobs? The first step in answering this question was taken in chapter 2, where four hypotheses implicit in the literature were teased out and stated in testable form. The structure of the study required that the hypotheses be considered independently. The next step is to consider the joint effect of social structural and economic structural variables.

Even though this is hardly the final word on the subject, a few conclusions about the nature of United States underutilization are warranted. First, underutilization affects the socially marginal far beyond what can be attributed to economic structure. Nonwhites are hardest hit, but it is even worse to be both nonwhite and female, handicapped, or uneducated. On the other hand, some "common sense" expectations were not met. Nonwhite youths were not significantly more underutilized than older nonwhites, although unemployment rates alone would lead one to believe the opposite. The lower educational attainment of nonwhites, and lower mismatch as a consequence, probably help to account for this.

Among whites, young persons are more likely to be underutilized. Handicapped persons and poorly educated persons are somewhat more likely to be underutilized, at least in certain categories.

The findings for economic structure are somewhat difficult to interpret. In agriculture, the unemployment rate is misleading, for underutilization is quite high. The relation of high underutilization to agriculture requires further research; I expect that small family farms, worked by older people, and migrant worker households are the sites of underemployment. The evidence for major occupational groups is slender but points to the importance of worker organization (unions, professional associations) for promoting adequate utilization. Further research based on firm size, type of technology, competitive positions, and comparable variables is badly needed. From the large number of under-utilized white men in the prime working ages one can conclude that there are marginal jobs existing apart from marginal groups. This conclusion would be further strengthened by research testing the effect of other possible sources of social marginality—for example, ethnic prejudice and the inability to speak English.

The persistence of substantial labor inadequacy in the United States points to a sizable loss of potential production—probably a greater loss than that from unemployment, which is a smaller proportion. How is this loss distributed within the class structure? Are the mismatched principally the first-generation college graduates of their families? Are they more likely to have graduated from small colleges or urban commuter schools?

Can the extent and type of underutilization distinguish the "stable poor" from the "disreputable poor"? The break between the underutilized by hours of work and the underutilized by level of income may reflect a cleavage between the unstable worker, who is more prone to personal and family disorganization, and the stable working poor.

These are questions that have not been answered by the usual studies of occupational and educational attainment. If economists have been too concerned to analyze the labor force in terms of income, sociologists have been perhaps too eager to analyze it in terms of occupational prestige. The argument here is that neither study is sufficient. A prestigious occupation may bring low income; but a low-prestige blue-collar worker may earn more than many professors' annual salaries. To understand the full impact of jobs on people, it is necessary to relate several dimensions of the job.

Many more substantive research issues could be mentioned. Wherever work has been an important explanatory variable—for example, in studies relating increased female participation rates to declining fertility—the *adequacy of work* may be investigated as an intervening variable.

One area for further technical research is adding and analyzing new variables. Further work would profit from using a black-nonblack distinction in preference to the white-nonwhite dichotomy. Better measures of economic organization, and particularly of unionization, are badly needed to continue the line of research begun here. And finally, longitudinal research on employment histories is necessary to establish the relationship of underutilization to the life cycle. Much of the underutilization of young or inexperienced workers may be a kind of subsidy for work experience. The need to relate underutilization measures to social surveys has already been mentioned.

A different line of research involves changing the unit of analysis. The role of underutilization in household labor supply may be a fruitful inquiry. Among other things, it would permit a refinement of secondary worker theory and would provide better data about the labor force participation of minorities and teenagers. Much of the current discussion about labor force "commitment" might be recast in terms of economic and cultural motivations to work conditioned by sex and age roles and household position.

Finally, for international comparison, national trends in underutilization may prove to be an important and sensitive social indicator with policy implications for taxation, internal migration, and manpower development. The empirical findings of this study argue strongly for the further analysis of the quality of work. .

Data Adequacy and Methods

Errors in data can lead to meaningless or misleading findings. For example, the confusion about "total disability" mentioned in chapter 5 makes it difficult to cross-classify disability status by labor force status. The labor force definition itself excludes some workers who should perhaps be counted (for example, discouraged workers) and includes others whose voluntary participation is quite minimal. Ambiguities in the labor force definition are carried over into the Labor Utilization Framework, and the data given here should be viewed in that light.

Besides problems of definition, the data presented here are subject to other sources of error. Three are discussed here: census underenumeration, sampling variability, and response error.

Census Underenumeration

One in every thousand *uncounted* Americans is also omitted from the Public Use Samples, and a faulty census count is transmitted to CPS labor force data through sampling and the ratio estimation to the national population. The undercount affects this study if the missed persons differ from counted persons in marginality or underutilization.

Available census estimates do show that some marginal workers are likely to be undercounted. About one-eighth of Negro males were missed both in 1960 and 1970, and the undercount among young persons was high, especially in 1960. The 1960 census enumerated 90% of nonwhites, and in 1970 about 92% of Negroes were enumerated. By contrast, 98% of whites were counted in each census. Both censuses were more likely to undercount Negro males, especially those aged 20–24. Although the undercount was much improved by 1970, it seems fair to conclude that the estimated number of young Negroes, especially young Negro males, is too small.[1]

It is more difficult to find evidence about the labor utilization of missed persons. A Census Bureau study in two ghetto areas found the labor force status of missed persons to be similar to that of counted persons. Trained interviewers conducted a series of "casual" interviews with passers-by in bars and on street corners in New Haven, Connecticut, and Trenton, New Jersey. Census personnel concluded that the undercount did not affect the unemployment rate, although uncounted workers differed in residence and family patterns from counted workers.[2] The methodology does not permit replication or statistical inference, but the Wirtz study, a few years later, assumed that the missed workers were more likely than counted ones to be "subemployed."[3] Of course, many undercounted workers live outside the inner city, and no assumption about their underutilization is warranted. On balance, it is probably safe to assume that the underutilization figures given here do not overstate the problem.

Sampling Variability

An inflation factor of 1,000, the reciprocal of the sampling rate, may be used to estimate the number that would be obtained from a complete census count. Sampling variability is the chance difference between the Public Use Sample figure and the figure that would be given by a complete count. The standard error for the 1970 civilian labor force estimate is 155,200. This means that in 95% of the samples drawn, the civilian labor force figure would lie between 79,588,600 and 80,209,400. The size of the labor force estimated from the 5% neighborhood characteristics sample is 79,899,000; the published figure is 80,051,046.

In some tables that present cross-classification by several control variables, the estimated entries are quite small. Small magnitudes might fall outside the 95% confidence intervals and should be interpreted cautiously. Table A.1 presents standard errors for several variables of interest.[4] These standard errors were based on generalized approximate standard errors for the percentage size and the 1/1000 sample, and on the homogeneity of the classification variable.

No estimates are available for coding, tabulation, and other technical errors besides sampling.

Response Error

In large samples, sampling variability is a less important source of error than response error.

Response error is accidental or tendentious misreporting by the respondent. The level of response error for every variable is not known. Some response error can be detected because it is logically inconsistent—for example, see the discussion of disability data in chapter 5. Some 1960 response errors were estimated by matching census data with CPS data and a check of employer records, and similar checks are underway for 1970 data.[5]

Occupation is a variable susceptible to response error. The 1960 employers record check showed large underreporting among laborers (index of inconsistency = 41.7) and managers (32.4), with slight underreporting of clerical and service workers. Overreporting occurs predominantly among sales workers

Table A.1. *Approximate standard error of percentages based on estimate of the civilian labor force, by variable, for 1970 data*

Variable	Estimated percentage					
	1% or 99%	5% or 95%	10% or 90%	15% or 85%	20% or 80%	
Marginality variables						
Race[a]	0.04	0.09	0.12	0.14	0.17	
Schooling	0.03	0.08	0.11	0.13	0.15	
Age	0.03	0.07	0.09	0.09	0.12	
Underutilization variables						
Unemployed	0.04	0.09	0.12	0.14	0.17	
Hours of work	0.03	0.07	0.09	0.09	0.12	
Level of income	0.06	0.14	0.20	0.23	0.27	
Mismatch	0.06	0.14	0.20	0.23	0.27	

Note: The largest applicable standard error should be used.

[a] Standard errors for disability and class of worker are the same.

and professional workers. Comparisons of CPS with 1970 data show that the census tends to overestimate the number of salesmen and underestimate the number of managers.[6] Inaccuracy in reporting occupation data among white-collar workers—especially the downgrading of managers—may bias mismatch estimates upward. Inaccuracy in lower blue-collar categories—e.g., the underreporting of laborers—may affect the count of economically marginal workers, but this appears to be a more serious problem with 1960 data than with 1970 data.

Nonresponse, a related source of error, is corrected in Public Use Samples by an allocation procedure. In 1970, 34.7% of all persons had at least one item allocated. Employment status was allocated for 5.1% of 1970 respondents, down from 6.1% in 1960. Income was allocated for 12.5% of the 1970 records but only 6.3% of 1960 records.[7] Allocation is an editing process subject to its own error, but it is the best available method of supplying missing data. In this study, allocated occupation or education were excluded in setting mismatch cutoffs for the entire labor force. Allocations were used in tabulating individual records.

Methods

For each variable, labor force underutilization is described by a percentage distribution, which is more reliable than absolute frequencies. Adequate and inadequate participation rates (discussed below) relate underutilization to the general population. The marginal and nonmarginal levels of the independent variable are compared by the index of dissimilarity or chi-square. Sample sizes are so large that most differences are significant, and so measures of association are presented to show the strength of the relations. The conventional measures of association based on χ^2, as well as other measures, are used. In some cases, if it appears that the relationship between the independent variable and utilization might be spurious, artificial controls are introduced through standardization and decomposition of differences between rates. Where several levels of an independent variable may be labeled "marginal" statuses, nonparametric measures analogous to multiple-sample comparisons or analysis of variance are used.

LEVELS OF MEASUREMENT AND THE LUF

As a nominal (qualitative) variable, the LUF may be a dichotomy (adequate-inadequate), a trichotomy (unemployed-underemployed-employed), or a polytomy with five components. The hierarchical tabulation scheme also permits one to think of the LUF as an ordinal variable ranging from unemployment to adequate utilization. Finally, percent or proportion underutilized could be used as an interval level variable.

Because the LUF is an experimental measure, it seemed most conservative to use it as a dichotomous qualitative variable (nominal level). This approach loses considerable information, because the labor force has been conceptualized in three dimensions. However, for exploratory work the nominal level of measurement seems justifiable. To use LUF as an ordinal variable presumes more conceptual consensus than the literature suggests. To use it as an interval variable assumes a validity and reliability for the components which this preliminary study could not establish. Although a few findings are supported with correlation analysis—e.g., percent underutilized correlated with percent Negro in regions—the multivariate analysis uses the adequate-inadequate dichotomy. The independent variables are also qualitative, and this limits the methods available.

Most multivariate methods require quantitative variables. Multiple regression and correlation require quantitative variables, although dummy regression analysis may be done with independent qualitative variables. Multiple classification analysis may be used with a dependent dichotomous variable but requires quantitative independent variables. Our data do not meet the level of measurement assumptions of these methods, and in addition do not meet the assumptions of homoscedasticity and independence of error terms. For these reasons, Goodman's hierarchical log-linear models are used. These are discussed later in this appendix.

UTILIZATION RATES

Each component C_i of underutilization, divided by the size of the labor force L, gives the component rate of underutilization for the reference week. The underutilization rate is:

$$\left[\sum_{i=1}^{4} C_i / L \right] \times 100,$$

where 1 = unemployed
      2 = underutilized by hours of work
      3 = underutilized by level of income
      4 = mismatch

This rate may also be thought of as a partial dependency rate. The adequately utilized are the complement of the underutilized.

By analogy to labor force participation rates, one can derive rates of adequate and inadequate participation. The adequate participation ratio is the ratio of adequately utilized persons to the noninstitutionalized population aged 16 and over. Similarly, J-specific rates may be derived where J is age, education, occupation, or another variable. In some tables, full-time underutilization rates have been computed. These are discussed in more detail in appendix B.

GOODMAN'S HIERARCHICAL LOG-LINEAR MODELS

The observed frequencies f_{ijkl} of a cross-classification may be expressed as a function of the observed odds for and against utilization and the total observed frequency n_{ijk}. If F_{ijkl} is the expected frequency under some specified model, then F_{ijkl} can also be expressed as a function of τ parameters for the "main effects" and "interactions effects" of variables Y, R, and S.[8] The "model" includes significant main effects and interaction effects, and the "fit" of the model is assessed through chi-square. The models used here are expressed as natural logarithms, and this makes the model additive rather than multiplicative. If $G_{ijkl} = \log_e F_{ijkl}$ and $\lambda = \log_e \tau$, then table 8.1 may be modeled as $G_{ijkl} = \theta + \lambda_i^Y + \lambda_j^R + \lambda_k^S + \lambda_l^U + \lambda_{ij}^{YR} + \lambda_{ik}^{YS} + \lambda_{il}^{YU} + \lambda_{jk}^{RS} + \lambda_{jl}^{RU} + \lambda_{kl}^{SU} + \lambda_{ijk}^{YRS} + \lambda_{ijl}^{YRU} + \lambda_{jkl}^{RSU}$. (Subscripts i, j, k, l are omitted in chapter 8 to simplify the presentation.)

If the λ parameter is nil, the standardized value of the parameter estimate will be approximately normally distributed with zero mean and unit variance for large samples. The absolute size of λ parameters is a guide to their relative importance. Single-variable effects reflect marginal distributions. The two-variable effects reflect an association between a pair of variables. Three-variable effects show an interaction among variables. Combinations of two- and three-variable effects may be ordered into a series of hierarchical hypotheses. The hierarchical hypotheses are then used to demonstrate the fit of the model and the significance of the contribution of each effect. A comparison of the hierarchical hypotheses is used to partition χ^2 and to estimate multiple-correlation coefficient analogues.

Measuring Involuntary Part-time Employment

After the unemployed members of the labor force have been identified, the employed workers who were "at work" during the reference week are classified by hours of work. (Employed persons who were "not at work" during the reference period [e.g., those sick or on vacation] were assumed to be adequately utilized by hours of work.) Involuntary part-time workers are the underutilized by hours of work. This classification requires a definition of part-time employment, a definition of involuntary part-time employment, and an adjustment of census data to reflect involuntary part-time work.

Defining Part-time Employment

Public Use Samples include the number of hours worked by all respondents aged 14 and older who were "at work" in the week preceding the census. Thirty-four hours is the upper limit used by the Census Bureau for part-time workers. This cutoff prevents the misclassification of workers in entire occupations in which the average weekly hours vary from 35 to more than 40. In 1970, male statisticians worked a mean 38.6 hours a week and female proofreaders worked a mean 35 hours a week.[1] A higher cutoff, say a "standard" 40-hour workweek, would overcount part-time workers. The variation in full workweeks is also recognized in government computations of "labor force time lost." Unemployed persons are considered to have lost 37.5 hours (35 + [40−35/2]), and involuntary part-time workers are assumed to have lost the difference between 37.5 hours and the actual number of hours they worked.

The 35-hour cutoff also prevents the misclassification of the occasional worker who missed the bus, took a long lunch break, and so forth. Hours worked at all jobs are recorded, but the total hours are attributed to the main job. A more detailed study might investigate multiple-job holders with insufficient hours of work in their principal occupation. Throughout this study, 34 hours is the cutoff point for part-time work.

Defining Involuntary Part-time Employment

Many workers, especially students and women, prefer part-time work. Conceptually, the underutilized by hours of work are working part-time despite their preferences to work full-time. Census data do not indicate whether part-time workers are voluntarily or involuntarily part-time. The voluntary part-time labor force can be identified from Current Population Survey (CPS) data. Unemployed persons are asked whether they are seeking full-time or part-time work, and part-time workers are asked their usual hours of work and their reasons for not working full-time. Respondents are classified as "part-time, for economic reasons" if their part-time work is involuntary due to slack work, material shortages, partial layoff, or an inability to find full-time work. This classification includes workers who are usually full-time and those whose part-time hours were further reduced for economic reasons, as well as those unable to find full-time work. Workers whose short hours were caused by illness, vacation, conflicting personal obligations, and so forth, are not included.

Monthly Labor Review, Employment and Earnings, and the *Employment and Training Report of the President* are among the sources of published data concerning those working part-time for economic reasons. Individual records on CPS tapes contain hours of work, reasons for part-time work, usual hours of work, and a recode item for part-time work for economic reasons.

Adjusting Census Data

The census date is April 1. The Current Population Survey is taken during the week in which the twelfth of the month falls. March CPS tapes and published April CPS data were used to adjust census data, but at the risk of introducing up to one month's difference in reference periods. The CPS sample results were used only to determine percentage distributions. Absolute numbers were obtained by multiplying the percentage distributions by independent estimates of the population. The independent estimates of population used in this study were the 1960 and 1970 census samples, respectively.[2]

Only published sample percentages were available for adjusting 1960 data, and this limits the 1960 data reported here. For 1970, sample percentages were taken from the data tape, and so it was possible to combine more variables of interest. Estimates were made both of involuntary part-time workers and of voluntary part-time workers. The percentage of voluntary part-time workers was used in the calculation of part-time mismatched workers.

The major shortcoming of this method is that it limits the analysis of part-time workers to adjusted aggregates. Individual records could not be adjusted. This limits the analysis of multiple underutilization. An attempt to provide case-by-case adjustments using a stepwise regression program did not produce a sufficiently high R^2.

"Full-time" Rates

Because of the difficulty in adjusting for involuntary part-time work, some tables in the text report "full-time" underutilization rates. In most tables, the full-time rate is computed by expressing the unemployed, working poor, and full-time mismatched as a percent of *all* workers. In some cases, the rate is computed as a percent of all full-time workers—that is, part-time workers are excluded from the denominator. "Full-time" rates include all of the unemployed as full-time, although some 887,000 unemployed in 1970 sought part-time work.[3] However, this is balanced by the exclusion of 1,021,000 part-time mismatched workers.

Measuring Underutilization by Level of Income

The unemployed, part-time workers, students, entrants, and reentrants to the labor force were omitted from the income adequacy analysis. The unemployed were omitted because they are already included among the underutilized. Part-time workers may be partitioned into the involuntary and the voluntary part-time workers. The involuntary part-time workers are already included among the underutilized. Voluntary part-time workers are assumed to earn lower wages in proportion to their shortened hours, and so they are excluded. Students, even those working more than 35 hours a week, are presumed to be subsidizing their on-the-job training and earning lower wages than nonstudents.[1] The same argument may be used for entrants and reentrants; in addition, there is the practical problem that entrants and reentrants had no work-related income to report in the year preceding the census. Consequently, the persons analyzed for income adequacy were those nonstudents who reported work-related income for the previous year and who were: (1) at work for more than 34 hours in the reference week, or (2) with a job and not at work in the reference week.

Assumptions

The procedure used to assess underutilization by level of income required classifying the pool of eligible workers—as described above—with respect to a poverty cutoff. This involved several assumptions that will be made explicit.

The first assumption was that income reported for the previous year could be used as a proxy for the current year. This assumption is an accommodation to the data available. The ideal data would be current annual earnings, or earnings for the reference week.

The second assumption was that only work-related income should be included. Underutilization by level of income is designed to measure labor-market–related economic hardship, and not general welfare. The work income measure used was the net sum of wages, salaries, profits or losses from self-employment, and profits or losses from one's own business or farm. Transfer payments, interest, dividends, rents, and other forms of income were excluded.

The third assumption concerned the proportion of the poverty level set as the cutoff for the worker. The poverty level is based on household size. If a worker were the chief income recipient of the household, it was assumed that the poverty level for the household was the appropriate cutoff for his income. This procedure is similar to that used by Levitan and Taggart, although their analysis of the working poor was limited to household heads.[2]

It seemed inappropriate to make the household poverty cutoff the cutoff for secondary earners.[3] For male secondary earners, the cutoff used was the poverty cutoff for a single, urban male in the prime working ages. For female secondary workers, the cutoff was that used for a single, urban female in the prime working ages. Secondary earners may work irregularly, and even if the secondary earner had worked full-time in the reference week, it was possible that the previous year's earnings reflected only a few weeks' work. Consequently, the poverty cutoff for secondary workers was translated into a minimum weekly wage. For 1969, this wage was $39.50 for males and $36.00 for females. Weekly earnings were approximated by dividing work-related income by the number of weeks worked.[4]

The Poverty Index

Cutoff points for 1970 were taken from the Social Security Administration index. The base for this index is a minimally adequate diet derived from a U.S. Department of Agriculture study made in 1955.[5] The average food-cost-to-income ratio in the 1955 study was one to three, and this ratio was retained in the poverty index for families of three or more members. In smaller families, larger factors were used to compensate for higher fixed expenses. The base year was 1963, and the Consumer Price Index (CPI) was used to adjust subsequent annual indices. Through the 1960's, the CPI rose faster than the cost of the basic food plan, and so the use of the CPI reflects the impact of inflation more accurately.[6]

The poverty index has been criticized for the one-to-three food/income ratio. Some critics argue that by 1960, the ratio had declined to one to four. This would cause the poverty level to be set unrealistically low. Even adjustments made with the CPI would be insufficient because the assumption of a constant composition of commodities could not be met.[7]

A second criticism cuts the other way. The CPI is based on a standard market basket, the items of which are selected from consumer production surveys. The items are not limited to necessities and do not allow for the substitution of inferior goods. It is not a true "cost-of-living" index.[8] This would be a damaging criticism if the poor were the most astute shoppers, always limiting their purchases to necessities and making the most economical selection of inferior goods. But it is probably more reasonable to assume that the CPI reflects prices affecting low-income shoppers. And there are data to indicate that prices may be even higher in urban ghetto areas.

On balance, it seems fair to conclude that the poverty index represents a reasonable series of cutoff points for identifying the working poor. However, the poverty index did not exist in 1960, and so the extension of the poverty cutoff to the 1960 data required a few additional assumptions.

Special Assumptions for 1960 Data

Establishing a poverty level for 1960 assumes that the ratio of food to income used in 1970 also held in 1960. It further assumes that the ratios of poverty cutoffs among households of differing characteristics were as valid in 1960 as they were in 1970. The CPI was used to deflate the 1963 poverty level back to 1959, just as it had been used to inflate it forward to 1969. This was a reasonable assumption in 1969 because the CPI was rising faster than the basic food basket. For the 1959–60 biennium, however, the index for the food basket rose faster than the CPI. The difference was slight and does not imply extensive bias in the 1960 levels. The 1960 cutoff levels were assigned case-by-case by examining the sex, age, and urban-rural residence of the household head and the size of the household. This cutoff level was the criterion only for the chief income recipient. The adjusted weekly figure for secondary earners was $32.40 for males and $30.00 for females.

Further Comments

The sex differential in poverty cutoffs came about because of the smaller food requirements for most females. This raises the possibility that a woman earning just over the female cutoff might be omitted from the inadequately utilized, while a man earning the same wage would be included. The 1970 data revealed no such cases. However, 50% of the male working poor (544,000) earned less than the female cutoff. The differentials within the poverty index make other borderline cases possible—for example, the urban worker who would not be underutilized if he lived in a rural area, or the parent of a large family who would not be underutilized with fewer dependents.

A second objection to the use of the poverty index is that it is not an adequate welfare measure. This is true; total family income, transfer payments, and the like are not included in work-related income. However, the charge is unfair, because the Labor Utilization Framework is not designed to measure welfare. The 1970 data were analyzed for the effects of total personal income and total family income. Of those underutilized by income, 1,007,000 fell below the poverty level even when all forms of personal income were counted. Even when all forms of family income were added in, no further improvement was made. Although not designed as a welfare measure, the Labor Utilization Framework seems to reflect economic hardship in the labor force very well. Many of the poor are not in the labor force, and so the Labor Utilization Framework does not reflect their welfare.

If the preceding objection hinted at an overcount of the poor, a third objection hints at their undercount. Poverty in the United States, this objection runs, is a matter of relative deprivation. The point at which one begins to "feel" poor is much higher than the absolute figure in the poverty index. This objection leads to the suggestion that the lowest decile of the income distribution be used for the cutoff.[9] Such a procedure has also been suggested for developing countries, where response error on income questions is especially likely to be high—however, it was suggested for operational, not theoretical, reasons.[10] The relative approach does not seem to be suitable for the United States. It may be the case that all of the underemployed feel relatively deprived, but not all of the relatively deprived are underemployed. A relative criterion seems to have very little to do with underutilization, and the labor utilization approach is not designed to be a measure of poverty per se.

An absolute cutoff is more solidly rooted in the concept of underutilization. The poverty index is based on food consumption, and so it is directly related to human capital. Were their survival to depend solely on the labor market, the underutilized by level of income could not maintain their human capital for long.

Finally, the treatment of unpaid workers deserves some comment. The underutilization of unpaid workers—the overwhelming majority of whom work in a family enterprise—is difficult to measure and is a particular concern in developing countries where the unpaid worker class is very large. Several methods have been suggested for apportioning total household income among unpaid family workers. These include per worker income, per person income, and weighted per person income.[11] No adjustment was made for unpaid workers in this study. In 1960, unpaid workers comprised only 1.03% of the labor force (695,000); in 1970, there were 444,000 unpaid workers or 0.6% of the labor force. Many of these workers reported earnings for the previous year and could be classified by income. Of these workers, 327,000 or 47.1% of the unpaid workers in 1960 fell below the poverty level. In 1970, 21,000 or 4.7% of the unpaid workers were underutilized by income. The 1960 figure indicates a large percentage of unpaid workers with income in 1959, albeit a low income. The 1970 figure is more difficult to interpret. It is possible that unpaid workers in 1970 were also unpaid or out of the labor force in 1969. This ambiguity indicates that a procedure for analyzing unpaid workers by imputed income would be desirable.

Such a procedure might use household income from family-owned enterprises for establishing per worker income figures. Of the unpaid workers in 1970, 60.1% lived in rural areas. It is likely that many of them worked on farms. Roughly 19.4% lived in central cities of 50,000 or more, and 20.5% lived in urbanized areas outside central cities. Urban unpaid workers may have worked in family shops or services. A small number are unpaid apprentices.

The inadequate classification of unpaid workers flaws the data. It is probably not a serious error, both because of the small number of unpaid workers and the even smaller number of unpaid workers subject to misclassification. The maximum number of workers who could have been misclassified is 301,000 in 1970 and 187,000 in 1960, excluding any students or entrants among them.[12]

Measuring Mismatch

Workers who were not already classified as unemployed, underutilized by hours of work, or underutilized by income were sorted for mismatch. The pool of persons analyzed for mismatch included the following:

1. full-time workers earning an adequate income
2. voluntary part-time workers
3. employed persons "not at work" during the reference period who earned an adequate income in the preceding year
4. full-time workers who are students, entrants, or reentrants to the labor force

Workers in this pool who were not mismatched were classified in the residual category, the "adequately utilized."

A worker is defined as mismatched if his education is greater than one standard deviation above the mean education in his current occupation. Three variables are required to determine mismatch for any worker: current occupation, completed years of schooling, and mismatch cutoff for the occupation. A three-digit occupational code is included in census and CPS tapes. Completed years of schooling, the proxy variable for skill level, was computed from total years of schooling by adjustments for current school attendance and noncompletion. The procedure for associating a mismatch cutoff with every occupation required four stages:

1. stratifying the three-digit occupational codes into a manageable two-digit code, a process done by using median education for the predominant sex within the three-digit occupation group
2. determining the mean and standard deviation for years of schooling within each stratum (i.e., two-digit code)
3. reassociating the cutoff for the two-digit code with the three-digit occupations
4. placing the cutoff for his own three-digit occupational code on each worker's record

Then completed years of schooling for every worker could be compared with the cutoff level. Those falling above the level were mismatched.

The four-step procedure used in establishing a cutoff is discussed in some detail below.

Establishing Mismatch Cutoffs

DEVELOPING A TWO-DIGIT CODE

A three-digit occupational code is used to report census and CPS data. The 1960 census and March 1970 CPS used 297 codes. As a result of a far-reaching overhaul of the classification, 441 codes were used in the 1970 census.[1] Many of these three-digit codes contained too few workers to provide a mismatch cutoff. Consequently, it was necessary to use a two-digit recode.

Two recodes of two digits are readily available for census data. The smaller of the two is the major occupational group recode, of which there were 12 codes in 1970 and 11 codes in 1960. This code was unsatisfactory because of the educational heterogeneity within some major occupational groups. For example, the "professional, technical, and kindred workers" group contains dancers and athletes as well as physicians, lawyers, and university professors.

The more complex two-digit recode, called the "intermediate classification," classified occupations by industry and sex. In 1960, there were 161 intermediate classes for men and 70 for women. In 1970, men were classified into 170 intermediate codes and women into 103 codes. This two-digit code was abandoned because a unique stratum for each occupation, and not a sex-specific stratum, was considered preferable. The choice of a unique set rather than parallel sets of strata will be discussed in more detail below.

The three-digit code was unusable, and neither of the two-digit codes was satisfactory. A two-digit code based on median education within major occupational groups was used for the data presented here.[2] The major advantage of this procedure is that it creates strata that are relatively homogeneous for education.[3] This is a conservative approach when overeducation is being measured.

Median education is published correct to tenths of years, but completed years of schooling is the variable used to assess mismatch. Median years of schooling were rounded down to completed years for purposes of classifying strata.

Women tend to be concentrated in fewer occupations than men, although more dispersion is taking place. For example, the census two-digit "intermediate classification" codes for women increased from 70 in 1960 to 103 in 1970. Further, women workers as a whole are somewhat better educated than men. The median educational attainments for occupations contained in census reports PC(2)-7a are given by sex. Which median should be used?

Three courses of action were possible. First, either the male or the female median could be used consistently. The use of the male median might lead to an overstatement of mismatch among males.

Second, two median levels might be used for every occupation, one for males and one for females. A caste system could be created for some occupations. A man might be mismatched with three years of college, while for a woman in the same occupation, four years of college might be the cutoff for mismatch.

The strata, and consequently the cutoff levels, would become artifacts of the propensity for schooling and not of the occupation.[4]

To make this point more clearly, consider adding race-specific median education. Blacks tend to have less education than whites. Consequently, a level of inferior training in some strata might become the nonwhite standard, and any nonwhite who had attained the white standard might be "mismatched." Nonwhites with education and occupation equivalent to that of whites would show a higher rate of mismatch merely by virtue of the generally disadvantaged position of nonwhites. This would have the effect of changing the variable of analysis from the occupation to the occupation-race group.

It might be objected that a whole range of cutoffs is used in measuring income inadequacy. The poverty index is based on a minimal food plan, which does vary according to nutritional needs. The difference with a range of mismatch cutoffs would be the implication that a group's current education is a "proper" level of education. This is arbitrary and it enshrines the effects of past discrimination.[5]

Nevertheless, occupational composition must be taken into account, particularly when there is danger of biasing the count of mismatched persons too high. For that reason, I have adopted a third solution that incorporates composition. Under this solution, the sex of the majority of the occupation is the reference group for the median. Sex composition is included lest the higher female educational attainment lead to an overcount of female mismatch in general, and particularly in some major occupational groups. An overcount would be especially likely among clerical workers and private household workers, and to a lesser extent among professional, technical, and kindred workers. (On the other hand, because nonwhites have a lower educational attainment than whites, occupations in which nonwhites are a majority would overstate white mismatch. So race composition is not included.)

THE STRATA CREATED FOR CENSUS DATA

As described, median education for the majority sex was used to stratify the detailed three-digit occupational code. In 1970, 89 of 441 coded occupations had a female majority, and so the female median education was used for them. Sixty-three occupations were classified into the same stratum using either the male or the female median education. In 13 occupations, the female median lowered the male median by one year, and in 3 occupations, the male median was lowered by two years. Males in these occupations are subject to an overcount of mismatch, but they compose a very small fraction of the labor force. Together, these 13 occupations accounted for 0.02% of the civilian labor force, and of this small percentage, 26.7% were male. Table D.1 presents further information.

In 1960, women were a majority in 48 occupations. In 38 of these, the male and female medians (rounded to complete years) were the same. In the remaining 10, the female median was higher in 4 occupations and lower in 6.

With this solution for education there were 47 strata for 1960 census data and 57 for 1970 census data. A slightly different procedure had to be used for March, 1970 CPS data, and it is discussed below.

CPS DATA

The 1970 CPS tape used the 1960 occupation classification. The 1960 occupation classification had been stratified by the 1960 education distribution, and the 1970 occupation classification by the 1970 education distribution. The problem with the CPS data was to match the 1960 occupation classification with the 1970 education distribution. The 1970 occupation codes were more detailed than the 1960 codes, so the following decisions were made.

For all codes except the "not elsewhere classified" (n.e.c.) codes, I tried to match the 1960 and 1970 codes. If an identical code were used in 1960 and 1970, it was assigned to the 1970 education-occupation stratum.

Sometimes the 1960 code was broader. For example, "apprentices, metal trades" was subdivided in 1970 to molder apprentices, sheetmetal apprentices, and so forth. If the multiple 1970 codes all had the same stratum, it was the stratum assigned to the broad 1960 code. If the multiple codes fell into different strata, the 1970 education levels for the strata were checked. For example, the 1960 code for "funeral directors and embalmers" was split into the 1970 codes "funeral directors," in the managers and proprietors group, and "embalmers," in the professional, technical, and kindred workers group. The median educational level was the same for both 1970 codes, but "embalmers" were in a stratum with other technical workers of the same education, and "funeral directors" were in a stratum with other managers of their educational level. The choice of stratum makes no difference for measuring mismatch in this instance.

In some cases the multiple 1970 codes represented not only different strata but also different levels of education. The 1960 code "artists and art teachers" would seem to include the more specific 1970 codes "painters and sculptors" and "university art, drama, and music teachers." The median educational levels of painters and university art teachers were quite different in 1970. It was not possible to make an accurate assignment of 1970 stratum, and so the 1960 stratum and the 1960 median education were used. This expedient was a last resort in two other circumstances: 1960 codes which were more narrow than the 1970 code, and 1960 codes which did not exist in 1970 (e.g., student professional nurses).

The n.e.c. codes were a problem particularly for new, rapidly expanding occupations. Three different occupational codes were used to classify computer specialists in the census in April, 1970. But if any of these computer specialists were respondents in the March, 1970 CPS, they were coded as "professional, technical, and kindred workers, n.e.c." Consequently, n.e.c.

Table D.1. *Occupations in which females are a majority but in which the female median may lead to an over-statement of male mismatch (1970)*

Occupation	Number (1)	Number female (2)	Percent female (3)	Male median education—female median[a] (4)
All occupations, this table	1,740,927	1,471,962	84.6	...
Librarians	123,144	100,325	81.5	1
Radiologic technicians and technologists	53,511	36,609	68.4	1
Health technicians, n.e.c.	60,174	33,764	56.1	2
Religious workers, n.e.c.	35,450	19,728	55.7	2
Prekindergarten and kindergarten teachers	128,224	125,884	98.2	1
Enumerators and interviewers	71,261	56,872	79.8	1
Secretaries, legal	87,700	86,369	98.5	1
Secretaries, medical	70,729	69,925	98.9	1

Teacher aides, excluding school monitors	135,020	120,938	89.6	1
Winding operatives, n.e.c.	63,670	33,375	52.4	1
Nursing aides, orderlies, attendants	751,983	636,626	84.7	1
Boarding and lodging housekeepers	7,549	5,577	73.9	1
Personal service apprentices	1,457	853	58.5	1
Cooks, private household	34,215	32,243	94.2	1
Housekeepers, private household	105,111	101,640	96.7	1
Laundresses, private household	11,729	11,234	95.8	2

[a]Male and female median education adjusted as described in text.

Source: U.S. Bureau of the Census, *1970 Occupational Characteristics*, table 5, pp. 59-86.

categories were too heterogeneous for education. To avoid overstating mismatch, a special tabulation of mean education was done on the n.e.c. categories, and they were assigned to strata on this basis.[6]

EDUCATION DISTRIBUTION WITHIN STRATA

Median education was chosen for stratifying occupations because it is a measure of central tendency. However, because mismatch involves the standard deviation, it was necessary to see how the strata were distributed with respect to education. A multimodal distribution would indicate a problem in identifying the stratum and/or a problem in the use of a measure of central tendency. The distribution was also analyzed for skewness and kurtosis lest the standard deviation be misleading.

Skewness indicates "bunched up" or "stretched out" tails of the distribution. A positive coefficient of skewness would indicate a distribution with a "stretched out" right tail. This would be of some concern because it would indicate that the values of education associated with the stratum were bunched close to the mean for low values, while high values stretched far above the mean. Hence, positive skewness would imply that every highly educated person in the stratum would probably be mismatched, and even intermediately high scores would be mismatched because of the bunching around the mean. A negative skew, or a skew to the left, would indicate a few very low scores. We might expect this in a stratum with a few older, less-educated workers. It would not indicate a likely overstatement of mismatch.

Kurtosis measures the "flatness" or "peakedness" of a curve. A leptokurtic curve has an excess of values near and far from the mean. The sides of the curve are depleted. In a "flat" or platykurtic curve, there are more values under the flanks of the curve.

Occupational strata representing 60% of the 1970 labor force were selected and examined for normality. A random sample of all the workers in each stratum was taken to yield at least one hundred cases for observation. In a normal curve, the mean, mode, and median are all the same. In all the strata examined except for three, the maximum distance among any pair of the median, mode, or mean was seven-tenths of a year of schooling or less. In the remainder, the mode was a completed high school education, while the mean and median were one to two years below this. In these three strata, the standard deviation was quite large, as might be expected, and extended beyond the mode.

Every distribution was somewhat leptokurtic; all except one were skewed to the left. This indicates an excess of lower educational scores. (The exception had a very small positive coefficient of 0.013.) Thus, while none of the distributions may be described as "normal," the deviations from normality do not seem to be such that they would lead to an overstatement of mismatch.

THE CUTOFFS

The preceding steps document the stratification of the occupation codes. Mean and standard deviation of education were computed, by sex, for each stratum. In every stratum in which females were in the majority—13 in 1970—the female mean and standard deviation were used. In all other strata, the male mean and standard deviation were used. The cutoff level was the first standard score, that is, the mean plus one standard deviation. If the standard score included fractions of a year, it was rounded up to the next highest year. For example, if the standard score for a stratum were 13.2 years, the mismatch cutoff would be 14 years. A person in this stratum who had reported 13.2 years would have had only 13 years of completed schooling and would otherwise be shown as mismatched. Rounding up is a conservative measure which counteracts overcounts in borderline cases.

The cutoff level and the level for 1.5 standard scores corresponding to the worker's current occupations were assigned to every worker's record. After the comparison with completed years of schooling, the worker was classified as mismatched or adequately matched. The education level of every worker who reported an occupation was used in the determination of cutoff levels, and every worker record included the information about mismatch. Records for which occupations had been allocated were excluded from the cutoff determination. The only workers reported as mismatched in net private underutilization are those who were not "caught" in the earlier tabulation for unemployment, short hours, and low income.

Part-time Mismatched Workers

Voluntary part-time workers are by definition excluded from underutilization by hours of work. Underutilization of income as used here is a measure of the working poor, those who work full-time for an inadequate income. Consequently, the voluntary part-time worker is not analyzed for income adequacy. It is possible, however, for the voluntary part-time worker to be mismatched. This is readily understood at the conceptual level, but difficult to calculate with census data.

Although the Public Use Samples give hours of work, they do not tell us whether the respondent is voluntarily or involuntarily working a part-time schedule. The March, 1970 CPS data tell us what proportion of these workers were also mismatched. I estimated that the same proportion of voluntary part-time mismatched workers would have been found in the census, and so a proportionate number of part-time mismatched were added to the full-time mismatched.

For 1960, the problem was more complicated. The only data available were the proportion of all part-time workers who were voluntary part-time, from published CPS tabulations and the proportion of all part-time workers who were also mismatched, from the 1960 census tape. (The 1970 figures could be used if one assumed that the relationships which held in 1970 also held in 1960.) Four different sets of assumptions were used to derive four estimates, and the most conservative estimate was used. This estimate assumed that the proportion of all *voluntary* part-time workers who were mismatched was the same as the proportion of *all* part-time workers who were also mismatched.

This is a rather rough-and-ready measure. As a crude check of the 1960 estimate, I used the same assumption to reestimate the 1970 voluntary part-time mismatched. The result was an overestimate of about 3% of all mismatched workers, so it is possible that the 1960 mismatch figure is also overestimated. However, part-time mismatched workers are a small fraction of all mismatched workers, so an overestimate here should not distort the data too badly. The absolute number of part-time workers estimated for 1960 was 193,000, and of course this includes the possible overestimate.

Further Considerations

The procedure used here may be criticized on several grounds. The use of a unique cutoff rather than several has already been mentioned. Two other significant criticisms deserve examination.

INSTABILITY OF CURRENT OCCUPATION

One of the problems in the gainful worker approach to labor statistics was the instability of occupation. Unemployed persons may or may not report an occupation. Unemployed entrants to the labor force, unless they have received specialized training, are especially unlikely to have an occupation to report. Entrants may take "just any job" while waiting for one that suits their talents. The occupation reported for a multiple-job holder is the one in which he has the longest hours of work, although it may not be the occupation for which his training best suits him. Some voluntary part-time workers, such as the semi-retired or mothers of young children, may take jobs that they would not consider their regular occupation. Seasonal occupations may make greater or lesser use of skills. All of these imperfections, it might be argued, are incorporated into the mismatch measure.

Nevertheless, a cross-sectional look at occupations actually pursued, even if only temporarily, tells us a great deal about current labor conditions. The multiple-job holder whose inferior occupation takes up more of his working hours probably experiences poor conditions in his preferred occupation. The semi-retired craftsman who can find only unskilled part-time jobs experiences low demand for his skills. These cases fit in very well with the conceptual notion of mismatch.

The 1970 census included data on 1965 occupation. A retrospective mismatch figure might be useful for a case-by-case analysis of occupation stability. If the mismatched of five years ago are now adequately employed, then mismatch may be a problem of entry- and exit-level jobs. This sort of pseudopanel study would help settle the dispute on use of current occupation. However, there is reason to believe that the level of response error to this question may be quite high.

The measurement of mismatch used here required that education be at least an ordinal scale. A second method of mismatch might resolve some of the dispute about using current occupation, but at the expense of requiring an ordinal scale of occupation. Such a method would use completed education as the basis for mismatch. The reasoning is that adults may change their occupations several times, but their schooling is usually completed by age 25 or earlier. A distribution of occupations would correspond to every education level, and a cutoff would be established among occupations.

This method provides only cold comfort to the critic. Even within a range of "adequate" occupations attached to every grade level, the multiple-job holder and semiskilled craftsman are likely to show up mismatched. This method would have the advantage of ignoring the sex composition of occupations, although it may be argued that any ordinal scaling of occupations implicitly includes a prestige factor, and women's occupations tend to have lower prestige than men's. It might also be argued that this alternate method involves some circular reasoning, for education is likely to be a component in the ordinal ranking. Further, this alternate method does not differ conceptually from the method used here. Theoretically the two methods should produce identical results, although the crudeness of the measures makes this unlikely.

USING COMPLETED EDUCATION

Another criticism of the approach is that completed years of education is too imprecise a proxy for skill level. On-the-job training, years of seniority, years of labor force experience, and specialized training courses outside regular schools are all indicators of improved skill.

Completed years of schooling does not translate directly into job skills, although it may indicate the general level of having "learned how to learn." It may indicate greater ability to integrate ideas and to cope with complex issues. Nevertheless, years of schooling is a crude measure.

Many competent workers have supplemented a limited formal education with substantial on-the-job training and experience. The use of completed years of education does not overstate mismatch among these workers. Does it possibly understate mismatch? There is no indication that it does.

It is true that mismatch will appear higher among the young who seek more education. On the other hand, the use of a proxy for experience may shift mismatch disproportionately to the old. Mismatch measured by education reflects the changing education within the occupation. Mismatch measured by experience would reflect length of time and occupational stability in the occupation.

Certainly more work with alternate measures of mismatch would be appropriate. One promising line of research lies in using functional requirements of jobs, such as those found in the *Dictionary of Occupational Titles*, as a basis for evaluating the match between education and occupation. The National Longitudinal Surveys, which contain measures of school quality and intelligence, could be used to refine completed education.

Notes

1. Approaching Labor Underutilization and Labor Marginality

1. Matt. 20:6–7.
2. Pub. L. No. 93-203, sec. 302(b), (c), 87 Stat. 876 (1973), 29 U.S.C., sec. 882(b), (c) (Supp. III, 1973).
3. Federal Register, 41, 124, June 25, 1976, pp. 26346–47.
4. For example, see the comments of Jason Luby, pp. 1278–85, in U.S. Congress, House of Representatives, Committee on Education and Labor, Subcommittee on Manpower, Compensation, and Health and Safety, *Oversight Hearings on Comprehensive Employment and Training Act*, part 4-B. Both parts 4-A and 4-B of the hearings contain a number of references to the current allocation formula.
5. U.S. President, *Manpower Report of the President*, 1975, p. 189.
6. Sar A. Levitan and Robert B. Taggart, "Do Our Statistics Measure the Real Labor Market Hardship?" Paper delivered at the American Statistical Association Annual Meeting, Boston, August 23, 1976.
7. Pub. L. No. 94-444, 13, 90 Stat. 1483 (1977), (codified as note to 29 U.S.C. 952 [1977] Supp.).
8. Talcott Parsons, *The Structure of Social Action*, 1:141.
9. Early interest in this field is reflected in Philip M. Hauser, "The Labor Force as a Field of Interest for the Sociologist," *American Sociological Review* 16 (August 1951): 530–38; Philip M. Hauser, "The Labor Force and Gainful Workers—Concept, Measurement, and Comparability," *American Journal of Sociology* 54 (January 1949): 338–55. For recent work on women's participation rates, see James A. Sweet, *Women in the Labor Force*; Valerie Kincade Oppenheimer, *Female Labor Force in the United States: Demographic and Economic Factors Governing Its Growth and Changing Composition.*
10. For example, underemployment is not mentioned in two recent summaries: Ann R. Miller, "Labor Force Research and the 1970 Census of Population," in *Research and the 1970 Census*, ed. Abbott L. Ferris, pp. 109–19; Jeanne C. Biggar, "Needed Research on Sex and Racial Differentials in the U.S. Labor Force, 1970."
11. For example, Kenneth B. Clark, "Sex, Status, and Underemployment of

the Negro Male," in *Employment, Race, and Poverty*, ed. Arthur M. Ross and Herbert Hill, pp. 138–48.

12. In their landmark study, Blau and Duncan asked, "Please think about the first *full-time* job you had after you left school" (emphasis added). Unemployment and part-time work were thus excluded. Peter M. Blau and Otis Dudley Duncan, with the collaboration of Andrea Tyree, *The American Occupational Structure*, p. 446. Other studies have tended to limit themselves to the middle class and/or to persons currently employed. This often gives their findings a skew in the direction of higher-status occupations. See Eugene Litwak, "Occupational Mobility and Extended Family Cohesion," *American Sociological Review* 25 (February 1960): 9–21.

13. David M. Gordon, *Theories of Poverty and Underemployment: Orthodox, Radical and Dual Labor Market Perspectives*, p. 101. For similar comments, see William Spring, "Underemployment: The Measure We Refuse to Take," *New Generation* 53 (Winter 1971): 23. In chapter 3 some proposed indices are compared.

14. Donald W. Tiffany, James R. Cowan, and Phyllis M. Tiffany, *The Unemployed: A Social-Psychological Portrait*, p. 2.

15. Raymond Owens, "Disguised Unemployment and Underemployment in Urban India." Paper presented at the 73rd Annual Meeting of the American Anthropological Association, Mexico City, 20–24 November 1974.

16. Frequent attempts are made to improve unemployment data, but most are not fundamental. For example, see U.S. President's Committee to Appraise Employment and Unemployment Statistics, *Measuring Employment and Unemployment*.

17. Daniel Bell, "The 'Invisible' Unemployed," *Fortune* 68 (July 1958): 198.

18. Emile Durkheim, *The Division of Labor in Society*, trans. George Simpson, p. 389.

19. Ibid., p. 370.

20. A. D. Smith, *Concepts of Labour Force Underutilisation*, p. 6.

21. Joan Robinson, "Disguised Unemployment," *Economic Journal* 46 (June 1936): 225.

22. Alfredo Navarrete, Jr., and Ifigenia M. De Navarrete, "Underemployment in Underdeveloped Economies," trans. Elizabeth Henderson, *International Economic Papers* 3 (1953): 235–39.

23. I sampled the most current entries in a 513-article underemployment bibliography for the geographic origin of the data. Although 32% were not specified by origin, 24% referred to Africa, 20% each to Asia and Latin America, and 4% to the Middle East. No "advanced countries" were included, if one excludes Puerto Rico. Von Frithjoh Kuhnen, "Bibliographie Über 'Ländliche Unterbeschäftigung,'" *Zeitschrift für ausländische Landwirtschaft* 11 (January–March 1972): 74–83.

Some studies were done in Italy in the 1950's and in Southeastern Europe before World War II. See Berdj Kenadjian, "Disguised Unemployment in Underdeveloped Countries," Ph.D. dissertation, Harvard University, 1957. More recently there has been a trend to more comparative work within developing countries. See Erik Thorbecke, "The Employment Problem: A Critical Evaluation of Four ILO Comprehensive Country Reports," *International Labour Review* 107 (May 1973): 393–423; Felipe Pazos, "Development and the Underutilization of Labour," *International Labour Review* 111 (March 1975): 235–49.

24. Karl Marx, *Capital: A Critique of Political Economy*, ed. Frederick Engels, trans. Samuel Moore and Edward Aveling; vol. 1: *A Critical Analysis of Capitalist Production*; vol. 2: *The Process of Circulation of Capital*; vol. 3: *The Process of Capitalist Production as a Whole*; quotation, 1:633.

25. Robinson, "Disguised Unemployment," p. 237.

26. To follow Parsons, the economy is the adaptive institution of society (A) and kinship is the pattern-maintenance institution (L). The economy itself has an adaptive imperative (A_A), for every economic organization must acquire land, capital, and labor. Its goal-attaining function (A_G) is production of goods and services. The household's adaptive imperative (L_A) is acquiring goods and services, and its goal-attainment (L_G) consists in maintaining the flow of goods and services. Most households obtain goods and services in exchange for labor offered to the economy. A household does have alternatives: crime, public doles, inheritance, and other nonwork revenues. In other words, the labor market is an A_G–L_G interface, and the commodity market is an A_G–L_A interface (Talcott Parsons and Neil J. Smelser, *Economy and Society*, pp. 55–70).

27. Curtis L. Gilroy, "Supplemental Measures of Labor Force Underutilization," *Monthly Labor Review* 98 (May 1975): 13–23; Philip M. Hauser, "The Measurement of Labour Utilization," *Malayan Economic Review* 19 (April 1974): 1–17.

2. Who Are the Marginal Workers?

1. Gideon Sjoberg and Roger Nett, *A Methodology for Social Research*, p. 244.

2. Eli Ginzberg, Foreword to *The Peripheral Worker*, by Dean Morse, p. v.

3. Morse, for example, defines the "peripheral worker" as the part-time or part-year worker; *Peripheral Worker*, p. 5.

4. Marginal status is probably a matter of degree, and persons with more than one sufficient condition could be "more marginal." One empirical question to be addressed is whether multiple marginality implies greater underutilization.

5. Marx, *Capital*, 1:644; Harry G. Johnson, "The Economic Approach to Social Questions," *Economica* 35 n.s. (February 1968): 19.

6. Tiffany, Cowan, and Tiffany, *Unemployed*, pp. 23–26; David N. Saunders, "Labor Force Behavior: A Longitudinal Perspective," *Review of Public Data Use* 1 (July 1973): 7–13; Charles T. Stewart, Jr., *Low-Wage Workers in an Affluent Society*, pp. 56–59.

7. Gunnar Myrdal, *Asian Drama: An Inquiry into the Poverty of Nations*, 2:1017; David M. Turnham, *The Employment Problem in Less Developed Countries*, pp. 80–91; Edgar O. Edwards, "Employment in Developing Countries," in *Employment in Developing Nations: Report on a Ford Foundation Study*, ed. Edgar O. Edwards, p. 11.

8. National Committee against Discrimination in Housing, "The Impact of Housing Patterns on Job Opportunities."

9. Marx, *Capital*, 1:635.

10. This fact alone does not determine the status set, especially for married women and for those who define their most important activities in non-work terms. But recent trends seem to indicate an increasing work-identification even among women.

11. Ross M. Stolzenberg, "Education, Occupation, and Wage Differences between White and Black Men," *American Journal of Sociology* 81 (September 1975): 299–323; Brigitte Mach Erbe, "Black Occupational Change and Education," *Sociology of Work and Occupations* 2 (May 1975): 156.

12. Herbert S. Parnes et al., *The Pre-Retirement Years*, p. 118.

13. *International Encyclopedia of the Social Sciences*, 1968 ed., s.v. "Labor Force Participation," by Jacob Mincer; Stewart, *Low-Wage Workers*, p. 35; Eleanor G. Gilpatrick, *Structural Unemployment and Aggregate Demand: A Study of Employment and Unemployment in the United States, 1948–1964*, with Foreword by William H. Miernyk, pp. 191–94.

14. Sar A. Levitan and William B. Johnston, *Work Is Here To Stay, Alas*, p. 73.

15. Melvin L. Kohn and Carmi Schooler, "Class, Occupation, and Orientation," *American Sociological Review* 34 (October 1969): 659–78.

16. Charles C. Killingsworth, "The Continuing Labor Market Twist," *Monthly Labor Review* 91 (September 1968): 12–17; Gilpatrick, *Structural Unemployment*, p. 190; E. Waldman and B. J. McEaddy, "Where Women Work: An Analysis by Industry and Occupation," *Monthly Labor Review* 97 (May 1974): 3–13.

17. Allan G. King, "Occupational Choice, Risk Aversion, and Wealth," *Industrial and Labor Relations Review* 27 (July 1974): 586–96.

18. Cited in Morse, *Peripheral Worker*, p. 85.

19. Robert Averitt, *The Dual Economy*, pp. 1–2.

20. Glen C. Cain, "The Challenge of Dual and Radical Theories of the Labor Market to Orthodox Theory," *American Economic Review* 65 (May 1975): 19.

21. Stewart, *Low-Wage Workers*, pp. 15–22.

22. Eliot Liebow, *Tally's Corner: A Study of Negro Streetcorner Men*, with a Foreword by Hylan Lewis; Harland Padfield and Roy Williams, *Stay Where You Were: A Study of Unemployables in Industry*; Leonard Goodwin, *Do the Poor Want to Work?*.

23. Gordon, *Theories*, p. 50.

24. Ibid., p. 44. Gordon refers to work by Vietorisz and Harrison in Harlem.
25. Ibid., p. 52.
26. Ibid., p. 52.
27. Ibid., p. 78.
28. Ibid., p. 44.
29. Sar A. Levitan and Robert B. Taggart, "Employment and Earnings Inadequacy: A New Social Indicator," *Challenge* 16 (January–February 1974): 28.
30. Gordon, *Theories*, p. 74; Morse, *Peripheral Worker*, p. 39, allows a "bridging" effect for raising commitment levels.
31. Stewart, *Low-Wage Workers*, p. 54.
32. Ann R. Miller, "Migration Differentials in Labor Force Participation: United States, 1960," *Demography* 3 (1966): 58–67; Morse, *Peripheral Worker*, pp. 57–67; Stewart, *Low-Wage Workers*, pp. 91–93. Contrast this with a case of migration in the career line: Ward S. Mason and Neal Gross, "Intra-Occupational Prestige Differentiation: The School Superintendency," *American Sociological Review* 20 (June 1955): 326–31.
33. Biggar, "Needed Research"; Sookon Kim, Roger D. Roderick, and John R. Shea, *Dual Careers: A Longitudinal Study of Labor Market Experience of Women*. Migrant farm workers are a special case of "career-line" migration. They are marginal in the sense that farm workers are unprotected and structurally marginal.
34. Charles C. Killingsworth, *Jobs and Income for Negroes*; Phyllis A. Wallace, *Pathways to Work: Unemployment among Black Teenage Females*.

3. How Do You Measure Underutilization?

1. See, for example, U.S. President's Committee, *Measuring Employment*; U.S. Congress, Senate, Committee on Labor and Public Welfare, Subcommittee on Employment and Manpower, "Unemployment and the Tax Cut," by Charles Killingsworth, in *Nation's Manpower Revolution*, 88th Cong., 1st sess., pt. 1, 1963, pp. 1787–94.
2. For example, see Gerald P. Glyde, David L. Snyder, and Anthony L. Stemberger, "Underemployment: Definition, Causes, and Measurement," pp. 57–94.
3. A qualification to this generalization needs to be made. Some economists who are primarily interested in building models of development are not interested in conceptual niceties of underutilization nor in direct empirical verification. Their work, while somewhat peripheral to this study, often posits a dual-economy structure, and this requires relating disguised unemployment to urban industrial employment. See, for example, W. A. Lewis, "Economic Development with Unlimited Supplies of Labour," *Manchester School of Economic and Social Studies* 22 (May

1954): 139–91; W. A. Lewis, *The Theory of Economic Growth*; Gustav
Ranis and J. Fei, "A Theory of Economic Development," *American
Economic Review* 51 (September 1961): 533–65.

4. Spring, "Underemployment," pp. 23–24.

5. R. S. Eckaus, "The Factor-Proportions Problem in Underdeveloped Areas,"
American Economic Review 45 (September 1955): 539–65; Harvey
Leibenstein, "The Theory of Underemployment in Backward
Economies," *Journal of Political Economy* 45 (April 1957): 91–103.

6. M. Desai and D. Mazumdar, "A Test of the Hypothesis of Disguised Unemployment," *Economica* 37 n.s. (February 1970): 39–53.

7. Turnham, *Employment Problem*, p. 68.

8. Theodore Schultz, *Transforming Traditional Agriculture*.

9. A criticism derived from William L. Kean, "Disguised Unemployment,"
paper read at the Conference on Labor Anthropology, Tepotzlan,
Mexico, May 18–21, 1975.

10. Yong Sam Cho, *"Disguised Unemployment" in Underdeveloped Areas,
with Special Reference to South Korean Agriculture*; Myrdal, *Asian
Drama*.

11. Lewis, "Unlimited Supplies," p. 142; Kean, "Disguised Unemployment,"
p. 7.

12. Stanislaw Wellisz, "Dual Economies, Disguised Unemployment and the
Unlimited Supply of Labour," *Economica* 35 n.s. (February 1968): 45.

13. Lewis, "Unlimited Supplies." But the average farm labor product is not a
floor to the urban wage market, as Smith shows, *Concepts of Underutilisation*, pp. 36–37.

14. Jacob Viner, "Some Reflections on the Concept of 'Disguised Unemploy-
ment,'" *Indian Journal of Economics* 38 (July 1957): 17–23; Clifford
Geertz, *Agricultural Involution: The Processes of Ecological Change in
Indonesia*.

15. Smith documents the arguments, *Concepts of Underutilisation*, pp.
35–36.

16. John W. Mellor and R. D. Stevens, "The Average and Marginal Product of
Farm Labor in Underdeveloped Economies," *Journal of Farm Economics* 38 (August 1956): 783. Their data and assumptions are challenged
by Harry T. Oshima, "The Ranis-Fei Model of Economic Development:
Comment," *American Economic Review* 53 (June 1963): 450.

17. Myrdal, *Asian Drama*, 3:2058.

18. Though Smith notes an Indian exception, *Concepts of Underutilisation*,
p. 2.

19. See, for example, Wellisz, "Dual Economies," for such a taxonomy.

20. Turnham, *Employment Problem*, pp. 64–65; P. N. Rosenstein-Rodan,
"Problems of Industrialization of Eastern and Southeastern Europe,"
Economic Journal 53 (June–September 1943): 202–11.

21. For an application of this approach in Pakistan, see M. H. Khan, *The Role
of Agriculture in Economic Development: A Case Study of Pakistan*, pp.

88–91; cited in United Nations, Department of Economic and Social Affairs, *Manual V: Methods of Projecting the Economically Active Population*, p. 54.

22. Turnham, *Employment Problem*, p. 65.
23. Smith, *Concepts of Underutilisation*, p. 43.
24. The unpublished field study from the United Arab Republic is cited in United Nations, *Manual V*, p. 53.
25. For examples, see the following: Peter J. Bertocci, "The Labor Impact of the Green Revolution in Bangladesh: Some Problems in Explanation and Implications for the Concept of Disguised Unemployment"; Barrie H. Michie, "Disguised Unemployment, Labor Productivity and the Peasant Mode of Production in Indian Agriculture"; Jane Granskog, "A Critique of Disguised Unemployment: Labor Allocation and Economic Alternatives in a Peasant Corporate Community." Each of these papers was presented at the 73rd Annual Meeting of the American Anthropological Association, Mexico City, 20–24 November 1974.
26. Herman P. Miller, "Measuring Subemployment in Poverty Areas of Large U.S. Cities," *Monthly Labor Review* 96 (October 1973): 14; Hauser, "Gainful Workers."
27. Turnham, *Employment Problem*, pp. 23–30; Myrdal, *Asian Drama*, 2:1019; Wilbert E. Moore, "The Exportability of the 'Labor Force' Concept," *American Sociological Review* 18 (February 1953): 68–72.
28. Miller, "Subemployment," p. 10.
29. At least one author uses "subemployment" rather than "underemployment" because his index takes no account of "the skills of workers in relation to the work they are actually doing" (Miller, "Subemployment," p. 17).
30. W. Willard Wirtz, "A Sharper Look at Unemployment in U.S. Cities and Slums: A Summary Report Submitted to the President by the Secretary of Labor."
31. Spring, "Underemployment," pp. 23–24.
32. Miller, "Subemployment," p. 11, citing press release, Senate Subcommittee on Employment, Manpower, and Poverty, May 1972.
33. William Spring, Bennett Harrison, and Thomas Vietorisz, "Crisis of the Underemployed," *New York Times Magazine*, Nov. 5, 1972, pp. 42–60.
34. Miller, "Subemployment," p. 10.
35. Sar A. Levitan and Robert B. Taggart, "Employment and Earnings Inadequacy: A Measure of Worker Welfare," *Monthly Labor Review* 96 (October 1973): 19–27; also see their *Employment and Earnings Inadequacy: A New Social Indicator*.
36. Thomas Vietorisz, Robert Mier, and Jean-Ellen Giblin, "Subemployment: Exclusion and Inadequacy Indexes," *Monthly Labor Review* 98 (May 1975): 3–12.
37. Ibid., p. 5.
38. Ibid., pp. 9–10.

39. Hauser, "Measurement"; idem, "The Working Force in Developing Areas," in *Human Resources and Economic Welfare: Essays in Honor of Eli Ginzberg*, ed. Ivar Berg, pp. 141–61; idem, "The Measurement of Labour Utilization—More Empirical Results," *Malayan Economic Review* (1977), in press.
40. Miller, "Subemployment," p. 12.
41. Levitan and Taggart, "Worker Welfare," p. 20.
42. Paul O. Flaim, "Discouraged Workers and Changes in Unemployment," *Monthly Labor Review* 96 (March 1973): 8–16; Joseph L. Gastwirth, "Estimating the Number of 'Hidden Unemployed,'" *Monthly Labor Review* 96 (March 1973): 17–26; Jacob Mincer, "Determining Who Are the 'Hidden Unemployed,'" *Monthly Labor Review* 96 (March 1973): 27–30; see the related bibliography in the same issue, pp. 31–37.
43. Gertrude Bancroft, "Alternative Indexes of Employment and Unemployment," *Monthly Labor Review* 85 (February 1962): 167–74. For full documentation to the controversy, see footnote 10 of Gilroy, "Supplemental Measures," p. 23.
44. Levitan and Taggart, "Worker Welfare," p. 20.
45. A weighted index proposed by the Eleventh International Conference of Labour Statisticians (although not to my knowledge used) would weight every component, x, by the average degree of underemployment, y. Σxy gives social underutilization; Σx is gross private underutilization because the components are not mutually exclusive. This index omits unemployment. Smith, *Concepts of Underutilisation*, pp. 44–45. Smith recommends a "categorisation" approach similar to the LUF.
46. Smith reviews these in *Concepts of Underutilisation*, pp. 63–65.
47. See Hauser, "The Working Force"; Wilhelm Flieger and Teresa A. Sullivan, under the general direction of Philip M. Hauser, "Manual of Work Force Measurement and Utilization," Chicago, 1974 (typewritten), chap. 5; Teresa A. Sullivan, "New Approaches to Labor Force Measurement," *Asian and Pacific Census Newsletter* 1 (August 1974): 5–8.
48. Ethel B. Jones, "The Elusive Concept of Underemployment," *Journal of Human Resources* 6 (Fall 1971): 520.

4. Data, Methods, and Time Effects

1. One-fifth of the 1960 detailed questionnaires were selected as an intermediate subsample, and one-fifth of this subsample was drawn, in turn, for the 1% Public Use Samples. The 1/1000 sample is a stratified, systematic subsample of the 1/100 sample. In 1970, six 1/1000 samples were made available. The one used in this study was the neighborhood characteristics sample drawn from the 1/100 sample of the 5% detailed questionnaire. All Public Use Samples suppress identifying data, including most geographic detail, to preserve confidentiality. U.S. De-

partment of Commerce, Bureau of the Census, *Public Use Samples of Basic Records from the 1970 Census: Description and Technical Documentation*; Lynda T. Carlson, *Technical Documentation for the 1960 Public Use Samples PUS-1960.*

2. The Comprehensive Employment and Training Act, cited in chapter 1, calls for study of involuntary part-time employment and the "working poor." It also includes discouraged workers.

3. U.S. Bureau of the Census, *1970 Public Use Samples*, p. 151.

4. Richard L. Rowan, "The Influence of Collective Bargaining on Hours," in *Hours of Work*, ed. Clyde E. Dankert, Floyd C. Mann, and Herbert R. Northrup, p. 27.

5. Herbert R. Northrup, "The Reductions in Hours," in *Hours of Work*, ed. Dankert, Mann, and Northrup, p. 10; David G. Brown, "Hours and Output," in *Hours of Work*, ed. Dankert, Mann, and Northrup, p. 153.

6. Clyde E. Dankert, "Automation, Unemployment, and Shorter Hours," in *Hours of Work*, ed. Dankert, Mann, and Northrup, p. 163 and table 1.

7. Sometimes it is the exclusive definition of underemployment (Claire C. Hodge and James R. Wetzel, "Short Workweeks and Underemployment," *Monthly Labor Review* 90 [September 1967]: 30–35).

8. For some recent discussions of the problem, see James O'Toole, *Work, Learning, and the American Future,* and "The Reserve Army of the Underemployed," *Change* 7 (May 1975): 26; Richard B. Freeman, *The Overeducated American*; U.S. President, *Manpower Report of the President*, 1974, pp. 104–107; Thomas Vietorisz et al., "Subemployment: Concepts, Measurements, and Trends," in *Proceedings of the Twenty-Seventh Annual Winter Meeting of the Industrial Relations Research Association* (San Francisco, 28–29 December 1974), p. 118; Ivar Berg, *Education and Jobs: The Great Training Robbery.*

9. Levitan and Johnston, *Work, Alas*, p. 74.

10. This dynamic is discussed in Randall Collins, "Functional and Conflict Theories of Educational Stratification," *American Sociological Review* 36 (December 1971): 1002–19. For relevant Supreme Court decisions, see *Griggs v. Duke Power Company*, 401 U.S. 424, 91 S. Ct. 849, 28 L. Ed. 2d 158 (1971); *Albemarle Paper Company v. Moody*, 422 U.S. 405, 95 S. Ct. 2362, 48 L. Ed. 2d 280 (1975).

11. Vera C. Perrella, "Employment of Recent College Graduates," *Monthly Labor Review* 96 (February 1973): 41–50; Anne M. Young, "Labor Market Experience of Recent College Graduates," *Monthly Labor Review* 97 (October 1974): 33–40.

12. Jack Alterman, "The United States Economy in 1985: An Overview of BLS Projections," *Monthly Labor Review* 96 (December 1973): 3–7.

13. Harry Braverman, *Labor and Monopoly Capital*, p. 430.

14. See Stephen P. Dresch, "Demography, Technology, and Higher Education: Toward a Formal Model of Educational Adaptation," *Journal of Political Economy* 83 (March–April 1975): 535–71.

15. See the following papers by Leo A. Goodman: "A General Model for the Analysis of Surveys," *American Journal of Sociology* 77 (May 1972): 1035–86; "A Modified Multiple Regression Approach to the Analysis of Dichotomous Variables," *American Sociological Review* 37 (February 1972): 28–46; "The Analysis of Multidimensional Tables: Stepwise Procedures and Direct Estimation Methods for Building Models for Multiple Classifications," *Technometrics* 13 (February 1971): 33–61; "The Multivariate Analysis of Qualitative Data: Interactions among Multiple Classifications," *Journal of the American Statistical Association* 65 (March 1970): 226–56.

16. See James A. Davis, "Hierarchical Models for Significance Tests in Multivariate Contingency Tables: An Exegesis of Goodman's Recent Papers," in *Sociological Methodology, 1973–1974*, ed. Herbert L. Costner, pp. 189–231.

17. Table 8.1 can be analyzed for similar odds-ratios showing the decline of underutilization between 1960 and 1970 for other categories:

white females:	1.02	all nonwhites:	1.50
nonwhite males:	1.67	all males:	1.04
nonwhite females:	1.35	all females:	1.07

18. For a treatment of underutilization from 1969 to 1973, see Clifford C. Clogg, "Measuring Underemployment: Demographic Indicators for the U.S. Labor Force, 1969–1973," Ph.D. dissertation, University of Chicago, 1977.

5. The Idiosyncrasy Hypothesis: Employment of the Disabled

1. U.S. Department of Commerce, Bureau of the Census, *Census of Population: 1970. Subject Reports: Persons with Work Disability*, Final Report PC(2)-6C, table 1; U.S. Department of Health, Education, and Welfare, Public Health Service, *Disability among Persons in the Labor Force by Employment Status: United States, July 1961–June 1962*, National Center for Health Statistics Series 10, no. 7. Using a somewhat less restrictive definition, a 1972 survey of the disabled conducted by the Social Security Administration reported higher numbers of disabled than those in the text. For persons aged 20–64, 14.6% were disabled; 9.5% of those in the labor force were disabled (Sar A. Levitan and Robert B. Taggart, *Jobs for the Disabled*, p. 7). This survey also found slightly higher disability among females.

2. U.S. Bureau of the Census, *Persons with Work Disability*.

3. U.S. Department of Health, Education, and Welfare, Public Health Service, *Prevalence of Selected Impairments, United States, 1971*, by Charles S. Wilder, Vital and Welfare Health Statistics Series 10, no. 79; U.S. Public Health Service, *Disability, 1961–1962*.

4. Levitan and Taggart, *Jobs for the Disabled*, p. 23.

5. U.S. Public Health Service, *Prevalence of Selected Impairments*, tables 1–7.

6. Frederick B. Siskind, "Labor Force Participation of Men, 25–54, by Race," *Monthly Labor Review* 98 (July 1975): 40–42.
7. Tiffany, Cowan, and Tiffany, *Unemployed*, pp. 67–83.
8. Ibid., p. 63.
9. F. G. Lawlis, "Motivational Aspects of the Chronically Unemployed," Ph.D. dissertation, Texas Technological College (Ann Arbor, Mich.: University Microfilm, 1969), No. 69-6445, cited by Tiffany, Cowan, and Tiffany, *Unemployed*, p. 96.
10. Tiffany, Cowan, and Tiffany, *Unemployed*, p. 63.
11. For a study that supports this line of reasoning, see Chris Argyris, *Personality and Organization*. For a related argument, see Peter B. Doeringer and Michael J. Piore, *Internal Labor Markets and Manpower Analysis*.

6. The Discrimination Hypothesis: Age

1. Everett Hughes, "Dilemmas and Contradictions of Status," *American Journal of Sociology* 50 (March 1945): 353–59.
2. See Myles Hollander and Douglas A. Wolfe, *Nonparametric Statistical Methods*, pp. 120–23.
3. See Evelyn M. Kitagawa, "Components of a Difference between Two Rates," *Journal of the American Statistical Association* 501 (December 1955): 1168–94. The overall unemployment rate used for 1960 here is slightly higher than that of the census tapes; see the sources in table 6.3.
4. See Evelyn M. Kitagawa, "Standardized Comparisons in Population Research," *Demography* 1 (February 1964): 296–315.
5. Data from U.S. Department of Commerce, Bureau of the Census, *Statistical Abstract of the United States: 1976*, pp. 355–63.

7. The Discrimination Hypothesis: Race and Sex

1. See Edna Bonacich, "Advanced Capitalism and Black/White Race Relations in the United States: A Split Labor Market Interpretation," *American Sociological Review* 41 (February 1976): 34–51, and "A Theory of Ethnic Antagonism: The Split Labor Market," *American Sociological Review* 37 (October 1972): 547–59.
2. Norfleet W. Rives, Jr., "Effect of Census Errors on Labor Force Estimates," *Industrial Relations* 15 (May 1976): 252–56.
3. Charles C. Killingsworth, "Rising Unemployment: A 'Transitional' Problem?" Hearings of Senate Subcommittee on Employment, Manpower, and Poverty, re: Manpower Development and Training Legislation, 1970, part 3; reprinted as Research Reprint Series No. 122.
4. For discussions of this, see Sar A. Levitan, William B. Johnston, and Robert B. Taggart, *Still a Dream: The Changing Status of Blacks since 1960*,

pp. 69–74; Reynolds Farley, "Trends in Racial Inequalities: Have the Gains of the 1960's Disappeared in the 1970's?" *American Sociological Review* 42 (April 1977): 196–97. The 1940–50 decline is discussed in Ralph H. Turner, "The Nonwhite Male in the Labor Force," *American Journal of Sociology* 54 (January 1949): 356–62. The 1950 rate, 56.1, is the same as the 1970 rate.
5. See Freeman, *Overeducated American*, pp. 137–58.
6. U.S. Bureau of the Census, *Statistical Abstract: 1976*, p. 363.
7. Oppenheimer, *Female Labor Force*, chap. 3.
8. Occupations included in this percentage are engineering, law, medicine, nursing, and teaching at all levels. Librarianship is included although not all librarians are certified.
9. The rates in table 7.7 were computed in the same way as the rates in table 7.4, and for the same reasons.
10. For evidence of this trend, see Elizabeth M. Almquist, "Untangling the Effects of Race and Sex: The Disadvantaged Status of Black Women," *Social Science Quarterly* 56 (June 1975): 136–39; and Levitan, Johnston, and Taggart, *Still a Dream*, pp. 46–53.

8. The Discrimination Hypothesis: Interactions

1. Daniel Patrick Moynihan, "Employment, Income, and the Ordeal of the Negro Family," *Daedalus* 94 (Fall 1965): 761.
2. Farley, "Trends in Racial Inequalities," p. 193.
3. The contribution made by race is not due solely to its position as the first association entered into the table. When the order of entry was varied, the addition of race and utilization accounted for 75% to 78% of the total variation. For comments on forward selection, see Leo A. Goodman, "Guided and Unguided Methods for the Selection of Models for a Set of T Multidimensional Contingency Tables," *Journal of the American Statistical Association* 68 (March 1973): 165–75.

9. The Achievement Hypothesis: Effects of Training

1. Gary S. Becker, *Human Capital*, pp. 7–26; Otis Dudley Duncan, David L. Featherman, and Beverly Duncan, *Socioeconomic Background and Achievement*.
2. It is possible that some of the underutilized by level of income are subsidizing their on-the-job training, but that cannot be established with the available data.
3. U.S. Department of Commerce, Bureau of the Census, *Census of Population: 1970. Subject Reports: Educational Attainment*. Final Report PC(2)-5B, table 1.

11. Conclusions and Recommendations

1. There have also been other calls for measurement of underemployment. See U.S. President's Committee, *Measuring Employment*, p. 59; Bennett Harrison, "Education and Underemployment in the Urban Ghetto," *American Economic Review* 62 (December 1972): 796–812.
2. However, the International Labour Organization's three categories— visible, invisible, and potential underemployment—are roughly equivalent to the three components used here (International Labour Organization, *Measurement of Underemployment*, Report IV of the Ninth International Conference of Labour Statisticians).
3. These terms are not used in the same sense in which Glyde and his colleagues use "micro-underemployment" and "macro-underemployment." Micro-underemployment is due to some characteristic of the individual other than skill; macro-underemployment refers to an entire occupational level in comparison with other occupation clusters in the labor market (Gerald P. Glyde, David L. Snyder, and Anthony L. Stemberger, "Underemployment: Definition, Causes, and Measurement," pp. 36–37).
4. For example, see U.S. President's Committee, *Measuring Employment*, p. 58; Deborah P. Klein, "Exploring the Adequacy of Employment," *Monthly Labor Review* 96 (October 1973): 3–9. Glyde and his colleagues make the point that more intensive research on this component is needed. Longitudinal data, with greater detail than the census gives, would be ideal. Glyde, Snyder, and Stemberger, "*Underemployment*," consider extensively what is here called mismatch.
5. In general, labor statisticians need to give more thought to the content of jobs in preparing occupation codes. See James G. Scoville, *The Job Content of the U.S. Economy, 1940–1970*; and *Manpower and Occupational Analysis: Concepts and Measurements*.
6. See Herbert J. Gans, "Jobs and Services: Toward a More Labor-Intensive Economy," *Challenge* 19 (July–August 1977): 41–45.

Appendix A

1. Jacob S. Siegel, "Estimates of Coverage of the Population by Sex, Race, and Age in the 1970 Census," *Demography* 11 (February 1974): 1–24. Also see U.S. Department of Commerce, Bureau of the Census, *Census of Population and Housing: 1970. Estimates of Coverage of Population by Sex, Race, and Age: Demographic Analysis*, by Jacob S. Siegel.
2. Deborah P. Klein, "Determining the Labor Force Status of Men Missed in the Census," *Monthly Labor Review* 93 (March 1970): 26–32.
3. Wirtz, "A Sharper Look."
4. The standard errors were interpolated from U.S. Bureau of the Census,

1970 *Public Use Samples*, pp. 186–89. 1960 Standard errors may be computed from Carlson, *PUS-1960*, pp. 63–67.

5. There is reason to believe that CPS interviewers, who are full-time, well-paid, and highly trained workers, elicit more accurate data from respondents. Employers' records are also considered a highly reliable source of occupation data.

6. U.S. Department of Commerce, Bureau of the Census, *Census of Population and Housing: 1960. The Employer Record Check*; Levitan and Johnston, *Work, Alas*, p. 83. For a discussion of response error in age reporting, see U.S. Department of Commerce, Bureau of the Census, *Census of Population and Housing: 1960. Accuracy of Data on Population Characteristics as Measured by CPS-Census Match*.

7. Carlson, *PUS-1960*, pp. 135–36; U.S. Department of Commerce, Bureau of the Census, *Census of Population: 1970. General Social and Economic Characteristics*, Final Report PC(1)-C1, *U.S. Summary*, table C-2.

8. Leo A. Goodman, "A Model for the Analysis of Surveys," *American Journal of Sociology* 77 (1972): 1044–47.

Appendix B

1. U.S. Department of Commerce, Bureau of the Census, *Census of Population, 1970. Subject Reports: Occupational Characteristics*, Final Report PC(2)-7A, table 45.

2. For the conversion to 1970 Census data, see "Revisions in Current Population Survey," *Employment and Earnings* 18 (February 1972): 6–9.

3. U.S. Bureau of the Census, *Statistical Abstract: 1976*, table 360.

Appendix C

1. In 1970, approximately 129,000 students were entrants working 35 or more hours a week and living in households earning less than the poverty level. Of these, 96,000 were primary individuals or chief income recipients.

2. Levitan and Taggart, "New Social Indicator," pp. 23–25.

3. Wirtz, "A Sharper Look," makes an adjustment for secondary work.

4. For a similar procedure, see Victor Fuchs, "Differentials in Hourly Earnings by Region and City Size."

5. U.S. Department of Agriculture, "Food Consumption and Dietary Levels of Households in the United States," ARS 626 (August 1957).

6. "Review in Poverty Statistics, 1959 to 1968," *Current Population Reports*, Series P-23, no. 28, August 12, 1969, pp. 1–7. See also Mollie Orshansky, "Counting the Poor: Another Look at the Poverty Profile," *Social Security Bulletin* 28 (January 1965): 3–29; idem, "Who's Who

among the Poor: A Demographic View of Poverty," *Social Security Bulletin* 28 (July 1965): 3–32.
7. Gordon, *Theories*, p. 99.
8. Julius Shiskin, "Updating the Consumer Price Index: An Overview," *Monthly Labor Review* 97 (July 1974): 3–20.
9. Gordon, *Theories*, pp. 4–5.
10. Flieger and Sullivan, "Manual," p. 51.
11. Ibid., pp. 52–53.
12. In 1970, 143,000 or 32.2% of unpaid workers were already tabulated among the unemployed or the part-time labor force. The comparable figure for 1960 was 508,000 (73.1% of unpaid workers). The unemployed, the part-time workers, and those already counted with the working poor are not subject to the misclassification at issue here.

Appendix D

1. John E. Bregger, "Revisions in Occupational Classifications for 1971," *Employment and Earnings* 17 (February 1971): 5–8.
2. Median education was taken from published census tabulations. U.S. Department of Commerce, Bureau of the Census, *Census of Population and Housing: 1960. Subject Reports: Occupational Characteristics*, Final Report PC(2)-7A, pp. 116–29, table 9. For 1970, see U.S. Bureau of the Census, *1970 Occupational Characteristics*, pp. 59–86, table 5.
3. For a somewhat similar procedure in stratifying occupations by income, see Valerie K. Oppenheimer, "The Life Cycle Squeeze: The Interaction of Men's Occupation and Family Life Cycles," *Demography* 11 (May 1974): 227–46.
4. An argument can be made that a single occupational prestige scale is appropriate for men and women. See Donald J. Treiman and Kermit Terrell, "Sex and the Process of Status Attainment: A Comparison of Working Women and Men," *American Sociological Review* 40 (April 1975): 176. However, mismatch is not appropriately measured by an indicator of occupational prestige. Mismatch is a concept that recognizes that persons with high educational attainments may still be absorbed into occupations with lower prestige than they might expect. Why some occupations are "absorptive" is an issue for another study. Certainly occupational segregation, licensing requirements, and other issues are involved. This reconceptualization of occupational attainment seems appropriate at a time when there is a kind of "credential inflation."
5. The same reasoning used to justify a single stratification of occupations may be used to justify a unique cutoff level for every occupation.
6. Other matches of census codes have been made for other purposes. See David Snyder and Paula M. Hudis, "Occupational Income and the Effects of Minority Competition and Segregation: A Reanalysis and Some

New Evidence," *American Sociological Review* 41 (April 1976): 227–28; U.S. Department of Commerce, Bureau of the Census, "1970 Occupation and Industry Classifications in Terms of Their 1960 Occupation and Industry Elements," by John A. Priebe, Joan Heinkel and Stanley Greene.

Bibliography

Books and Monographs

Argyris, Chris. *Personality and Organization*. New York: Harper & Bros., 1957.

Averitt, Robert. *The Dual Economy*. New York: W. W. Norton, 1968.

Becker, Gary S. *Human Capital*. New York: National Bureau of Economic Research, 1964.

Berg, Ivar. *Education and Jobs: The Great Training Robbery*. New York: Praeger, 1970.

Blau, Peter M., and Duncan, Otis Dudley. With the collaboration of Andrea Tyree. *The American Occupational Structure*. New York: John Wiley & Sons, 1967.

Braverman, Harry. *Labor and Monopoly Capital*. Washington, D.C.: Monthly Review Press, 1974.

Carlson, Lynda T. *Technical Documentation for the 1960 Public Use Samples PUS-1960*. Rosalyn, Va.: National Data Use and Access Laboratories, 1973.

Cho, Yong Sam. *"Disguised Unemployment" in Underdeveloped Areas, with Special Reference to South Korean Agriculture*. Berkeley: University of California Press, 1963.

Dankert, Clyde E.; Mann, Floyd C.; and Northrup, Herbert R., eds. *Hours of Work*. Industrial Relations Research Association Publication No. 32. New York: Harper & Row, 1965.

Doeringer, Peter B., and Piore, Michael J. *Internal Labor Markets and Manpower Analysis*. Lexington, Mass.: Heath Lexington, 1971.

Duncan, Otis Dudley; Featherman, David L.; and Duncan, Beverly. *Socioeconomic Background and Achievement*. New York: Seminar Press, 1972.

Durkheim, Emile. *The Division of Labor in Society*. Translated by George Simpson. New York: Free Press, 1964; London: Collier-Macmillan, 1964.

Freeman, Richard B. *The Overeducated American*. New York: Academic Press, 1976.

Geertz, Clifford. *Agricultural Involution: The Processes of Ecological Change in Indonesia*. Berkeley: University of California Press, 1971.

Gilpatrick, Eleanor G. *Structural Unemployment and Aggregate Demand: A Study of Employment and Unemployment in the United States, 1948–1964.* Foreword by William H. Miernyk. Baltimore: Johns Hopkins Press, 1966.

Goodwin, Leonard. *Do the Poor Want to Work?* Washington, D.C.: Brookings Institution, 1972.

⭐ Gordon, David M. *Theories of Poverty and Underemployment: Orthodox, Radical, and Dual Labor Market Perspectives.* Lexington, Mass.: Heath Lexington, 1972.

Hollander, Myles, and Wolfe, Douglas A. *Nonparametric Statistical Methods.* Wiley Series in Probability and Mathematical Statistics. New York: John Wiley & Sons, 1973.

Khan, M. H. *The Role of Agriculture in Economic Development: A Case Study of Pakistan.* Wageningen: Centre for Agricultural Publications and Documentation, 1966. Quoted in United Nations, Department of Economic and Social Affairs, *Manual V: Methods of Projecting the Economically Active Population,* p. 54. Population Studies no. 46. New York: United Nations, 1971.

Killingsworth, Charles C. *Jobs and Income for Negroes.* Policy Papers in Human Resources and Industrial Relations No. 6. Ann Arbor: Institute of Labor and Industrial Relations at the University of Michigan, 1968.

Kim, Sookon; Roderick, Roger D.; and Shea, John R. *Dual Careers: A Longitudinal Study of Labor Market Experience of Women.* 2 vols. Columbus: Ohio State University, Center for Human Resource Research, 1972.

Lenski, Gerhard E. *Power and Privilege: A Theory of Social Stratification.* New York: McGraw-Hill, 1966.

Levitan, Sar A., and Johnston, William B. *Work is Here to Stay, Alas.* Salt Lake City, Utah: Olympus Publishing Co., 1973.

——; ——; and Taggart, Robert B. *Still a Dream: The Changing Status of Blacks since 1960.* Cambridge, Mass.: Harvard University Press, 1975.

——, and Taggart, Robert B. *Employment and Earnings Inadequacy: A New Social Indicator.* Policy Studies in Employment and Welfare No. 19. Sar A. Levitan, gen. ed. Baltimore: Johns Hopkins Press, 1974.

——, ——. *Jobs for the Disabled.* Policy Studies in Employment and Welfare No. 28. Sar A. Levitan, gen. ed. Baltimore: Johns Hopkins Press, 1974.

Lewis, W. A. *The Theory of Economic Growth.* Homewood, Ill.: Richard D. Irwin, 1955.

Liebow, Eliot. *Tally's Corner: A Study of Negro Streetcorner Men.* Foreword by Hylan Lewis. Boston: Little, Brown & Co., 1967.

Marx, Karl. *Capital: A Critique of Political Economy.* Vol. 1: *A Critical Analysis of Capitalist Production.* Vol. 2: *The Process of Circulation of Capital.* Vol. 3: *The Process of Capitalist Production as a Whole.* Edited by Frederick Engels. Translated by Samuel Moore and Edward Aveling. New York: International Publishers, 1967. [From English ed. of 1887.]

Morse, Dean. *The Peripheral Worker.* Foreword by Eli Ginzberg. New York: Columbia University Press, 1969.

Myrdal, Gunnar. *Asian Drama: An Inquiry into the Poverty of Nations.* 3 vols. New York: Pantheon, 1968.

Oppenheimer, Valerie Kincade. *Female Labor Force in the United States: Demographic and Economic Factors Governing Its Growth and Changing Composition.* Population Monograph Series, No. 5. Berkeley: Institute of International Studies, University of California, 1970.

O'Toole, James. *Work, Learning, and the American Future.* San Francisco: Jossey-Bass, 1977.

Padfield, Harland, and Williams, Roy. *Stay Where You Were: A Study of Unemployables in Industry.* Philadelphia: J. B. Lippincott Co., 1973.

Parsons, Talcott. *The Structure of Social Action.* 2 vols. New York: Free Press, 1968; London: Collier-Macmillan, 1968.

——, and Smelser, Neil J. *Economy and Society.* New York: Free Press, 1956.

Schultz, Theodore. *Transforming Traditional Agriculture.* New Haven: Yale University Press, 1963.

Scoville, James G. *The Job Content of the U.S. Economy, 1940–1970.* New York: McGraw-Hill, 1969.

——. *Manpower and Occupational Analysis: Concepts and Measurements.* Lexington, Mass.: D. C. Heath, 1972.

Sjoberg, Gideon, and Nett, Roger. *A Methodology for Social Research.* New York: Harper & Row, 1968.

Stewart, Charles T., Jr. *Low-Wage Workers in an Affluent Society.* Chicago: Nelson-Hall, 1974.

Sweet, James A. *Women in the Labor Force.* New York: Seminar Press, 1973.

Tiffany, Donald W.; Cowan, James R.; and Tiffany, Phyllis M. *The Unemployed: A Social-Psychological Portrait.* Englewood Cliffs, N.J.: Prentice-Hall, 1970.

Turnham, David M. *The Employment Problem in Less Developed Countries.* Development Centre Studies, Employment Series no. 1. Paris: Development Centre of the Organization for Economic Cooperation and Development, 1971.

Wallace, Phyllis A. *Pathways to Work: Unemployment among Black Teenage Females.* Lexington, Mass.: Heath Lexington, 1974.

Articles, Chapters, and Reports

Almquist, Elizabeth M. "Untangling the Effects of Race and Sex: The Disadvantaged Status of Black Women." *Social Science Quarterly* 56 (June 1975): 129–42.

Alterman, Jack. "The United States Economy in 1985: An Overview of BLS Projections." *Monthly Labor Review* 96 (December 1973): 3–7.

Bancroft, Gertrude. "Alternative Indexes of Employment and Unemployment." *Monthly Labor Review* 85 (February 1962): 167–74.

Bell, Daniel. "The 'Invisible' Unemployed." *Fortune* 68 (July 1958): 198.

Bertocci, Peter J. "The Labor Impact of the Green Revolution in Bangladesh: Some Problems in Explanation and Implications for the Concept of Disguised Unemployment." Paper presented at the 73rd Annual Meeting of the American Anthropological Association, Mexico City, 20–24 November 1974.

Biggar, Jeanne C. "Needed Research on Sex and Racial Differentials in the U.S. Labor Force, 1970." Oak Ridge, Tenn.: Southern Regional Demographic Group, 1973.

Bonacich, Edna. "Advanced Capitalism and Black/White Race Relations in the United States: A Split Labor Market Interpretation." *American Sociological Review* 41 (February 1976): 34–51.

———— "A Theory of Ethnic Antagonism: The Split Labor Market." *American Sociological Review* 37 (October 1972): 547–59.

Bregger, John E. "Revisions in Occupational Classifications for 1971." *Employment and Earnings* 17 (February 1971): 5–8.

Cain, Glen C. "The Challenge of Dual and Radical Theories of the Labor Market to Orthodox Theory." *American Economic Review* 65 (May 1975): 16–22.

Clark, Kenneth B. "Sex, Status, and Underemployment of the Negro Male." In *Employment, Race, and Poverty*, edited by Arthur M. Ross and Herbert Hill, pp. 138–48. New York: Harcourt, Brace & World, 1967.

Clogg, Clifford C. "Measuring Underemployment: Demographic Indicators for the U.S. Labor Force, 1969–1973." Ph.D. dissertation, University of Chicago, 1977.

Collins, Randall. "Functional and Conflict Theories of Educational Stratification." *American Sociological Review* 36 (December 1971): 1002–19.

Davis, James A. "Hierarchical Models for Significance Tests in Multivariate Contingency Tables: An Exegesis of Goodman's Recent Papers." In *Sociological Methodology, 1973–1974*, edited by Herbert L. Costner, pp. 189–231. San Francisco: Jossey-Bass, 1974.

Desai, M., and Mazumdar, D. "A Test of the Hypothesis of Disguised Unemployment." *Economica* 37 n.s. (February 1970): 39–53.

Dresch, Stephen P. "Demography, Technology, and Higher Education: Toward a Formal Model of Educational Adaptation." *Journal of Political Economy* 83 (March–April 1975): 535–71.

Eckaus, R. S. "The Factor-Proportions Problem in Underdeveloped Areas." *American Economic Review* 45 (September 1955): 539–65.

Edwards, Edgar O. "Employment in Developing Countries." In *Employment in Developing Nations: Report on a Ford Foundation Study*, edited by Edgar O. Edwards, pp. 1–46. New York: Columbia University Press, 1974.

Erbe, Brigitte Mach. "Black Occupational Change and Education." *Sociology of Work and Occupations* 2 (May 1975): 150–68.

Farley, Reynolds. "Trends in Racial Inequalities: Have the Gains of the 1960's

Disappeared in the 1970's?" *American Sociological Review* 42 (April 1977): 189–208.

Flaim, Paul O. "Discouraged Workers and Changes in Unemployment." *Monthly Labor Review* 96 (March 1973): 8–16.

Flieger, Wilhelm, and Sullivan, Teresa A. "Manual of Work Force Measurement and Utilization." Under the general direction of Philip M. Hauser. Chicago, 1974. [Typewritten.]

Fuchs, Victor. "Differentials in Hourly Earnings by Region and City Size." Occasional paper no. 101. New York: National Bureau of Economic Research, 1967.

Gans, Herbert J. "Jobs and Services: Toward a More Labor-Intensive Economy." *Challenge* 19 (July–August 1977): 41–45.

Gastwirth, Joseph L. "Estimating the Number of 'Hidden Unemployed.'" *Monthly Labor Review* 96 (March 1973): 17–26.

Gilroy, Curtis L. "Supplemental Measures of Labor Force Underutilization." *Monthly Labor Review* 98 (May 1975): 13–23.

Glyde, Gerald P.; Snyder, David L.; and Stemberger, Anthony L. "Underemployment: Definition, Causes, and Measurement." Report prepared for National Institute of Education. University Park, Pa.: Pennsylvania State University, Institute for Research on Human Resources, January, 1975.

Goodman, Leo A. "The Analysis of Multidimensional Tables: Stepwise Procedures and Direct Estimation Methods for Building Models for Multiple Classifications." *Technometrics* 13 (February 1971): 33–61.

――――. "A General Model for the Analysis of Surveys." *American Journal of Sociology* 77 (May 1972): 1035–86.

――――. "Guided and Unguided Methods for the Selection of Models for a Set of T Multidimensional Contingency Tables." *Journal of the American Statistical Association* 68 (March 1973): 165–75.

――――. "A Model for the Analysis of Surveys." *American Journal of Sociology* 77 (1972): 1044–47.

――――. "A Modified Multiple Regression Approach to the Analysis of Dichotomous Variables." *American Sociological Review* 37 (February 1972): 28–46.

――――. "The Multivariate Analysis of Qualitative Data: Interactions among Multiple Classifications." *Journal of the American Statistical Association* 65 (March 1970): 226–56.

Granskog, Jane. "A Critique of Disguised Unemployment: Labor Allocation and Economic Alternatives in a Peasant Corporate Community." Paper presented at the 73rd Annual Meeting of the American Anthropological Association, Mexico City, 20–24 November 1974.

Harrison, Bennett. "Education and Underemployment in the Urban Ghetto." *American Economic Review* 62 (December 1972): 796–812.

Hauser, Philip M. "The Labor Force and Gainful Workers—Concept, Measurement, and Comparability." *American Journal of Sociology* 54 (January 1949): 338–55.

———. "The Labor Force as a Field of Interest for the Sociologist." *American Sociological Review* 16 (August 1951): 530–38.

✗ ———. "The Measurement of Labour Utilization." *Malayan Economic Review* 19 (April 1974): 1–17.

✗ ———. "The Measurement of Labour Utilization—More Empirical Results." *Malayan Economic Review* (1977), in press.

———. "The Working Force in Developing Areas." In *Human Resources and Economic Welfare: Essays in Honor of Eli Ginzberg*, edited by Ivar Berg, pp. 141–61. New York: Columbia University Press, 1972.

✓ Hodge, Claire C., and Wetzel, James R. "Short Workweeks and Underemployment." *Monthly Labor Review* 90 (September 1967): 30–35.

Hughes, Everett. "Dilemmas and Contradictions of Status." *American Journal of Sociology* 50 (March 1945): 353–59.

Johnson, Harry G. "The Economic Approach to Social Questions." *Economica* 35 n.s. (February 1968): 1–21.

✓ Jones, Ethel B. "The Elusive Concept of Underemployment." *Journal of Human Resources* 6 (Fall 1971): 519–24.

✓ Kean, William. "Disguised Unemployment." Paper presented at the Conference on Labor Anthropology, Tepotzlan, Mexico, May 18–21, 1975.

✗ Kenadjian, Berdj. "Disguised Unemployment in Underdeveloped Countries." Ph.D. dissertation, Harvard University, 1957.

Killingsworth, Charles C. "The Continuing Labor Market Twist." *Monthly Labor Review* 91 (September 1968): 12–17.

———. "Rising Unemployment: A 'Transitional' Problem?" Hearings of the Senate Subcommittee on Employment, Manpower and Poverty, re: Manpower Development and Training Legislation, 1970, part 3; reprinted as Research Reprint Series No. 122. East Lansing: School of Labor and Industrial Relations, Michigan State University, 1970–71.

King, Allan G. "Occupational Choice, Risk Aversion, and Wealth." *Industrial and Labor Relations Review* 27 (July 1974): 586–96.

Kitagawa, Evelyn M. "Components of a Difference between Two Rates." *Journal of the American Statistical Association* 501 (December 1955): 1168–94.

———. "Standardized Comparisons in Population Research." *Demography* 1 (February 1964): 296–315.

Klein, Deborah P. "Determining the Labor Force Status of Men Missed in the Census." *Monthly Labor Review* 93 (March 1970): 26–32.

✗ ———. "Exploring the Adequacy of Employment." *Monthly Labor Review* 96 (October 1973): 3–9.

Kohn, Melvin L., and Schooler, Carmi. "Class, Occupation, and Orientation." *American Sociological Review* 34 (October 1969): 659–78.

Kuhnen, Von Frithjoh. "Bibliographie über 'Ländliche Unterbeschäftigung.'" *Zeitschrift für ausländische Landwirtschaft* 11 (January–March 1972): 74–83.

Leibenstein, Harvey. "The Theory of Underemployment in Backward Economies." *Journal of Political Economy* 45 (April 1957): 91–103.

Levitan, Sar A., and Taggart, Robert B. "Do Our Statistics Measure the Real Labor Market Hardship?" Paper delivered at the American Statistical Association Annual Meeting, Boston, August 23, 1976.

———. "Employment and Earnings Inadequacy: A Measure of Worker Welfare." *Monthly Labor Review* 96 (October 1973): 19–27.

———. "Employment and Earnings Inadequacy: A New Social Indicator." *Challenge* 16 (January–February 1974): 22–29.

Lewis, W. A. "Economic Development with Unlimited Supplies of Labour." *Manchester School of Economic and Social Studies* 22 (May 1954): 139–91.

Litwak, Eugene. "Occupational Mobility and Extended Family Cohesion." *American Sociological Review* 25 (February 1960): 9–21.

Mason, Ward S., and Gross, Neal. "Intra-Occupational Prestige Differentiation: The School Superintendency." *American Sociological Review* 20 (June 1955): 326–31.

Mellor, John W., and Stevens, R. D. "The Average and Marginal Product of Farm Labor in Underdeveloped Economies." *Journal of Farm Economics* 38 (August 1956): 780–91.

Michie, Barrie H. "Disguised Unemployment, Labor Productivity and the Peasant Mode of Production in Indian Agriculture." Paper presented at the 73rd Annual Meeting of the American Anthropological Association, Mexico City, 20–24 November 1974.

Miller, Ann R. "Labor Force Research and the 1970 Census of Population." In *Research and the 1970 Census*, edited by Abbott L. Ferris, pp. 109–19. Oak Ridge, Tenn.: Oak Ridge Association Universities, 1971.

———. "Migration Differentials in Labor Force Participation: United States, 1960." *Demography* 3 (1966): 58–67.

Miller, Herman P. "Measuring Subemployment in Poverty Areas of Large U.S. Cities." *Monthly Labor Review* 96 (October 1973): 10–18.

Mincer, Jacob. "Determining Who Are the 'Hidden Unemployed.'" *Monthly Labor Review* 96 (March 1973): 27–30.

———. "Labor Force Participation." In *International Encyclopedia of the Social Sciences*, 1968 ed.

Moore, Wilbert E. "The Exportability of the 'Labor Force' Concept." *American Sociological Review* 18 (February 1953): 68–72.

Moynihan, Daniel Patrick. "Employment, Income, and the Ordeal of the Negro Family." *Daedalus* 94 (Fall 1965): 745–70.

National Committee against Discrimination in Housing. "The Impact of Housing Patterns on Job Opportunities." New York: The Committee, 1968.

Navarrete, Alfredo, Jr., and De Navarrete, Ifigenia M. "Underemployment in Underdeveloped Economies." Translated by Elizabeth Henderson. *International Economic Papers* 3 (1953): 235–39.

Oppenheimer, Valerie K. "The Life Cycle Squeeze: The Interaction of Men's Occupation and Family Life Cycles." *Demography* 11 (May 1974): 227–46.

Orshansky, Mollie. "Counting the Poor: Another Look at the Poverty Profile."

Social Security Bulletin 28 (January 1965): 3–29.

———. "Who's Who among the Poor: A Demographic View of Poverty." *Social Security Bulletin* 28 (July 1965): 3–32.

Oshima, Harry T. "The Ranis-Fei Model of Economic Development: Comment." *American Economic Review* 53 (June 1963): 448–52.

✦ O'Toole, James. "The Reserve Army of the Underemployed." *Change* 7 (May 1975): 26.

Owens, Raymond. "Disguised Unemployment and Underemployment in Urban India." Paper presented at the 73rd Annual Meeting of the American Anthropological Association, Mexico City, 20–24 November 1974.

✶ Pazos, Felipe. "Development and the Underutilization of Labour." *International Labour Review* 111 (March 1975): 235–49.

Perrella, Vera C. "Employment of Recent College Graduates." *Monthly Labor Review* 96 (February 1973): 41–50.

Ranis, Gustav, and Fei, J. "A Theory of Economic Development." *American Economic Review* 51 (September 1961): 533–65.

"Revisions in Current Population Survey." *Employment and Earnings* 18 (February 1972): 6–9.

Riley, Matilda White. "Membership of the American Sociological Association, 1950–1959." *American Sociological Review* 25 (December 1960): 914–26.

Rives, Norfleet W., Jr. "Effect of Census Errors on Labor Force Estimates." *Industrial Relations* 15 (May 1976): 252–56.

Robinson, Joan. "Disguised Unemployment." *Economic Journal* 46 (June 1936): 225–37.

Rosenstein-Rodan, P. N. "Problems of Industrialization of Eastern and Southeastern Europe." *Economic Journal* 53 (June–September 1943): 202–11.

Saunders, David N. "Labor Force Behavior: A Longitudinal Perspective." *Review of Public Data Use* 1 (July 1973): 7–13.

Shiskin, Julius. "Updating the Consumer Price Index: An Overview." *Monthly Labor Review* 97 (July 1974): 3–20.

Siegel, Jacob S. "Estimates of Coverage of the Population by Sex, Race, and Age in the 1970 Census." *Demography* 11 (February 1974): 1–24.

Siskind, Frederick B. "Labor Force Participation of Men, 25–54, by Race." *Monthly Labor Review* 98 (July 1975): 40–42.

Snyder, David, and Hudis, Paula M. "Occupational Income and the Effects of Minority Competition and Segregation: A Reanalysis and Some New Evidence." *American Sociological Review* 41 (April 1976): 209–34.

✦ Spring, William. "Underemployment: The Measure We Refuse to Take." *New Generation* 53 (Winter 1971): 20–25.

✶ ———; Harrison, Bennett; and Vietorisz, Thomas. "Crisis of the Underemployed." *New York Times Magazine*, Nov. 5, 1972, pp. 42–60.

Stolzenberg, Ross M. "Education, Occupation and Wage Difference between

White and Black Men." *American Journal of Sociology* 81 (September 1975): 299–323.

✶ Sullivan, Teresa A. "New Approaches to Labor Force Measurement." *Asian and Pacific Census Newsletter* 1 (August 1974): 5–8.

✶Thorbecke, Erik. "The Employment Problem: A Critical Evaluation of Four ILO Comprehensive Country Reports." *International Labour Review* 107 (May 1973): 393–423.

Treiman, Donald J., and Terrell, Kermit. "Sex and the Process of Status Attainment: A Comparison of Working Women and Men." *American Sociological Review* 40 (April 1975): 174–200.

Turner, Ralph H. "The Nonwhite Male in the Labor Force." *American Journal of Sociology* 54 (January 1949): 356–62.

Vietorisz, Thomas, et al. "Subemployment: Concepts, Measurements, and Trends." In *Proceedings of the Twenty-seventh Annual Winter Meeting of the Industrial Relations Research Association*, San Francisco, 28–29 December 1974, pp. 117–28.

————; Mier, Robert; and Giblin, Jean-Ellen. "Subemployment: Exclusion and Inadequacy Indexes." *Monthly Labor Review* 98 (May 1975): 3–12.

✶ Viner, Jacob. "Some Reflections on the Concept of 'Disguised Unemployment.'" *Indian Journal of Economics* 38 (July 1957): 17–23.

Waldman, E., and McEaddy, B. J. "Where Women Work: An Analysis by Industry and Occupation." *Monthly Labor Review* 97 (May 1974): 3–13.

✶ Wellisz, Stanislaw. "Dual Economies, Disguised Unemployment and the Unlimited Supply of Labour." *Economica* 35 n.s. (February 1968): 22–51.

Young, Anne M. "Labor Market Experience of Recent College Graduates." *Monthly Labor Review* 97 (October 1974): 33–40.

Government Documents

Albemarle Paper Company v. Moody, 422 U.S. 405, 95 S. Ct. 2362, 48 L. Ed. 2d 280 (1975).

Comprehensive Employment and Training Act of 1973. Statutes at Large, vol. 87 (1973). *U.S. Code*, vol. 29 (Supp. III, 1973).

Federal Register, 41, 124, June 25, 1976, pp. 26346–47.

Griggs v. Duke Power Company, 401 U.S. 424, 91 S. Ct. 849, 28 L. Ed. 2d 158 (1971).

International Labour Organization. *Measurement of Underemployment*. Report IV of the Ninth International Conference of Labour Statisticians. Geneva: International Labour Office, 1957.

Parnes, Herbert S., et al. *The Pre-Retirement Years*. U.S. Department of Labor, Manpower Research Monograph No. 15. Washington, D.C.: Government Printing Office, 1970.

Pub. L. No. 93-203, sec. 302(b), (c), 87 Stat. 876 (1973), 29 U.S.C., sec. 882(b), (c) (Supp. III, 1973).

Pub. L. No. 94-444, 13, 90 Stat. 1483 (1977), (codified as note to 29 U.S.C. 952 [1977] Supp.).

"Review in Poverty Statistics, 1959 to 1968." *Current Population Reports.* Series P-23, no. 28, August 12, 1969.

❉ Smith, A. D. *Concepts of Labour Force Underutilisation.* Geneva: International Labour Office, 1971.

United Nations. Department of Economic and Social Affairs. *Manual V: Methods of Projecting the Economically Active Population.* Population Studies no. 46. New York: United Nations, 1971.

U.S. Congress. House of Representatives. Committee on Education and Labor. Subcommittee on Manpower, Compensation, and Health and Safety. *Oversight Hearings on Comprehensive Employment and Training Act,* part 4-B. Washington, D.C.: U.S. Government Printing Office, 1977.

———. Senate. Committee on Labor and Public Welfare. Subcommittee on Employment and Manpower. "Unemployment and the Tax Cut," by Charles Killingsworth. 88th Cong., 1st sess., pt. 1, 1963. In *Nation's Manpower Revolution,* pp. 1787–94. Washington, D.C.: U.S. Government Printing Office, 1964.

U.S. Department of Agriculture. "Food Consumption and Dietary Levels of Households in the United States." ARS 626 (August 1957).

U.S. Department of Commerce. Bureau of the Census. *Census of Population and Housing: 1960. Accuracy of Data on Population Characteristics as Measured by CPS-Census Match.* Evaluation and Research Program of the U.S., Series ER-60, No. 5. Washington, D.C.: U.S. Government Printing Office, 1964.

———. ———. *Census of Population and Housing: 1960. The Employer Record Check.* Evaluation and Research Program of the U.S., Series ER-60, No. 6. Washington, D.C.: U.S. Government Printing Office, 1965.

———. ———. *Census of Population and Housing: 1960. Subject Reports: Occupational Characteristics.* Final Report PC(2)-7A. Washington, D.C.: U.S. Government Printing Office, 1963.

———. ———. *Census of Population: 1970. General Social and Economic Characteristics.* Final Report PC(1)-C1, *U.S. Summary.* Washington, D.C.: U.S. Government Printing Office, 1972.

———. ———. *Census of Population: 1970. Subject Reports: Educational Attainment.* Final Report PC(2)-5B. Washington, D.C.: U.S. Government Printing Office, 1973.

———. ———. *Census of Population: 1970. Subject Reports: Employment Status and Work Experience.* Final Report PC(2)-6A. Washington, D.C.: U.S. Government Printing Office, 1973.

———. ———. *Census of Population: 1970. Subject Reports: Occupational Characteristics.* Final Report PC(2)-7A. Washington, D.C.: U.S. Government Printing Office, 1973.

———. ———. *Census of Population: 1970. Subject Reports: Persons with Work Disability*. Final Report PC(2)-6C. Washington, D.C.: U.S. Government Printing Office, 1973.

———. ———. *Census of Population and Housing: 1970. Estimates of Coverage of Population by Sex, Race, and Age: Demographic Analysis*, by Jacob S. Siegel. Evaluation and Research Program PHC(E)-4. Washington, D.C.: U.S. Government Printing Office, 1974.

———. ———. "1970 Occupation and Industry Classifications in Terms of Their 1960 Occupation and Industry Elements." By John A. Priebe, Joan Heinkel, and Stanley Greene. Technical Paper No. 26. Washington, D.C.: U.S. Government Printing Office, 1972.

———. ———. *Public Use Samples of Basic Records from the 1970 Census: Description and Technical Documentation*. Washington, D.C.: U.S. Government Printing Office, 1972.

———. ———. *Statistical Abstract of the United States: 1976*. 97th ed. Washington, D.C.: U.S. Government Printing Office, 1976.

U.S. Department of Health, Education, and Welfare. Public Health Service. *Disability among Persons in the Labor Force by Employment Status: United States, July 1961–June 1962*. National Center for Health Statistics Series 10, no. 7. Public Health Service Publication no. 1000. Washington, D.C.: National Center for Health Statistics, 1964.

———. ———. *Prevalence of Selected Impairments, United States, 1971*, by Charles S. Wilder. Vital and Welfare Health Statistics Series 10, no. 79. Washington, D.C.: National Center for Health Statistics, 1975.

U.S. Department of Labor. Bureau of Labor Statistics. *Handbook of Labor Statistics, 1973*. Washington, D.C.: U.S. Government Printing Office, 1974.

U.S. President. *Manpower Report of the President*. Washington, D.C.: U.S. Government Printing Office, 1973, 1974, and 1975.

U.S. President's Committee to Appraise Employment and Unemployment Statistics. *Measuring Employment and Unemployment*. Washington, D.C.: U.S. Government Printing Office, 1962.

Wirtz, W. Willard. "A Sharper Look at Unemployment in U.S. Cities and Slums: A Summary Report Submitted to the President by the Secretary of Labor." Washington, D.C.: U.S. Department of Labor, n.d. [ca. 1967.]

Index